BEYOND THE HIGGS BOSON

Beyond the Higgs Boson

The W Boson and Dr Ashutosh Kotwal's Quest for the Unknown

MANIK KOTWAL

Translated from the Marathi by
Jerry Pinto

HarperCollins *Publishers* India

First published in India by HarperCollins *Publishers* 2024
4th Floor, Tower A, Building No. 10, DLF Cyber City,
DLF Phase II, Gurugram, Haryana – 122002
www.harpercollins.co.in

2 4 6 8 10 9 7 5 3 1

In grateful acknowledgement of the permission given by
Rajhans Prakashan, Pune 411030, for translation of their
Marathi book *Putra Whava Aisa* into English.

Copyright © MANIK KOTWAL 2024
English translation copyright © Jerry Pinto 2024
Image on page 133 courtesy of Edupedia Publications Pvt. Ltd.
and Pen2Print Reproduced with permission.

P-ISBN: 978-93-6213-594-0
E-ISBN: 978-93-6213-075-4

The views and opinions expressed in this book are the author's own
and the facts are as reported by her and the publishers are
not in any way liable for the same.

Manik Kotwal asserts the moral right
to be identified as the author of this work.

All rights reserved. No part of this publication may be reproduced,
stored in a retrieval system, or transmitted, in any form or by any
means, electronic, mechanical, photocopying, recording or otherwise,
without the prior permission of the publishers.

Typeset in 11.5/16 Dante MT Std at
Manipal Technologies Limited, Manipal

Printed and bound at
Manipal Technologies Limited, Manipal

This book is produced from independently certified FSC® paper to ensure
responsible forest management.

To
Gautam, Ashwini and Papa
The three near and dear ones to me and Ashutosh

Contents

Author's Note	xi
Prologue	xxvii

THE NEST

1.	Legacy	3
2.	The Waxing Moon	12
3.	Lucknow—A Time to Cherish	21
4.	Minuses and Pluses	25
5.	Destination Delhi	36
6.	Wandering at Will	42
7.	Mumbai—New Games, New Rules	47
8.	Passage to England	54
9.	Enterprise and Accomplishment	61

OUT OF THE NEST

10.	New Horizons	71
11.	Prof. Fortune, a Remarkable 'Guru'	77
12.	Visiting India, Living in Scotland	83
13.	Los Alamos and Harvard	92
14.	Summer Job at IBM	102

15. Iraq–Jordan–Egypt	106
16. … And America	111
17. The Immersive Education Experience	116
18. Ashutosh's PhD Thesis—and World Fame	124

SPREADING WINGS

19. The Science of Particle Physics	135
20. In the Beginning	149
21. Standard Model Theory	158
22. Post-Doctoral Work	164
23. A Heavy Particle	170
24. Duke University and Collider Detector at Fermilab	180
25. A Herculean Effort	192
26. The Higgs Boson	204

HOME SWEET HOME

27. Jab We Met	225
28. A Happy Family	229

THE LIMITLESS SKY

29. Tireless Traveller	249
30. In Search of Supersymmetry	255
31. Back to the Future	259

EDUCATION: A NOBLE GIFT

32. Quick March in New Avenue	271
33. Ashutosh as Educator	277
34. A Benevolent Teacher	283

WORDS OF ADULATION

35. In the Eyes of Others	293
36. His Hidden Talent	305
37. Ashutosh and Indian Scientific Organizations	315
38. Ashutosh's Reflections	333
Epilogue	343
Appendix 1: Ashutosh V. Kotwal's Career	346
Appendix 2: Research Interests of Dr Ashutosh Kotwal	352
Appendix 3: Upsetting the Standard Model of Physics	358
Additional Sources	366
Glossary	367

Author's Note

It was Dr K.K. 'Nana' Kshirsagar who first suggested that I write about my son, Ashutosh. Nana Kshirsagar is a founding member of Vigyan Bharati, an organization dedicated to the promotion of science. He thought that it might be a good idea for someone close to Ashutosh, from the family even, to write about those aspects of his personality and mental make-up that led him to take up science as a vocation. This suggestion left me in a dilemma. I could scarcely believe that my son was indeed important enough to merit a biography. Would I be able to be objective or would my natural affection as a mother get in the way?

But when I began to think about it, my instinctive refusal was inflected by two ideas. I can only hope that Ashutosh will go from strength to strength even after this, but the young people of today might like to read an account of his work up to this point; such an account might prove to be a guidepost of sorts for some of them. And then I thought if anyone should write about him, perhaps it would be best for that person to be me. I hesitate to say that I know him fully but in the first seventeen years, his father and I were the people who knew him best. I can describe with some confidence how he got to be the way he is and the formative influences and events that shaped his character.

And so, I decided to give it a shot. Ashutosh's father greeted Nana's suggestion with delight, for his son is the apple of his eye. I knew I would have to be careful.

Although his achievements are many, I am much prouder that Ashutosh is a good human being. I began this book with the idea that I should include such incidents from his childhood that might help the reader understand his nature better. After I decided that I would be writing this, his father initiated the project and began the actual writing.

Ashutosh and I began a series of telephone conversations. As I cannot write too fast, his father took notes and offered suggestions. Often when Ashutosh and I were chatting, my mind would simply fill with amazement.

At the age of seventeen, my son left us to go to what was a completely new environment. At the time, I gave him no indication of the mix of emotions—pride and worry—that I felt. But it is also true that he never gave us any cause for concern. These conversations shed new light on his life at the time and made me even more proud of him. He only spoke of those things he felt might be useful in the writing of this book, always talking in a calm fashion, with never a trace of self-promotion.

That one's child has chosen to transcend the rat race, forsaking the pursuit of money or fame, can only be a source of pride for a parent. I experienced the satisfaction of seeing those conversations turn into this book. I was given the opportunity to listen to Ashutosh recount some of the major incidents of the last thirty-nine years of his life. In my child, I got a glimpse of what a magnificent obsession is, what it means to commit oneself to a goal and to work at it with complete dedication. Often I would feel a pang of sorrow that I did not know all this about my own son earlier. But now those pangs have been replaced by a sense of satisfaction. I began to see that God had given me a seed, a truly different seed to protect; I had not known this and in my ignorance, I could have made any number of mistakes along the way. That I did not make any of them is something in which I can now take pride.

Human intelligence has the important ability to adapt and create its own identity in each environment. Ashutosh did change a great deal. Each time he confronted a new space and a new challenge, he would use the learnings of the old to help him deal with it. He did not forget the old, nor did the new frighten him. This wealth of experience stood him in good stead. Each time he faced up to a challenge and overcame it, he converted it into a lesson for future use.

Today, I am proud that Ashutosh studied in nationally recognized schools like the Delhi Public School and the Cathedral & John Connon Anglo-Scottish School and in each one, he shone.

According to a survey published by *India Today*, IIT Bombay is one of Asia's top ten educational institutions. The University of Edinburgh is one of Europe's top ten universities. The University of Pennsylvania (UPenn) is an Ivy League institution, and again is one of the top ten in the US. Its Wharton Business School is also recognized as one of the world's best schools. Harvard, of course, needs no introduction.

Ashutosh studied at all these institutions. Now he is a professor at Duke, also a university often ranked among the top ten US universities.

Perhaps this introduction to Ashutosh's personal and intellectual development will prove to be an inspiration to young men and women who are on the threshold of life. This was the impulse that made me begin writing. I would like to introduce the young to the way Ashutosh took delight in science and the excitement he felt at confronting its basic questions and investigating its fundamental concepts. I would like to infuse the young with some of this feeling. The youth of today are fascinated by modern technology. I would like them to know that science, which forms the basis of technology, is just as exciting and intellectually stimulating.

The Marathi edition of this book coincided with Ashutosh's fiftieth birthday. His career has been a series of successes. He is looked up to with respect and admiration in his field. I have often heard it said of him: 'His best is yet to come.' He is young at heart—I have seen him have free and frank conversations even with teenagers. They seek him out in his office to talk to him and clear their minds.

∽

I believe Ashutosh is Ganapati Bappa's prasad to me. His intelligence, his level-headedness and his talent are all gifts from Bappa. His ability to keep his balance in trying circumstances, his skill at working out his own path, and the energy with which he made his way through life were all his inherent gifts.

This made my role as a mother easy and trouble free. He did not let me behave like an overindulgent mother pampering her only child. I never had to play tiger mom or helicopter mother.

This book has been my labour of love. I have tried to present Ashutosh's journey through his formative years up to his becoming a world-renowned particle physicist. Being his mother, I could read some of his traits, which were instrumental in his becoming what he is. I have put those salient aspects on paper.

The Almighty appoints a good gardener who takes good care of the seeds with water and compost so they grow healthy and flower. The gardener with the green thumb was Ashutosh's father. Father and son were of a similar temperament and it did not take much effort for them to strike up a harmonious relationship; even so, I have to say, I have seen few fathers who are so devoted. As a committed and capable railway officer who was often given challenging assignments, Ashutosh's father was busy throughout Ashutosh's growing years, but he never allowed his son to slip down the list of his priorities. To my mind, this is proof that a child will respond when given the right encouragement, support and trust by his father. My husband would interact at the cognitive level of his son, and so would help him grow. He would set aside the role of the teacher and become a student again. He showed a great deal of interest in his son's education. He would discuss Ashutosh's work on the phone or in person and read his essays and papers with interest. When the material went over his head, he would accept this candidly. Father and son drew a great deal of joy from this dialogue, and made a unique world together.

Ashutosh's father can be somewhat authoritarian at times. The phrase 'appearances are deceptive' could have been written about him. But he never demonstrated this side of his nature in his dealings with his son. He encouraged Ashutosh to develop his ability to think for himself and make his own decisions and then trusted him fully. When Ashutosh left us at a rather young age to study abroad, his father did not offer mundane advice about daily behaviour. When he was asked, he would give his opinion according to his lights; but Ashutosh always carried the feeling that his father's eyes were upon him and this belief guided his existence.

I thought it might be difficult for any young person to go to the US for undergraduate studies, right after the twelfth standard, but for Ashutosh, it was not a decision, it was a quest.

People often ask me if I am proud of my son, the famous scientist. Of course, I feel proud, who wouldn't? More than that, I am delighted to see the relationship between my son and his father, who share a special bond, based on mutual trust.

It is said that marriages are made in heaven. And it is also said that opposites attract. Ashutosh's wife Ashwini is not the same as he is but is a perfect match for him. Both of them believe in giving a 100 per cent to their work and so achieving success; and both also believe in enjoying life to the full. She has an incredible knowledge of accounting and business. She is his consiglieri, his trusted lieutenant, his friend. In her company, he relaxes and opens up. But when they do have a fight, which is a rare thing, it seems to me as if Ashutosh's deeply felt but rarely expressed sense of not having siblings is now being fulfilled by squabbling with his wife.

By this time, Ashutosh has spent more time with Ashwini than he has with me. He has shared all the important moments in his career with her. Over the phone and through letters, she has brought us into this golden circle.

The apex of our pentagonal family, the jewel in its crown, is our grandson, Gautam. Ashwini has brought him up well. It seems to me when I look at Gautam that he is another of Bappa's little schemes to bring joy to our family.

Ashutosh went to the United States of America when he was only seventeen. The US welcomed Ashutosh with open arms, offered him respect for his talents and gave them their due. In the educational and research spheres, he was lucky to encounter mentors such as Profs. Terry Fortune, Francis Pipkin, Richard Wilson, Richard Nickerson and Heidi Schellman, Dr Hugh Montgomery and Profs. Michael Tuts, Paul Grannis, Harry Weerts, Young-Kee Kim, Alfred Goshaw, Melvyn Shochet and Nigel Lockyer, the kind you could only meet there. He was lucky to have the support of people like G. P. 'Kaka' Patil and his wife, Ashutosh's Lalit Maushi, Reena-Prashant Vankudre and Desai Kaka. They made a safe space for him in their nest. He also received family-style love and affection from the brothers, Parimal–Parag–Pavan; friends like Jasvir–Tejvir (Jassi–Teji), and Arijit–Dhiman–Satyadev. He found a home away from home with Ashok Kaka and Truus Kaki, and with Abhijit–Sangeeta.

The United States' educational culture not only presented Ashutosh with new challenges but also with new directions. New vistas were thrown open to him. The United States of America is called 'the Land of the Free'; here, the Statue of Liberty raises her torch to proclaim freedom. And Ashutosh was led to take American citizenship. I feel I should bow my head in respect to the land that has offered him so much.

And science, the field to which Ashutosh gave his heart, his mind, his being and his life? Here too I should bow my head in gratitude:

Poornamadaha poornamidam poornat poornamudachyate
Poornasya poornamaadaaya poornamevavishishyate.

(God is Absolute. The world is Absolute. The Absolute evolves from The Absolute.
If the Absolute is removed from the Absolute only the Absolute remains.)

Our ancient rishis had profound wisdom coupled with insights into the outer world. Modern science is catching up only now, trying to figure out the essences of which these sages spoke so many centuries ago.

Particle physics, the field of Ashutosh's endeavour, concerns itself with everything; from the infinite expanses and enormous masses of the nebulae down to the fundamental particles that can never be perceived by the human senses. It ranges from the infinitely huge to the unbelievably minute. It is cutting-edge science which scythes its way through ideas of the ageless and timeless universe, taking us back to the moment of Creation. At the time of the Big Bang, an unimaginably enormous burst of energy emanated from a point in space at a tremendous speed; this burst threw out elementary particles and the forces that affect them. One might call particle physics an attempt to understand the mind of God.

The twentieth century saw the rapid rise of this very exciting branch of fundamental science. It is full of mystery and profundity; it is awe-inspiring and enjoyable. Ashutosh and others of his ilk have given an abject lesson of their deeply meditative mind, their vision and their intellectual prowess while pursuing this science.

The Higgs Boson—or the 'God Particle' in common parlance—was detected in 2012 at the accelerator known as the Large Hadron Collider (LHC), which is located at CERN, the international laboratory in Geneva, Switzerland. Ashutosh's research predicted the mass of the Higgs boson, which facilitated its detection and gave a new direction to particle physics.

The march does not stop here. Any scientist worth his salt is averse to becoming complacent with success or getting deterred at failure. His motto is 'Excelsior!' So, Ashutosh has moved on to investigate the mysteries of dark matter and the origin of the Higgs boson. His meticulous analysis of data collected at the Fermi National Accelerator Laboratory has brought forth some amazing findings, generating renewed interest in probing the Higgs field further with a much larger collider of a 100 km circumference.

Dark matter might well be dark galactic clouds of heavy particles, produced at the time of the Big Bang. There is a chance that these particles will show up at the LHC. The challenge is their detection: since they are invisible, much ingenuity is required. Ashutosh is developing a very fast electronic circuit that will use artificial intelligence techniques to detect a particular kind of dark-matter signature very fast—as fast as the LHC collisions occur at intervals of 25 billionths of a second. No other method has been developed that can match this extreme speed.

Ashutosh has received a special grant from the Department of Energy, USA, to probe the Higgs boson deeper and to use silicon chip-based artificial intelligence to trace links to the mysterious dark matter forming 84 per cent of the total matter in the universe.

If dark matter production is proven, it will revolutionize our understanding of how the galaxies took their present form, the nature of the cosmic void, the vacuum and perhaps of space and time itself.

For centuries humans have tried to fathom the beginning and evolution of the universe. This has been a long journey, undertaken by visionary scientists. Now, Ashutosh has had the honour of joining this caravan. Science inspired him to add tenacity, diligence and perseverance to his innate intelligence. I can only thank science for these qualities. In his field, he is at the very peak. I have had the good fortune to write about the challenges, struggles and vision of unwavering hope that went into his success.

This could only happen through the grace of Bappa.

Before this book, I wrote biographies of two of the greatest scientists of all time—Galileo and J. Robert Oppenheimer. Both of them influenced the course of human history with their fundamental research which has had a huge impact on human lives, whether for good or for evil. While I was engaged in this work, I experienced the struggle, the interactions between the individual and society, the joys and griefs, the dramatic moments and all the grey areas in the souls of these men of extraordinary talent. My protagonists were both intelligent scientists. As a writer, it was thus my duty to understand their scientific theories and write about them as clearly as possible. I had a passing acquaintance with Galileo's work. But it was a strenuous climb to get to that moment in the twentieth century when quantum theory exploded onto the scene, bringing with it the atom bomb to which Oppenheimer's work also contributed. In the preface of these books, I wrote about my regret that my knowledge of science was limited and that I was in a way indifferent to it.

World-class scientists are exercising their minds and their intellects to understand the mysteries of particle physics. It is a branch of physics which studies the building blocks of the universe. To put it another way, it is the branch of science that seeks to describe the indescribable; scientists are beginning to realize that it has the power to unlock the secrets of the millions of universes that might exist. Their thirst for knowledge drives them to find answers.

It is an unending quest. One might say that their motto is 'miles to go before I sleep'; now Ashutosh has joined this trail. For him this is as much a labour of the intellect as it is a labour of love. Of his work, I have written as much as I could say that I understood.

The writing of this book has made clear what I once knew through a glass darkly—that humankind as a species is infinitely curious about itself and about its surroundings. It was a startling realization.

∽

While Writing

There was great cheer around the house when I finished the groundwork and began writing the book. I felt as if I were floating on a sea of happiness. All human beings have many aspects to their personalities. Every mother carries around with her images of her children, at various stages, each inscribed in her mind.

I saw Ashutosh again as a child—peaceful, happy and innocent. This image of Ashutosh was one of him in a talkative mood, chatting away with me. It may seem surprising but every moment of his life, from the time he was born to the time he went to the US, is inscribed in my mind. These memories are complete: filled with his words, his body language, his behaviour, even his exclamations, all these were in my head. And so, when I started writing, I initially concentrated on those early years.

As one of the persons closest to him, I undertook to unravel the various facets of his personality, as tenderly as I could, but I also had to make readers know at least the basics of his scientific work. In my view, this was a risky business. I had to try and understand it as best as I could. My problem is that I respect the value of objectivity and rationality in science, but I don't understand much of it. But I kept at it, reading as much as I could. I would pay careful attention to the conversations between father and son. I asked Ashutosh questions and he answered them in easy terms to help me understand his work. Sometimes, I would talk to Ashutosh's father and he would try to clear my concepts.

Over the years, Ashutosh's father has collected and carefully stored many of Ashutosh's documents, both educational and work-related. I read through all of these as well.

Once the book began to take shape, I began to look for a good publisher. In May 2015, there was a family celebration. The occasion was my husband's eightieth and my seventy-fifth birthday. Speaking at the celebration event, Ashwini mentioned that Ashutosh's fiftieth birthday was coming up in December. When I went to invite Anand Hardikar, a friend of ours and the well-known editor of Rajhans Publication, I happened to mention in passing that I was working on this book. He was delighted at the news. He offered much support and encouragement.

In our first meeting, Mr Hardikar asked me to complete the book before Ashutosh's birthday. Hence, I accelerated my process and completed the book. Then I met Rajhans Prakashan's publisher, Dilip Majgaonkar. He was very supportive of the idea and soon agreed to publish the book.

When Anand read the draft, he made many suggestions. He asked me to open up certain areas. He suggested new lines of inquiry, such as our backgrounds as his parents; Ashwini, Ashutosh and Gautam's family life; Ashutosh's opinions and feelings towards India and his reading habits. All these were duly incorporated into the book.

I had worked with Rajhans before and knew them as having an appetite for good work and a comfortable and harmonious working style. Their attitude to this book made me very happy indeed. I had many long fruitful and frank discussions with them.

Ashutosh's father and I cannot thank them enough for the hard work they put into this book.

In 2014, between September to November, I stayed at Ashwini and Ashutosh's place in Chicago. During that time, I had long conversations with Ashwini that were both free-spirited and wide-ranging. She would talk about her experiences in America, her marriage and relationship with Ashutosh, their affection for Gautam and their work. When Gautam heard that 'Mo' was writing a book about his father, he was thrilled. He then demanded that I write about him too. I happily agreed. It was a great time.

Spending time with Ashutosh, sitting with him and talking, proved invaluable. Discussing subtleties in person provided me with insights that were never possible in phone conversations. He also told me stories about his students, friends, colleagues, and his mentors. I got to hear Ashutosh's friends, Dr Arijit Banerjee and Dr Pasha Murat describe his perspectives on research and on societal issues, and his own style of working and interacting with people.

I was in Chicago with Ashutosh when I started writing about the origin of the universe. I asked him, 'How are galaxies and stars formed?' He said, 'When there are irregular densities in the gravitational field, dark matter aggregates around these high-density fluctuations. The focal point of this aggregation becomes the centre where visible matter begins to accumulate, and it is out of these concentrations of matter that galaxies and stars form.'

On 12 February 2016, I was reading the newspaper when I saw the news about the discovery of gravitational waves. I remembered our conversation about gravitational waves. I picked up the phone and called Ashutosh. He was happy to see the contribution of Indians in the project; scientists from the Inter-University Centre for Astronomy and Astrophysics (IUCAA) in Pune, Tata Institute of Fundamental Research (TIFR) in Mumbai and Bengaluru, Chennai Mathematical Institute, Raja Ramanna Center for Advanced

Technologies (RRCAT) Indore, IIT and Institute of Plasma Research in Gandhinagar, Indian Institute of Science Education (IISER)—Trivandrum and Kolkata, which along with many other institutes worldwide, were involved in the process.

Einstein's suggestion that gravitational waves must be generated when large revolving masses coalesce had just been proved. This was a huge discovery. It was now possible to go deeper into the history of our universe, back to the earliest times. Until Einstein came along, Newton's theory of gravity was considered to be perfect, but Einstein formulated a broader and more powerful theory. This was where we got the Theory of General Relativity and from then on, research into gravity has continued. Today it has translated into the discovery of these gravitational waves.

As a young researcher, Ashutosh realized that establishing the W boson's mass with a greater degree of accuracy would help to triangulate the Higgs boson's mass and aid in its discovery. Ashutosh saw the possibility of throwing open some more windows so that we might catch a glimpse of the deep past of the universe.

In a way, the discovery of the Higgs field and the Higgs boson is even more important than the discovery of gravitational waves. This is because the gravitational field was universally accepted. The Higgs field is neither a field of matter nor that of a force—it is a completely new kind of fundamental building block. The properties of the Higgs boson have been measured and agreed with the predictions based on Ashutosh's initial measurements of the W boson mass. This was huge.

In science, a theory is true only at the level of accuracy at which it is tested. Tests of the Higgs boson theory must continue at higher levels of accuracy and the experiments at the Large Hadron Collider are being improved for this purpose. Ashutosh continues to measure the W boson mass with higher accuracy because this measurement provides one of the most powerful tests of the Higgs boson theory. History has demonstrated that flaws in established theories can show up when examined more closely, with better observations of nature. Ashutosh's latest measurement, published in the world's leading journal *Science* in 2022, revealed a significant disagreement with the simplest version of the Higgs theory as encapsulated in the standard model of particle physics. It could be our biggest clue pointing towards future discoveries beyond the Higgs boson.

The book was being edited when I accidentally ran into Vinod Shirsath, the editor of the weekly Marathi magazine *Sadhana*. When he heard about the book, he offered to publish some chapters in the Diwali edition. Both Diliprao and Shri Hardikar agreed and the section which is titled 'Passage to England' in this version was published. It was a happy moment for me.

My husband gave his all to this book. He cross-checked facts in scientific texts. For years, he had collected Ashutosh's documents. Every now and then, he would recount his memories of Ashutosh and help flesh out the book. In the morning or late at night, Vijayrao would talk with Ashutosh over the phone. Once they began to talk, they both forgot about the time. I had always felt that his father should be the one to write a biography about Ashutosh, as he was the one who created and nurtured the scientist in him. I am indebted to Diliprao, Shri Hardikar and Vijayrao, otherwise known as VYK, for the rest of my life.

Before I conclude, I must express my gratitude to HarperCollins, who undertook to publish my book in English; Siddhesh Inamdar for his enthusiasm in initiating this project; Jerry Pinto, who undertook the laborious task of translation; and Suchismita Ukil, Amrita Mukerji and Kartik Chauhan for their hard work and commitment to bringing out the English edition.

I am also indebted to many readers and well-wishers. I would like to thank Nana Kshirsagar and Hematai for their loving encouragement. Ajit Thombre of 'Pratima Offset' made a great effort to get everything right. Shekhar Godbole and Raju Deshpande's aesthetic supervision resulted in a beautiful book. Trupti Deshpande of Rajhans also helped a lot. Thank you all very much from the bottom of my heart.

Manik Kotwal

Prologue

John F. Kennedy Airport, New York. Sunday, 1 July 2012, 10.30 a.m.

He sits at the departure gate for a flight about to leave for Melbourne, Australia. He is bubbling over with excitement. His fingers itch to send his colleagues a message about the 'great news'.

Prof. Laurie L. Patton, Dean of Arts and Sciences, Duke University, is a senior colleague. As someone who has studied the Marathi language and is a frequent visitor to Pune, she is also a good friend. He sends her a message saying, 'Please keep this confidential as there will be no mention of the following until official press releases from CERN (Conseil Européen pour la Recherche Nucléaire or the European Centre for Nuclear Research, in Switzerland, near Geneva), Fermilab, Brookhaven and other US national laboratories.'

He adds:

> As you know, the High Energy Physics (HEP) group at Duke has made significant contributions over more than two decades to

the high-energy collider experiments at Fermilab and CERN—in particular the CDF experiment at Fermilab and the ATLAS experiment at CERN. Faculty involved are Profs. Goshaw, Kruse, Oh and myself and Assistant Prof. Arce, who was recruited by Duke about three years ago. This week there will be press releases from CERN and Fermilab about their respective efforts on the search for the Higgs boson, the long sought-after hypothetical particle that manifests the mechanism by which all fundamental particles acquire the property of mass. It is one of the cornerstones of the fundamental theory called the Standard Model of particle physics.

HEP faculty, scientists, postdocs and students have made critical contributions to the detector construction, software algorithms, data analysis and physics leadership on these experiments. Some of us have direct leadership of key aspects of the data analysis leading to the Higgs results. This is a proud moment for us which I wanted to share with you, in advance of the official announcements.

Laurie replies with a message of congratulations, 'What a wonderful piece of news to greet me on my return from India. It is really thrilling to think that our HEP faculty have had a major hand in learning how all fundamental particles acquire the property of mass. This is the kind of thing I take on the road immediately.'

To which he responds, 'As the eminent physicist Richard Feynman would say, finding something new and definite in the data for the first time and telling others about it are both extraordinary moments of joy.'

Laurie asks him, 'Feynman wrote a lot about beauty and discovery. Would there be any different feeling if you were in nature rather than in an airport?'

He replies, 'That doesn't matter. The Higgs field, which spreads all through the universe and occupies even the vacuum, is still around the airport!'

He hears the boarding announcement for his plane. He shuts the laptop and joins the passenger line.

∽

Eureka! Eureka!

4 July 2012, 11 p.m.

The phone rings. We know who is calling this late at night. Both of us run to pick up the phone, more eager than usual. After saying 'Hello', there is a momentary silence and then, in the usual calm tone, a single word, 'Aai!'

My words spill over. 'It has been an exciting day. Excitement everywhere. Stream of breaking news on TV.' We hear his rollicking laughter now, his happiness pouring down the wire. His father says, 'It must be 3 a.m. there! Don't you have to read a paper tomorrow? Don't you want to sleep?'

The obedient son replies, 'Yes, Papa, I'm going to sleep now.'

I know there is a celebration going on. This is not a night to be sleeping. The night is still young for them. After fifty years of stumbling, hesitating, inching forward, a divine ray of hope breaks the darkness. That sneaky, elusive god particle had decided to reveal itself. On the world stage, a new play is about to begin, its prologue being uttered right now.

The game's afoot. How could anyone sleep? He speaks with us from Australia. Scientists from around the world are participating in the 'International Conference on High Energy Physics' to examine the evidence for the Higgs boson and the scientific activity that led up to that 'Eureka' moment.

This moment has him playing the guide, the navigator. On the morning of 4 July, at the inauguration event of the conference, the discovery of 'Higgs boson', the god particle, was announced; there was a simultaneous announcement in Geneva. Geneva and Melbourne were taken by a storm of happiness. But then that is only natural. The last forty years have been spent looking for this particle. Three generations of scientists and technologists have poured their reserves of knowledge and talent into this search. And finally, they were able to prove the existence of the particle.

As the research papers were being read, the atmosphere was joyous. Scientists cited a recent study, which helped establish with precision what mass might be expected for the Higgs boson. This was the research that established the precise mass of another particle, the W boson. The name of the scientist who was cited was Dr Ashutosh Kotwal! In February 2012, this was officially announced by the Fermi National Accelerator Laboratory in the United States and recognized across the world.

As Ashutosh, who conducted research into the mass of the W boson, which helped predict the mass of the Higgs boson, is an Indian by birth, it is interesting that boson particles themselves get their name from another Indian physicist, Dr Satyendra Nath Bose, who developed the concept of such particles. What a happy coincidence!

Ashutosh led the team of scientists measuring what are known as 'W boson events'—the fleeting traces of the particle's momentary presence after being produced in the beam collisions. After observing a million events, he used innovative concepts and techniques and came up with the mass of the W boson. This was now found to be 80.387 billion electron-Volts (GeV), a figure with an unprecedented accuracy of ±0.02 per cent.

According to the Standard Model theory of particle physics, the W boson and the top quark are two particles that are closely related to the Higgs boson. Ashutosh and others had already measured the mass of the top quark accurately. From these two masses, he could predict the mass of the Higgs boson. By using triangulation, Ashutosh found out the maximum and minimum mass of the Higgs boson and it was discovered to be within this range.

On the night of 4 July 2012, sleep eluded me too. A breeze rocked the branches of the jasmine creeper outside. Its scent came in through the window and with it, a flood of memories about Ashutosh. Its fragrance permeated my heart and Ashutosh's life unfolded before my eyes …

THE NEST

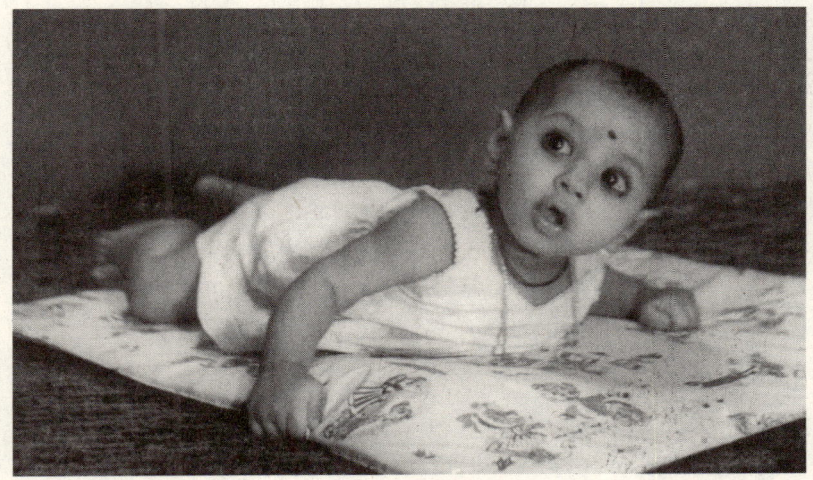

Ashutosh at three and a half months.

With Mothe Baba, Mothi Aai, Papa, and Aai after returning from his first trip abroad in July 1982.

There is no law that establishes how long a fledgling should continue to enjoy the warmth of the nest and the protection of the wings of its parents. Its parents must strengthen its wings to ready it for the inevitable moment of its departure. And at the right time, the parents must also undertake the job of tossing the fledgling out of the nest in order that it might fly ...

1

Legacy

Rewind to 29 May 1961, around 8 a.m. In a sprawling old bungalow on Puranik Painter Gully, off Tilak Road, Pune, young Manik Pradhan of Pile Wada is laughing up a storm with her friends. Two houses down, Sarojini Babar, otherwise known as Akka, calls out, 'Hey Manik, tell your Baba there's a call from Mumbai for him.'

Manik's father, Waman Krishna Pradhan, is a man who lives life to the fullest. He gets up only at 9 a.m. At home he is known as Balasaheb, but among his friends and acquaintances, he's Bappa. He is a jovial man, a lover of theatre and music, an expert bridge player, very proud of his culinary skills, a man who likes to cook for his friends and family. He has spent his life in the Military Engineering Services as a non-commissioned officer and lived in various places across the country, including Simla, Jabalpur and New Delhi.

Manik runs down the street and takes the call. The person on the other end is Bhaisaheb, the husband of Manik's Kusum Maushi. (Bhaisaheb is also the much older brother of noted theatre director and actor Vijaya Mehta.) He says: 'Tell Balasaheb that the boy is in Mumbai only for a couple of days.'

That Manik Pradhan was, of course, yours truly. I had no idea that this phone call was going to change my life. Without a care in the world, I returned home and gave the message to my mother. My mother, Indutai, roused her husband.

Balasaheb roared, 'Manikbai, let's go to Mumbai.'

Across a Crowded Room

I borrowed a Dhakai sari that belonged to my close friend, Sudha Chaphekar (Gowarikar) for this encounter. All three of Bhaisaheb's daughters were my friends. We chattered cheerfully all the time.

From the boy's side, my future sister-in-law Sudhatai Varde was an expert public speaker. My father-in-law, Yashwantrao Neelkantrao Kotwal, and his youngest son, Ashok, would sometimes chip in with a few words. Vijayrao's mother, Indirabai Kotwal, did not say much, only chiming in occasionally. Vijay Kotwal, on the other hand, seemed to have taken a vow of silence.

My father was delighted. 'Everyone should get a son-in-law like this,' he said, meaning a boy from a 'good' caste, who was handsome and had a career, a Class I officer in the Indian railways; all in all, a good catch.

The four of us continued to chat; Vijayrao, however, remained silent.

Then both Bhaisaheb and Balasaheb made another suggestion: the two of us should go out on a drive together.

The driver, a Mr Sheikh, was in front and the two of us at the back. Outside the windows, the crowds of Mumbai teemed. The car crawled along at an ant's pace; the silence in the back seat was unbearable to me at least, being the kind who said whatever came to her mind.

Vijay Kotwal asked me just two questions. I was a mathematics student, BA Honours. 'Are you going to study further?' As if the marriage had already been fixed, I said: 'I'd love to do my master's at Mahalanobis in Calcutta.'

I had also studied classical music formally up to the Visharad level. He asked, 'Can one continue with music if one has to move around?' Once again, I answered in the same manner: 'Yes, Calcutta has some very good teachers like A. Kannan, Malavika Kannan and Sandhya Mukherjee. I would be lucky to study with any of them.'

Easier said than done. But Vijayrao seemed to approve. He asked Mr Sheikh to drop me back and got off at Dadar to go home. He had to return to Calcutta the next evening by the Howrah Mail.

The next day, Baba told my father to take me to what was then the Victoria Terminus train station. All the Kotwals were fair and good-looking; even Mahadoo, the malwani help, was blue-eyed and curly haired. This startled me somewhat.

There were ten minutes left for the train to leave. It was then that my future father-in-law took Balasaheb's hands in his and, pressing them with a smile, said, 'It's on.' Then he told his son, 'Vijya, go take a walk on the platform!' The two of us began to walk down that platform. Vijayrao then asked me his third question: 'You want to do this, right?'

In true Manik Pradhan style I said, 'Who asks me for my opinion?'

Vijayrao seemed deeply disappointed. Many years later, I told this story to my son Ashutosh and my daughter-in-law Ashwini. Ashutosh said, 'What kind of stupid response was that?'

I wasn't trying to be irritating. I wasn't even against the marriage. I liked the fact that Vijayrao had completed degrees in electrical and mechanical engineering from the Victoria Jubilee Technical Institute[1] and was living in Calcutta. But I had just said what I was thinking. I might have been my father's favourite child, but he had not thought it necessary to ask my opinion.

Sudhatai's (who was now confirmed as my sister-in-law) father-in-law, Mr Daji Varde, also took me to one side and asked me, 'You do want to get married to him, right? Your parents are not forcing this on you, are they?'

His question left me shaken. I was not in the habit of talking back to elders. I did not know what to say. He said sharply, 'Look me in the eye and tell me.' I was put in a spot. My words dried up. My parents' home had been a traditional one, while my first encounter with my in-laws revealed them to be quite modern and progressive. I can't say whether Daji was really convinced by my response, but he did give the green signal to our marriage. His was the deciding vote in the Kotwal family.

The First Taste of Married Life

On 29 December 1961, we got married in high style in Pune. In January 1962, I set foot in Calcutta. I enjoyed the novelty of it all, but there were culture shocks in store. From childhood, I had been intrigued by Bengali culture, thanks to my readings of Bankim Chandra Chattopadhyay, Saratchandra Chatterjee and Rabindranath Tagore. But when I went to Calcutta, the upper class, the bhadralok women, foiled my plans to get close to them and to their culture. I

---

[1] The name was changed to Veermata Jijabai Technical Institute in 1997, thus ensuring the continuity of the name by which it is best known: VJTI, the premier engineering college in India in the 1950s.

realized very quickly that I would have to learn their language. I had to learn a new language to get along in the outside world, and I had to watch my words within the house, which was twice the work. This took several years.

Vijayrao and I were the perfect example of how a couple can be diametrically opposed. We differed in everything, in our ways of thinking, in our natures. These differences were clearest in our ways of talking and behaving. I believe in giving all the details and telling him everything when he asks a question. He would respond with: 'I don't want the history of the matter. Just say yes or no.' My thoughts and feelings were always nebulous; his were precise. My moods tended to change at the drop of a hat; he was temperate by nature, his responses slow and deep.

This new version of family life exposed many of my shortcomings. Vijayrao was very busy, engrossed in his work, and I began to feel lonely. My mind was full of confusion and doubt. I tried very hard to prove myself the perfect housewife, but I had been pampered at home and found it difficult to adjust to my new situation. In the middle of all this, I had two very serious miscarriages. I grew very depressed.

Appointments were made with the top doctors in Bombay and Calcutta. It was discovered that I was Rh negative; only 2 per cent of Indians have this blood group. My father was Rh positive, my mother Rh negative, and this was how I ended up being Rh negative. When the father and the mother are both of the same Rh group, there is no problem for the child. But in my case, Vijayrao was positive and I was negative. This can have a deleterious effect on the foetus, in which case, when the child is born, sometimes a blood transfusion becomes necessary. In acute cases, these transfusions have to continue throughout life. The child can also be differently abled.

In my case, there was another problem. In the case of Rh-negative women, two miscarriages are considered as if they have already given birth twice. When I had my second miscarriage, I had been admitted to the Calcutta Railway Hospital. I was lying unconscious, with Vijayrao sitting by my side, in tears. There was no one else with us. In that state, without checking my blood, the doctors gave me 300 cc of Rh-positive blood, or so the Bombay doctors guessed. Thus, there was the grave possibility that my body had already produced antibodies against Rh-positive blood. There were doubts about whether I would be able to carry another pregnancy to term. Most women have some concerns when they find themselves pregnant for the first time. But in my case, with the next pregnancy, there was a threat not only to the child's life but also to mine. And if the child were to be born, its future was uncertain.

Chaitra Poornima, 1965. I performed a strict fast on the advice of one of my mother's friends. (And I keep that fast even now.) I began to show signs of a new pregnancy. We were then at Kharagpur. The railway hospital there was beautiful, and the doctors were extremely capable. But as we had decided earlier, in April, I was brought to Mumbai. Through this pregnancy, I was looked after by Dr Chandrakant Saraiya, who insisted that I should have a blood check-up every month. Each time I went to KEM Hospital for these investigations, my heart was in my mouth. If the number of antibodies was high, it might be necessary to intervene and abort the foetus. But by some miracle, my Rh-negative blood did not affect this little one. Apparently, there was no exchange between my negative and the foetus's positive blood. And my mind calmed down. My grandmother would say at the time: the child looks like it will be an intelligent one. He will make you all very happy.

When my cousin Shirish Kanekar would come over in the afternoon for a chat, the afternoon would dissolve into the evening as we laughed and talked. Late at night, there would be a delicious 'Pradhan-style' non-vegetarian meal, cooked by Balasaheb.

In December 1965, I began to show signs of coming close to term, after Datta Jayanti.

Joyful Days

Ashutosh made his appearance on 20 December 1965. It was forty-three minutes into the new day when he showed up. Dr Chandrakant Saraiya had predicted that this would be the date.

The family was delighted. The bouncing baby weighed nine pounds; his face was a replica of his father's. From dawn, people started coming to see us. Some called him an apple, others said he looked like the full moon.

As a child, one of my favourite authors was Y.G. Joshi; he said somewhere: 'Grandchildren are like the cream on the milk of life.' This proved true for both sides of the family.

Vijayrao's father, Mothe Baba, came to see his new grandson. I was in bed, worn out, and my father-in-law sat by me and fed me warm milk from a saucer. Ashutosh is 'Balusha' (a kind of sweet) for all of us in the family. Even for the outsiders, Marathi or otherwise, who have known him since childhood, he is Balusha. Later in his life, he was called Ash, Ashu, Kotu, etc., by his schoolmates.

When he was three or three-and-a-half months old, his naming ceremony was celebrated in high style. Vijayrao's mother said, 'He has made us all happy, so his name should be Anand (which means happiness).' My father liked it initially, but changed Anand to Nandubal. And so the silver gifts Ashutosh was given on this occasion all have 'Nandubal' inscribed on them. I am a devotee of Lord Shankar, so I wanted to name him Ashutosh. Everyone liked the name although my mother and I continued to call him Balusha. Even now we have to make an effort to refer to him as Ashutosh.

I have only one elder brother, Major Bhalchandra, otherwise known as Dilip Vaman Pradhan. Ashutosh's Dilip Mama and Urmila Mami bought him a perambulator. Urmila Mami dressed him in a fine suit and put a beauty spot on his cheek to ward off the evil eye. Later, she took him to a reputed photographer in Colaba and had his first photograph taken. Vijayrao brought a big, illustrated book called *Animal World* (Life Books).

First Steps

As time passed, Ashutosh began to grow up, and his playfulness would delight me a lot. He was extremely active and full of fun. Even as a baby, he would giggle a lot. The only occasions he would cry were when there was a delay in satiating his hunger. At times it would lead to violent protests and anger, reminding me of Sage Jamadagni, when I would feel completely helpless.

Vijayrao was still posted in Kharagpur. At that time, the electrification of the railways was in full swing. This was of great importance to the triangle between Calcutta, Tatanagar and Durg, and the coal mines in Orissa. When I reached Kharagpur with little Ashutosh, I was welcomed with great enthusiasm and excitement. The railway colony there is a legacy of the British era. The quarters were comfortable and the grounds, spacious. Each home has staff quarters attached. In my absence, Vijayrao had planted a beautiful garden around the house to welcome his princeling.

As soon as Ashutosh could walk, he began to play football in this garden. This encouraged the development of his motor skills.

His teeth began to appear at four months. On the advice of Bengali doctors, he began to drink soups and juices, and eat boiled river fish. Dr Spock's *Baby and Child Care* was my Bible.

Bath time was a hugely enjoyable and elaborate event. His grandmother had given me a list of herbs to grind and apply all over him. Then he had to be massaged with almond milk. Egg whites and Johnson's Baby Oil were the *sine qua non*. On holidays, his father would happily take over these duties.

In those days, a high dining chair was used for children. I bought a lovely one from Calcutta's New Market, but Ashutosh never used it. For he would eat on the run, all over the house and garden.

He would be over the moon when his father was around. In that hot climate, Vijayrao was in the habit of taking a shower to freshen up after he returned from work. Then he would relax, lie back and his little son would sit by his side and powder his father, bringing to the task a deep concentration. This was as close to heaven as a man could get, Vijayrao remembers.

Ashutosh started speaking late. This economy with words was an augury of things to come. He would speak in sign language. I believe he felt that if he could get his mother to understand him, why go to the trouble to speak? When I understood this, I did not respond to signs, and this forced him to speak. By two-and-a-half years, he was speaking fluently.

The evening ritual of the powder became a time when father and son bonded, telling stories and jokes. And then they would fall asleep in each other's arms.

2

The Waxing Moon

Although Ashutosh was laconic as a child, we managed, the three of us, to have some wonderful conversations. We travelled a great deal. We beguiled the hours of many train journeys with word games and riddles. We played endless games of Three Nought Four, and even though his father and I played as a team and he alone, he would win. His face would shine with the childlike enjoyment of having defeated his parents.

'Come, Je, Come' was a favourite game of his. One person must choose a thing, a person or a place. The other team must try and guess it by asking questions. Answers could only be 'Yes' or 'No'. This game would be played for hours. Ashutosh had the knack of asking the right questions.

He enjoyed puzzles made out of paper and folded handkerchiefs, and unknotting and unravelling things. He also enjoyed noughts and crosses.

But most of all he loved telling jokes and riddles. He still does. It would begin with, 'Aai, tell me a joke.' I'd realize he wanted to tell a joke. I would start him off, and then my role was only to laugh until my sides split.

I still remember the jokes he told when he was four or five years old, the expressions on his face, the gestures he made, all of which were childlike and innocent. We enjoyed listening to these jokes, the kind that children in an English-medium school tell each other. One of these jokes ran so: Once upon a time there was a family of tomatoes, off somewhere in a rush. The Little Tomato couldn't keep up with his parents and was falling behind. Father Tomato looked behind, knocked Little Tomato on the head and said, 'Ketch up!'

Another one: Which part of the body travels the most? The two wrists (tourists)!

I would always feel I should reciprocate in kind and tell him some jokes. Only I couldn't manage to think of many. Whenever I heard or read a good joke, I would try and mug it up, but when it came to the crunch, I'd forget the punchline. He had the knack of telling a joke, I just didn't.

I have set down some of the riddles Ashutosh told us between the ages of five and twelve. These are the ones I remember:

The running dog: Peter, Sophia and their dog, Zorro, are out on a walk. Peter walks at the rate of four miles per hour while Sophia manages three miles per hour. Zippy Zorro runs between the two of them, back and forth. His speed is eight miles per hour. Peter and Sophia walk for an hour. How much has Zorro run?

Answer: No need to hurt your head with too much mathematics. Simple thinking will give you the answer. However he runs and wherever he runs, in an hour Zorro will run eight miles.

Who wins the race? There is a 100-metre race between John and Jack. When John reaches the 100-metre mark, Jack could cover only 90 metres. To make the race more competitive, John was made to run 110 metres and Jack 100 metres. Who wins this race?

Answer: John's speed is 10/9 times Jack's speed. So, when John reaches the 110-metre mark, Jack has reached the 99-metre mark. John wins again.

The well-boiled egg: Mrs Chandra is known to be finicky about her boiled eggs. She believes that an egg must be boiled for exactly nine minutes. Mr Chandra has two hourglasses. One empties in seven minutes and the other in four minutes. How can Mr Chandra use the hourglasses to ensure that his wife gets the perfect boiled egg?

Answer: Both are to be inverted simultaneously. When the four-minute hourglass is empty, it is to be turned over again. When the seven-minute hourglass is empty, that means one minute of the four-minute hourglass is left. Start boiling the egg now. After one minute, when the four-minute hourglass is empty, turn it over, and four minutes later, turn it over again. The egg will be boiled for precisely nine minutes.

Ashutosh's paternal grandmother was proud of his simple behaviour, lack of self-importance and his eating habits. They would play hide-and-seek for hours in the Kharagpur house. His grandfather always had a stock of sweets and chocolates. If Ashutosh were given one, he would run to find his grandmother and share it with her. This, too, made her very proud. He loved her puffed-rice laddoos.

My mother, Indutai, loved cooking. Ashutosh loved her non-vegetarian food, but her colocasia, cutlets, spicy buttermilk, sour and spicy lentils and sprouted pulses were his special favourites. Indutai loved English literature as much as she loved the language. She appreciated those who spoke English well. When we went to Pune to stay with her, Ashutosh would run off to play with the neighbour's children for hours. The children spoke chaste Marathi. That her grandson who lived in another state and studied in a convent school could still speak good Marathi was a source of pride for Indutai.

When I would take little Ashutosh to Pune, he would play with his cousin Deepa, who was a year his junior and Dilip Mama's daughter. They would be running about the backyard of the bungalow. From time to time, Deepa would wail, 'Hey Indu, look at what Balusha is up to.' And sometimes Indutai would get annoyed and yell at them, 'What's all this? You miss each other when one of you is not around and when you meet you start fighting?'

Then Deepa would weep even louder. And Ashutosh would reply with a straight face, 'That's part of the fun too.' Indutai's anger would fade, and she would have to hide a smile.

When Ashutosh was very young, his father went on a business trip to Japan. When he returned, he brought back many battery-operated toys, including a spaceship called Sputnik. One day, I settled Ashutosh down for a nap in the afternoon. Later, I realized that it was getting late, but he had not woken up. So, I popped my head around the door and the scene on the bed left me stunned. He had used a little screwdriver to open the toys and had dismantled them. He was examining the parts with great care. I watched silently. Once he had finished his examination, he put them together again. It was only when everything had been set right that he noticed my presence and grinned.

I cannot remember him ever being obstinate, complaining or whining, or asking for anything. He loved koshimbir, vegetables and fruit as much as he enjoyed non-vegetarian food. Whatever he was served, he ate with enjoyment. He just did not care for oily or spicy food. His basic temperament was sunny and content. He never threw tantrums, but he knew his own mind. I was not familiar with child psychology, but it did occur to me that no one should try and meddle with the basic nature of a child. Not even the child's mother.

Outsiders saw him as a quiet child. There may be many reasons for reticence: shyness, conceit, misanthropy, being a bookworm and self-centredness, among others. But I figured out that this was a trait he had received as his patrimony from his father and paternal grandmother. It was also a deliberate choice. Others would think of his silence as reticence, but if his bent of mind towards logical thinking and action therefrom led to his articulate and precise use of words, then how was he at fault? Since he would listen to what others had to say with tolerance and attention, since he spoke with politeness to his seniors and made appropriate responses to his equals, I did not think it necessary to see anything untoward in this trait of his.

On the other hand, I often thought I could learn something from him.

First School

When Ashutosh turned three, Vijayrao was transferred back to Calcutta, and so it was there that my son's education began in earnest. When he was three and a half, we admitted him to the Southpoint School in Ballygunje's Dover Lane. But his first guru was always his Papa. He enjoyed sitting on his father's lap at the dining table and tracing the letters and numbers. For the first three or four days of school, he cried a lot. This was rather distressing. His father had gone to Hyderabad for a fortnight. Before leaving, he had asked his son, 'Now you will go to school every day, right?' And so Ashutosh would go to school every day.

There was no trouble getting him out of bed, nor was he ever late. I would go and pick him up after class. His class teacher was a young woman by the name of Roma Nandy. When school let out, all the children would stream out and run to their ayahs. Only Ashutosh would stay where he was and would stare at me, unblinking. Only when Roma-di said, 'You can go now, Ashutosh', would he run up to me and kiss me.

At this time, I was always worried about Ashutosh's physical well-being. His tonsils gave him endless trouble. He would get high fevers that lasted a couple of days. These episodes would frighten me. Now I think back and feel I didn't know anything about bringing up a child. I often had to force him to eat, I feel bad about it even now. But we also laughed together, played together and roamed around together. Once his father had left for the office, Ashutosh and I would catch a tram and go shopping at Gariahat Market or visit some Marathi friends we knew.

Calcutta's trams were always packed; one never knew where they were going to stop. Our little one got rather good at running and jumping aboard a tram. The driver and conductor of the tram and the people on board were gentle souls. They would make room for us and ask us to sit down. There would be a chorus of enthusiastic shouts in Bengali—'Let Sister sit down!', 'Be careful while the kid is getting down!' In the evening, our son would recount all these sagas to Vijayrao. Now he could speak Bengali as well as he spoke Marathi. There were two domestic helpers, Parul and Sumitra, with whom he would chatter away in Bengali. He would sit on their laps and explain the stories from his illustrated Marathi books in Bengali. They would enjoy this tremendously and laugh a lot.

༺࿅༻

Story Time

Vijayrao had brought a fine tape recorder from Japan. Ashutosh's maternal great-grandmother (Panji) from Pune had told him stories.

These included 'The Pathan and the Sparrow', 'The Monkeys and the Berries' and 'The Old Lady's Rice', and Ashutosh could recount these with great flair and in the correct Konkani accent. But he was reluctant to perform them for his father. Then one day, we had a full recording session of these stories on the new tape recorder, just the two of us. These tapes are still in my safe custody.

That tender, sonorous voice, that clear diction; it gives us a lot of pleasure every time we play these tapes.

As he grew up, I felt there was a lacuna in my parenting, and this worried me for a long time. Until he was five or six, I would tell him stories. These were generally about birds and animals; some I invented myself, others I took from the tales my grandmother had told me, and a few came from the Puranas and other classical sources. I would throw in some verses and some acting as well to enhance the ones I had invented. But this ended after he got to be about six years old. His curiosity grew and my flair seemed to diminish. When I told him a story from the Puranas, some of the incidents I would describe or the behaviour of the characters in the story, or some elements of blind faith, would not sit well with him. I could not answer satisfactorily the incisive questions he began to ask. I grew diffident about telling him stories. I bought several books and began to do some reading myself to see if I could understand what was going on.

What surprised me was that he liked the stories my mother told. My mother loved English literature. Her favourite authors were W. Somerset Maugham, A. J. Cronin and Thomas Hardy, and she would tell him stories from their oeuvres with great enjoyment.

To my mind, these were not stories a boy his age would enjoy. Perhaps it was her skill at telling the stories that made him enjoy them. It was also possible that my mother was a stern woman who did not have the knack of talking to young children. But they were united by the love of stories. Although he did not speak much when he was young, Ashutosh always liked people.

In 1969–70, the Naxalbari movement was at its peak. Bombs were exploding across the city of Calcutta. Trams and buses were being burnt. Chief Minister Jyoti Basu's home was along the route we used every day. There was strict security along that road. Vijayrao would take Ashutosh to school at 9 a.m., and I would pick him up again at noon. And sometimes, suddenly during these three hours, a riot would begin. In those days, most homes did not have phones. If I somehow heard of a riot happening, I would be terrified. I would drop everything and rush to the school. Once I had him safe, I would calm down again. We would wait it out in the school and take a rickshaw home once things had calmed down and it was safe.

In 1970, Ashutosh was four-and-a-half years old. In Calcutta's Garden Reach Railway Community, there was a lovely couple, Sarla Ramchandran and her husband. Their children, a boy and a girl, were a little older than Ashutosh. We went to stay with them for a weekend. The children were romping about. We tried to call them for lunch, but when they paid no heed for a long time, I went out to bring Ashutosh in, physically if necessary. When I picked him up by his arms, my hands were nearly singed. The thermometer said he had a fever of 104 degrees Fahrenheit. I was frightened. When he had a fever, I would cradle Ashutosh in my lap. I did not need a thermometer to tell me when the fever was rising or falling. Sarla called the doctor. The medicines he prescribed brought the fever down for a while and then it would rise again to 105 degrees. The Bengali doctor recommended that we pour a bucket of water over his head if his fever increased. Sarla and Ramchandran kept vigil with me for three nights and three days, pouring water over him.

They would speak to each other in Tamil, and that would frighten me even more.

On the fourth day, pustules broke out all over his body and the doctor said he had measles. The couple said that they had been suspecting this all along. When the pustules erupted, his temperature became normal. When his fever broke, it was Ashutosh's habit to start playing in bed or to tell me jokes and riddles. Now he began to imitate the children in class for me. I knew what this was about, but Sarla was terrified.

She thought he was hallucinating since he was rolling his eyes and generally behaving strangely. After the ordeal of the last four days, I was feeling a bit relaxed. Now it was Sarla's turn of anxiety, and I had to calm her down.

We lived in Calcutta from March 1969 to September 1970. Before leaving the city, we had Maha Prasad at the famous Ganapati Bappa pandal in Maharashtra Niwas on Hajara Road, and then it was on to Vijayrao's new posting, Lucknow. Ashutosh was four years and nine months old then.

3

Lucknow—A Time to Cherish

We were in Lucknow for six years. Calcutta's humid air had caused Ashutosh frequent tonsillitis attacks with high fever. Lucknow's dry and cool air rid him of this problem. Ashutosh grew in grace and strength thereafter.

The Alambagh area in Lucknow had a huge housing community: the Research Design and Standards Organization of the Indian Railways. Surrounded by many trees and large maidans, the houses were lovely. The children could play freely and safely.

There was just one problem. There was only one school in the colony: St Mary's Convent. They had stopped allowing admission in the middle of the academic term. There were some famous schools in the city, but we had no car to take Ashutosh there and bring him back. I was in tears at the thought of him not getting into school. A new friend, Renu Pal, told me about City Montessori, a small school in one corner of the colony.

Ashutosh got admission there, but the school asked me if I would help with the teaching. The next year, the principal of St Mary's herself invited Ashutosh to join the school and asked me if I would teach there.

As a child, Ashutosh was always careful about his homework. The nuns of the school were very loving but strict disciplinarians. Ashutosh did not like being scolded in school. In the early morning, he would suddenly wake up from deep sleep, stretch and then turn to me, sleeping by his side, and say, 'Aai, homework!' I never had to push him to study. I did not like doing this, and I would not have been able to do it either. Until he went to the eighth or ninth standard, he would ask for my help with mathematics and the languages. But other than that, he was independent. I never had to supervise his work.

Lucknow was a relaxed time. Ashutosh made progress in all subjects. He was a quiet and obedient child and so the nuns loved him. I was always around, keeping an eye on him. At the same time, I could observe other children his age.

This brought a good balance to my relationship with him. I was relieved of the pressure of parenting and he could grow at his own pace in the pleasant surroundings of Lucknow. He would play table tennis at the club and win prizes. Cricket, of course, and now he added badminton. The Railway Club in Lucknow was beautiful and well-decorated and close to the houses in the community. We had lots of friends. Next door was the Desai family whose youngest, Nilesh, was Ashutosh's best friend. They played together and spent a lot of time with each other. Sucheta (Mickey) and Sundeep were Nilesh's elder siblings. They also liked Ashutosh. Vidyatai, Nilesh's mother, was a close friend. And so Ashutosh had a special place in the Desai family.

Realm of Fine Arts

There was a large maidan right in front of our house. Naseemji, a young and enthusiastic hockey coach, offered instruction there. Naseemji was a hero in the eyes of his young students, including Nilesh and Ashutosh.

Godbole Kaka, who was steeped in the fine arts, came home to teach painting and drawing. Ashutosh's painting of a golden oriole won a prize, and the community talked about it for days. While he was learning from Godbole Kaka, he was also compelled to listen to the songs of Pankaj Mullick and K.L. Saigal, which Godbole Kaka insisted were a good background score to these classes; Ashutosh had to listen to and appreciate these singers as well.

My father Balasaheb, too, was a fan of these singers. He had a complete collection of their 78 rpms. When I went home, I would love to listen to these songs again.

Ashutosh would sit with me and listen to '*Babul mora*' and '*Duniya rang-rangeelee*' and '*Piya milan ko jaanaa*'. We would sing Saigal's '*Ek raaje ka beta lekar udnewala ghoda*' and act it out as well. We also got to hear Bal Gandharva's immortal voice on Balasaheb's gramophone. Ashutosh listened with rapt attention.

As a child, Ashutosh had no liking for the cinema. But Vijayrao and I loved the cinema. And so we sometimes dragged him along. He liked the circus and we went many times but Ashutosh found the movie *Mera Naam Joker* a bore.

Lucknow had a vibrant cultural scene and so we got to hear many fine classical singers and watched many classical dancers of repute. At the Baradari of Lucknow, through the night of Holi, we watched Pandit Birju Maharaj dance and sing for us, an unforgettable performance. Ashutosh loved it. He was particularly impressed by the maestro's command of percussion.

Anup Jalota was a college-going youth who lived in Lucknow then. He would come to our Railway Club's programmes as an accompanist on the harmonium, which is how I got to know him. He recommended his tabla player Pradeep Acharya to us. Both Vijayrao and Ashutosh learnt the tabla under his guidance for a while. Unfortunately, Pradeep died in an accident and that put an end to the lessons.

We watched dancers of the stature of Sonal Mansingh, Yamini Krishnamurthi and Swapnasundari in Lucknow for the first time. Sitara Devi, the queen of Kathak, and her nephew Gopi Krishna would often dance together in Lucknow. Lucknow was the home of Kathak. The artistry of Pandit Lachhu Maharaj and Pandit Birju Maharaj is inscribed forever in our minds.

While in Lucknow, we heard the young Amjad Ali Khan on the sarod, Pandit Shiv Kumar Sharma on the santoor and Hari Prasad Chaurasia's flute in a jugalbandi, and Pandit Kumar Gandharva singing the folk songs of Malwa. Hemant Kumar who sang for many Hindi films regaled us with an evening of chaste Rabindra Sangeet ... these were unforgettable experiences, and Ashutosh absorbed them all and stored them away.

4

Minuses and Pluses

In Lucknow, I realized that Ashutosh had a flair for language. I would buy Marathi books for him, and Balasaheb would send them too. They would be read with great attention. Lucknow had a peculiar Nawabi style of speaking Hindi. Even though he was in an English-medium school, the language on the playground was generally this variant of Hindi. And there were many Bengali settlements too. I kept up with watching Hindi and Bengali plays, the latter being mostly by Tagore. Ashutosh enjoyed both of them. He also studied Sanskrit during this time.

There was a vibrant Marathi Mandal in Lucknow where cultural programmes of various kinds were held. It would often enter state-level theatre competitions, under my leadership. Ashutosh did not take part in the plays, but he won many prizes in the elocution competitions. He had learnt chapters nine and twelve of the Bhagavad Gita and many other shlokas (verses) as well. His pronunciation of Sanskrit was excellent. He would recite the shlokas when he was bathing and well scrubbed, he would sit cross-legged and recite the Gayatri Mantra. This made me happy.

However, it was at an elocution competition that Ashutosh had a moment. He had learnt a poem by heart and had recited it at home perfectly. But at the Rajdhani Hall, seeing a huge crowd, he got stage fright and blanked out. I was watching and gesturing to him from the wings. He was stumbling and faltering, but he would not give up nor would he return to the wings. Only when he had finished did he come off the stage and say to me, 'Don't ever ask me to take part again. That was awful.'

Another similar incident happened in Lucknow. He would spend all day with his friends. Around 6 p.m., it would grow dark, and the children would begin to return home. There were many brother-and-sister pairs among his friends. They would all run off home in each other's company, laughing and talking or fighting … but they were *together*. At these times, Ashutosh would walk home alone. And when he reached home, I would also be alone, because his father would often be on tour or working late at the office. In the cold weather, I would close the windows and doors tight to keep out the draughts. Then that large house would seem terribly cold and quiet. I would give him an oil massage and a hot bath, which we both enjoyed. But when he sat down to dinner, he was alone again. Then he would say, 'Aai, all my friends go home with someone. I'm the only one who comes home alone.' When his father was on long tours, he would miss him and repeatedly ask, 'When will Papa be back?'

Uncle Chandoke's predictions

From Lucknow we travelled to the Himalayas a lot. Once when we were in Srinagar, we went to have lunch with our friends, the

Chandokes. Mr Chandoke was an amateur astrologer and began to read Vijayrao's palm. Ashutosh was playing nearby with a young Chandoke. But little pitchers have big ears.

The first thing Mr Chandoke said was that a promotion was quite close for Vijayrao. We didn't see any possibility of that happening because it had not been very long since he had been promoted to Joint Director. But this prediction came true. In 1976, the railways established Rail India Technical and Economic Services (RITES). This company was created to liaise with other nations for the exchange of technology, to receive and give assistance and other such matters. Vijayrao was chosen as the first head of the electrical department, and we had to go to Delhi.

The second prediction was that we were going to buy a car and land in the near future, and that he would build a house. That too seemed laughable because one needs savings for these things, and Vijayrao was not in the habit of doing any such thing. If he felt like buying something, he went ahead and did it. And even that slowly began to come to pass.

The third prediction: we would have another child. Ashutosh was eight-and-a-half years old when these forecasts were being made. In the next two years, as he saw the first two of Chandoke's predictions coming true, Ashutosh asked me, 'Aai, Uncle Chandoke's third prediction will also come true, won't it?' I could see what he was thinking. And so I sat him down and explained to him what the matter was. When I explained the scientific basis of the problem, about the Rh-negative and Rh-positive blood groups and all the rest of that, he began to understand. After that, he never mentioned the lack of siblings again. One day, he said to me, 'Anyway, I'm all grown up now. If I had a brother or sister, they'd be so much younger than me. What good would that do me? You and I are doing fine together.'

He kept himself happy with daily school life and the holidays and trips we took together. And when we went to meet his grandparents, he would find a bunch of children to hang out with.

He loved both his grandfathers. He and Balasaheb would joke and laugh and tease for hours. A story from when he was five-and-a-half: Vijayrao had gone to Rourkee for six weeks for a training course, so I took Ashutosh to stay in Pune. Balasaheb had retired, and he had started building a house. He would go and buy the materials himself. He chose the labourers and supervised the work as well. When Balasaheb was giving his workers instructions, Ashutosh was all ears. He would watch as Balasaheb checked the purchases or when he was talking to the workers. After tea in the evening, we would all take a trip to the site. He would romp around on the piles of sand and mud, and he would look forward to these expeditions. 'When are we going to the site for discussions?' he would ask Balasaheb all day. Seeing his grandson's excitement would double the joy Balasaheb was taking in the construction.

His friendship with his paternal grandfather was a little different. Mothe Baba was a scientist (a chemist) and took a deep interest in scientific news and new inventions.

Both grandfathers had extensive libraries. Mothe Baba had a beautiful collection of books on outer space and the stars. Ashutosh loved looking at these books. Eventually, Mothe Baba gave them to Ashutosh.

∽

Our Triumvirate

Of course, he didn't have his grandparents around all the time. The three of us had become a unit unto ourselves as we moved around

India, from Kharagpur to Calcutta, Lucknow to Delhi, and Mumbai. The last word in the family was always Vijayrao's, but it was also true that all decisions of significance were made keeping Ashutosh's well-being in mind. Father and son were like friends from the very beginning. For years, Ashutosh would address him as 'Hey Pappa', and Vijayrao quite liked that. He still treats us as his equals, but you can see his love and his openness in this behaviour. But he never crossed the limits of politeness, decency and respect.

One day, when he was very young, he said to me, 'Aai, Pappa's work is in the office, yours is at home and mine is in school!' He had worked things out in his own childlike way. 'Since Aai and Pappa do their respective jobs with joy and pleasure, I too should do my schoolwork in the same way.' That he had internalized this idea was clear from his behaviour.

He was of course the apple of our eyes, but we never spoiled him nor did we pamper him. As he grew older, it became clear that he knew his own mind but he never threw a tantrum. He liked books, toys and travelling; but he never made a fuss about clothes, food or things like that. We were three musketeers. When it was time for a trip, he would make lists of important things to take along and plan the packing. He would make a budget for the trip and then write down the actual expenses incurred against that.

He had to understand how things worked and why things happened the way they did. This was a habit of mind he formed when he was very young. The principles behind everything were very important to him. These had to be explained even when he was seven or eight years old.

And then the time came for the roles to shift around. He began to grow in both intellectual and emotional ways, and I began to feel that it was he who was helping me grow up.

As he began to make strides and achieve milestones, I was certainly proud of him.

But when our friends would praise me for what he was doing, I would feel a little embarrassed. For if I thought about it clearly, I could not tell how, as a mother, I had contributed to his successes. I had fed him and clothed him; I had looked after him when he was unwell; I had taught him when he needed it and to the extent that I could. But there was nothing extraordinary in any of this. I brought him books to read. I got him to learn things by heart: poems, shlokas, prayers and such. His father's interests included travelling, nature trips, adventure sports, games, gardening and swimming. He drew Ashutosh into all these.

But more important than this was his involvement in his son's development; he instilled in his son a love for intellectual pursuits and objectivity. He guided him through the maze of higher education. He would try and understand everything his son was doing, studying or researching. They would discuss these for hours with evident enjoyment.

When they encounter the outside world, children ask hundreds of questions. I don't remember Ashutosh bombarding me with questions though. He would be making his own observations and would often be lost in his own thoughts. He liked to find out the meaning of things or events on his own. His desire to know was part of his make-up. His father would bring him little books of general knowledge on subjects like nature, birds and animals, fish, stars and constellations, herbs, minerals, human history, and true-life adventure stories. When his father went to Calcutta, he would go to a special shop in Dalhousie Chowk and buy whatever issues of the journal *Knowledge* were available.

One with Nature

Even as a child, it was clear that Ashutosh was deeply interested in the world around him. Children generally do enjoy nature, trees, birds, flowers, that sort of thing. As he grew older, he began to get interested in the serenity of the mountain peaks of the Sahyadris and the Himalayas, the profound songs of the sea, the unexplored areas of jungles. It was as if the stones and rocks spoke to him without words and gestures and Ashutosh was able to understand what they were saying.

Rocks and stones of different kinds were an obsession for him from childhood. Our living room was decorated with a host of specimens, drawn from different parts of the country, from the tops of mountains to the seashores. I can still see the young Ashutosh returning from school, his head bent down, scanning the ground for any interesting sample to add to his collection.

Perhaps it was this deep attraction to nature that made him silent on occasions.

Even as a child, he was overwhelmed by the grandeur of nature. He wanted to understand nature's workings, either in the beauty of its calm moments or in the Sturm und Drang of its rages. I believe that this is where his interest in science began; the inspiration lay in his relationship with nature.

When Ashutosh was five years old, we went to Rajgir. This was where Gautam Buddha lived for thirteen years, in a capital city built on seven hills. It is a very beautiful area. The Japanese have built a beautiful stupa on one of the hills; the first cable ropeway in the country was constructed to take people to it. When our turn came, Vijayrao scooped Ashutosh up and sat down. I was terrified; the chair looked tiny and would hang in the air, suspended from a cable. But I gathered up all my courage and got into another chair.

For half an hour we were dangling 20–25 feet above the ground. I kept my eyes firmly on my family; they were enjoying the view like free birds. I did not show my son my fear, and his father of course had no fear to show.

Wherever we went, father and son were lost in their own world. It became very late when we were returning from Chandanwadi in Kashmir. The road was rocky; snowcapped peaks on all four sides—after all this was the Himalayas—and then a cold wind began to blow. I was in a state of near collapse. Eight-year-old Ashutosh seemed unaffected by that bone-chilling mountain breeze. This seemed to happen everywhere we went in Pahalgam. We spent the whole day over riverbeds and bridges and had many adventurous moments! We lost all sense of direction. We couldn't find our way back. No one was in sight. We were somewhere on the road to Amarnath. It was now growing dark. Then Ashutosh spotted a cottage that looked exactly like the one featured in the *Bobby* song, '*Hum tum ek kamre mein bandh ho*' (You and me, in a locked room…) and taking his bearings from that, he gave us directions home. And so we got back, after walking in the mountain valleys for an hour and a half, laughing and talking, for all the world as if nothing had happened.

Who knows what was going on in his head at that time? Sometimes he would share his thoughts with me. He would try and explain what he meant, gesticulating to make his meaning clear. I have a vague recollection of him asking me once why there could not be other multi-dimensional worlds, just like ours, just like the one we experience, that intersected with our own, but I could not really understand what he meant.

Conversations with Mother

I had a liking for literature and art. As a child, I introduced Ashutosh to these subjects and he developed a liking for them, a penchant that continues to this day. But he seemed more inclined to appreciate than to create. He was tutored in painting as a child and drew well. Even today, I enjoy listening to him when he talks about the finer points of the paintings of the great masters.

I suppose I should at least mention the things I did as a mother, what I did and didn't do. I did not force him to do anything that went against his basic nature. I did not allow his basic temperament to be disturbed in any way.

From time to time, he would fall silent, and I have to confess that this disturbed me a little. But I learnt to take it in my stride. Although he didn't talk much, he did enjoy talking to me, and even as a child knew how to make me talk. On holidays, he would initiate conversation, with an elegantly worded question. And then we would talk for hours.

But then there would also be quiet times when he would not speak but from certain questions he asked, I would imagine that it was because he was pondering some deep and profound question.

A story from August–September 1975, around the time of the Ganapati celebrations. Ashutosh was just about ten years old. He had learnt and recited two chapters of the Bhagavad Gita in the previous year's celebrations. That year I was directing and setting Vidyadhar Pundalik's play *Mata Draupadi*. The rehearsals would happen at our house, which meant Ashutosh would overhear the dialogues. The play depicts the myriad shades of emotion—of surpassing joy, hot anger, deep dejection and sadness—that Draupadi goes through before she can arrive at the place where she understands the importance of compassion and forgiveness. It is also the moment that she is transformed into the universal mother, achieving motherhood in the fullest form. Krishna appears in that phase as a human being and a friend of Draupadi and He expounds the philosophy of the Bhagavad Gita.

When Ashutosh had been memorizing the chapters of the Bhagavad Gita, I had explained the broad themes to him. He had obviously understood the difference between karmasanyaas and sanyaas, between karmatyaag and karmaphalatyaag. At one point, he used these concepts to explain some lines in the play to me. I often felt that my own worldview had been clarified by our conversations.

He told me that even in the kitchen, there were scientific principles at work and that I should try and understand them and apply them. I didn't understand what he was saying. I would say, 'I'm simply using the wisdom of the ages. I work according to my convenience and make some compromises to accommodate my comfort. The food should be conducive to good health; things should not be destroyed by misuse; time should not be wasted; these are the rules by which I work. Why should I concern myself with anything more?' He would try and explain what he meant but I didn't get it; I still don't.

He must have seen that I had no interest in science at the time. I had been appointed a teacher at St. Mary's Convent, Lucknow, to teach Mathematics and English. But when the science teacher went on leave, they asked me to stand in and teach science too. Ashutosh was worried that my fundamentals were poor and that I would therefore mislead my students. So I would take tuition from him every day before I started planning my class.

On holidays, Ashutosh would get up early but instead of bathing, he would start doing something he enjoyed. I had to get after him to take his bath. Eventually, I had to actually push him into the bathroom. Then he would begin to play with the hot water and the cold and so it was equally difficult to get him out of there. I had to drag him out again.

At school, I had to teach the concept of inertia to the seventh standard. In other words, the property of matter by which it stays in a state of constant motion or at rest, unless acted upon by an external force or object. This was one of Newton's laws. I would use Ashutosh's bath antics as a way of explaining inertia. When I told him this, he said: 'Wah, wah, Aai. Your science is getting really good.'

Lucknow was good for Ashutosh. Between the ages of four and ten, he thrived in this environment. The air was clean, the water was good, the school was in the colony, he had a bunch of friends, the teachers were competent, there were facilities for sports and lots of cultural activities.

We had come to Lucknow in September 1970, after a Ganpati lunch in Calcutta. We left Lucknow in September 1976, after we had eaten Ganpati prasada in Lucknow and headed to Delhi.

5

Destination Delhi

After six years in Lucknow, Vijayrao had been sent on deputation to RITES in Delhi. Our three years in Delhi were different, but they were as good as Lucknow. The first job was to find a good school for Ashutosh and then to locate a suitable house nearby.

In September 1976, all the schools had completed three months of the course, and the first term examinations were soon to be held. We were turned down by every school to which we applied. On Mathura Road, there was a Delhi Public School (DPS), a famous institution. That was the school of our choice. We told them, 'Take whatever test you want of the child.' When the railway minister, Mohammed Shafi Qureishi, gave us a letter of recommendation, Principal Deendayal agreed to give Ashutosh a test.

A New School

The task of setting a test was given to a senior teacher, Mrs Madan. She had set question papers in all the subjects. Ashutosh was given these papers to answer, sitting alone in a room on the top floor. I was in the foyer downstairs. Every half an hour or so, I saw Mrs Madan coming down the stairs or climbing them, and I would look at her with my heart in my mouth. Each time, her chubby face looked a little brighter and more excited. She would say, 'The boy is still writing, he's hard at it.' He had found a place in her good books already, but the teachers were in no mood to cooperate. Taking a new student at this point in time would disrupt the dynamics of the class. 'Oh dear,' Mrs Madan would say, 'you have no idea what sort of child you are refusing!' She took ten-and-a-half-year-old Ashutosh by the hand, leading him from class to class, until finally, Mrs Kalpana Chaudhuri, a young teacher, accepted him into her class.

In eight days, he acquired some knowledge of algebra and French. He studied hard and in many subjects, he topped the class. Then the attitude of the teachers and the students improved. He now had some French too.

Ashutosh would go swimming with his father in the Railway Club swimming pool, but it was in the school's Olympic-size swimming pool and under the supervision of competent coaches that he learnt to swim well. DPS had a huge ground with some superb horses that had been retired from the army. These were taken care of by Jat subedars and so Ashutosh learnt how to ride here. The school required each student to take two extracurricular activities. Ashutosh chose horse-riding and public speaking with no prompting from us.

The school had an eight-day National Cadet Corps camp in Nainital, nestled in the foothills of the Himalayas. When Ashutosh returned, he was full of tales of the towering peaks, the various trees he had seen in the forest, and the famous Naini Lake. After a few days, I met one of his teachers. 'How come you never came to fight with us?' she asked. I didn't know what she was talking about. 'The excessive heat at the camp, the shortage of water, the bad food? All the other parents came to complain about the trip.' I asked Ashutosh and he said, 'You wouldn't have been able to bear it so I didn't want to tell you how bad things were.'

DPS had an annual survey of the students' marks and the best were put up on a list. In the sixth, seventh and eighth standards, Ashutosh topped the lists. He was awarded a green blazer, which the school called a scholar's gown.

In the eighth standard, Ashutosh won the Delhi Board scholarship. I never received a complaint from the school. I taught at St. Mary's Convent and at the Cathedral School; I knew the teachers at these schools quite well. I did not teach at DPS but when I went to pick him up from additional classes, I did meet some of his teachers. They would usually express their satisfaction about his behaviour. When he had just arrived in the sixth standard, his teacher, Kalpana Chaudhuri, told me: 'He is very quiet. I think he needs to talk a little more, feel a little free.'

When he was in the eighth standard, he came home one day and said, 'The physics teacher, Mathur Sir, wants to meet you.' He looked downcast so I was a bit alarmed. The next day when I went to meet Mr Mathur, he seemed a bit upset. After I introduced myself, he said nothing for a while and kept wiping the perspiration off his face. I thought he was going to make some terrible complaint about my son; I waited with bated breath. Finally, he picked up the courage, it seemed, and said, 'He talks far too much. He doesn't pay any attention to my teaching. He is the best student, but I wish he would be a little quiet during classes. The other children follow his lead.'

I had to control my laughter. I gave Mr Mathur my assurance that I would correct my son at home, but first, I went to meet Mrs Chaudhuri to tell her what progress her favourite student had made in just two years!

～

Adoration and Intimacy

Our home in Delhi was rather imposing and modern in style. All three of us loved it. If we did not go out for a picnic or a trip on the weekends, Vijayrao and Ashutosh would busy themselves, gardening or climbing trees. Kalindi Colony was right on the banks of the Yamuna River. It was a new construction with the houses wide apart, and we had really nice neighbours on either side. One of them was a Sikh family. Satnam Aunty and Tej Aunty were very fond of Ashutosh. In front of us, Sheila Aunty was my friend. She taught me to drive. She too was full of praise for Ashutosh. All these were business families and wealthy. Sheila would say, 'Your son is special. Even if we were to take bags of money with us, our children would not get admission in Delhi Public School.' We were the only ones in government service, and so in their eyes we were a special breed. Ashu was a model for all their children. Vijay and Pravin, Sheila's sons, were Ashutosh's friends.

Kalindi Colony had its own cricket team. Satnam Aunty's daughter Simran (Simi) would tie a 'Rakhdi' for her two brothers and for her Ashu Bhaiya every year.

Delhi's summer and winter are extreme. The wind off the Yamuna would bite into our bones in the winter. In the summer, we had to get Ashu to the bus stop at 6 a.m.; in the winter, it was six-thirty. The route the bus took went alongside the Yamuna before arriving at Nizamuddin. In the winter, the uniform was a blue long-sleeved sweater, grey flannel shorts and socks and shoes.

We had a stream of guests when we lived in Delhi. Ashutosh's 'Dada Kaka', his father's elder brother whom I knew as Shridhar Kaka, 'Anu Kaka' (Sadanand Varde), my brother 'Dilip Mama' and when Parliament was in session, Mrunaltai Gore, my husband's maternal cousin, would come and stay. Longer stays were made by Mothi Aai, Mothe Baba, Indutai and Balasaheb, Ashutosh's maternal cousin Deepa, my maternal cousin Vilas Kanekar (Shirish Kanekar's younger brother), and we would wander around Delhi and its environs with them. Vilas Mama became our great friend and still is. With Deepa, we had a fine time and much repartee was exchanged. Ashutosh loved it when the Pune crowd visited.

A story from March 1977. The annual examinations of the sixth standard were approaching, Ashutosh's first examination in that school. He was very happy that his paternal grandfather (Mothe Baba) was coming to stay. His paternal grandmother (Mothi Aai) had gone to Igatpuri for a month-long Vipassana course. Mothe Baba and Ashutosh began to make extensive plans about what they would do together after the examinations were over. On the last day of the examination, Mothe Baba fell very ill. He was eighty-one and had a slender physique, but he had not had any health issues before this. He was very uneasy and, in a short while, he was terribly uncomfortable. We were still new to Delhi, and that day I was alone at home with my father-in-law. We didn't even have a phone. At the time, there weren't many people living in Kalindi Colony.

We had an account in the Punjab National Bank, which was close by. I knew the manager there by face. I ran to the bank and asked for his advice. He directed me to Dr Sabharwal's Jeewan Hospital, about a mile-and-a-half away from our house. There wasn't much public transport in Delhi. Somehow, I managed to get a rickshaw and took Baba to the hospital. The doctor diagnosed an enlarged prostate and began treatment immediately. When Mothe Baba was a little better, I went home and started cooking for lunch. The time for Ashutosh's return from the examination and the time of my departure with lunch for Mothe Baba coincided. I caught him on the way from the bus stop, told him what had happened in brief, and went to the hospital. Four or five days later, Mothe Baba had to have an operation. He had to be in the hospital for the next fifteen days. Each day, Ashutosh would faithfully take the lunch I made to the hospital, sit with his grandfather and keep him company. In this, he demonstrated a great maturity. After Mothe Baba came home, we had to take great care of him for the next two months. It was only Ashutosh's company that helped him get through the heat of Delhi and his new disability and weakness. After a month and a half, Mothe Aai finished her course and came to us. By this time, Mothe Baba's health had improved tremendously.

6

Wandering at Will

When I was young, my parents had lived for some years in Delhi. Now that they had returned as guests with us, they wanted to rekindle old memories and revisit their old stomping grounds (Safdarjung's Tomb, Lodhi Gardens, Red Fort, Qutab Minar). When Ashutosh's father was driving, he would relax; but if I were at the wheel, Ashutosh would pay anxious attention.

Each winter weekend we would pack the car with lots of food, fruit, thermoses of tea and coffee, some toys and games, and set off for another destination.

We made unforgettable trips to Agra, Fatehpur Sikri and the Bharatpur National Park. When we set out from Delhi, we had only planned trips to the Taj Mahal, Agra and Fatehpur Sikri. We loved our old Fiat car, which was pretty much an antique. Vijayrao would be at the wheel, I would be next to him and at the window would be Ashutosh, map in hand. In the back would be my father and mother and Vilas Mama. In the winter, this wasn't uncomfortable; in fact, it made the car quite warm. We would laugh and talk and joke a lot. We would stop at will, if we saw some interesting sight or if the desire to eat something suddenly took hold of us. And then the backseat crowd would doze off.

Ashutosh had the knack of keeping the dialogue with his father alive just to keep him alert for driving. He would navigate and point out places of interest along the way.

Our car was a faithful trooper, but if a problem arose, it was always Ashutosh who would lend his father a hand when the bonnet was opened. Perhaps I should remind my reader that all this happened more than forty years ago. There weren't too many places on the roads where a private vehicle could find mechanics or help. But these two were never discouraged.

My parents and I were deeply fond of history. The two of them were voracious readers. This meant that they were always ready with the history of any place we visited and would add some fables or legends of the area as well. After listening for a while, Mr Kotwal and Junior would slip away, leaving their guests lost in their dream world. But then I knew that father and son would already have familiarized themselves with every detail from the architecture of the period to the specific properties of the design, the history of warfare and battles, the techniques and scientific principles of construction.

If we were to go and see something, the time was to be used to its fullest; that was the house rule. Hunger, thirst, fatigue—these problems were of the body and were not to be given much consideration.

And so it happened that as we completed a wonderful trip to Agra and its surroundings, the map seemed to indicate that the Bharatpur Bird Sanctuary was not too far off. If we had come so far, perhaps we should take the effort to go and see the pelicans, so the Kotwals felt.

The Pradhans, however, said they were tired after all the travelling, and they had not yet had a meal within the time stipulated by the traditions of their home. Vilas Mama was on the Kotwal side. I was half a Kotwal but also half a Pradhan and so I was of two minds. Finally, the enthusiasm of their grandson and son-in-law won the day, and my parents agreed that we should go to Bharatpur. But then I had to listen to comments like, 'Consider the poor little fellow. How he is neglected. Poor thing, he doesn't say a thing.' I refrained from pointing out that said 'poor little fellow' was the instigator of this entire excursion.

We spent the night at the hotel in Agra and left the next morning for Bharatpur.

Although we spent the entire day in the national park, the two Kotwals were not satisfied. It was a day of thrilling birdwatching, completely unforgettable. I remember thousands of cranes, like a pink-and-white garland, stretched across the sky. My husband and son lost all sense of time, while my father was beginning to worry about it getting late and dark. Balasaheb suggested gently that we should leave, but it was only after sunset that we left the park and began looking for a place to spend the night.

We could not find a single hotel that was up to Balasaheb's standards. It was dark now, and the cold weather meant that all the villagers were huddled indoors. Then, as we were trundling down a side road, we heard someone speaking Marathi! Three or four young men had come to eat paan. When they heard our predicament, they invited us home with them. We accepted their invitation only to find that they lived in a single room. They had no food but some dry snacks. The Kotwals were quite happy, but I found all this a bit much. But we were guests, we ate what was served somehow and the Kotwals went off happily to sleep.

The next day our trip from Bharatpur to Delhi was just as adventurous. At the border of Haryana and Delhi, around the villages of Palwal and Bandel, we got caught in a cloudburst. Mathura Road is a busy highway. The torrents of rain made it difficult to see the road in front of us. Vijayrao was an expert driver but reckless; his son sat by his side, offering silent empathy and obviously they found this thrilling. But I could tell that the denizens of the back seat were in a state of high discomfort.

It was nearly midnight when we reached home. I made a nice hot meal, Balasaheb went to give Vijayrao a tot of brandy but when he entered the bedroom, father and son were curled up under a green velvet quilt, fast asleep!

The Splendours of Delhi

As the national capital, Delhi is a city that is clearly aware of its own importance. Important people and celebrities from all over the country and the world would visit the city and some of them would come to the school to talk to the children.

Ashutosh enjoyed the grand programmes that were held in the capital, especially the parades on Independence Day and Republic Day. At the Vijay Chowk in front of Rashtrapati Bhavan, there was a VIP enclosure, and his father would get passes to this. I can still picture Ashutosh watching the Beating Retreat ceremony with complete attention every year. He would get lost in the aerial displays of the new fighter jets purchased by the Air Force. He could recognize all the models.

The first time he saw an airport was in May 1969 when his father went to Japan. It was natural that he should watch these huge objects lift off into the sky and fly like birds with eyes full of wonder. Seeing the enjoyment with which he watched the air display, his father bought him books on aeroplanes and flight, illustrated with all kinds of models and with descriptions of their working. He studied these with great care. He built aeroplane models out of balsa wood and elastic bands and flew these with delight.

Our being in Lucknow and Delhi was a golden opportunity for Ashutosh, I think now. The ambience and the social environment had a good effect on him. Mind and body were both strengthened.

In May 1979, Vijayrao was transferred to Bombay. We were all devastated at the thought of leaving Delhi. Our Sikh neighbours were also saddened at losing us but gradually we began to pack and plan our move to Bombay with renewed excitement.

7

Mumbai—New Games, New Rules

Ashutosh was born in Bombay and was now returning to the city at the age of thirteen and a half.

Once we arrived in the city, we had to start another search for his school. I had heard much about the Campion and Cathedral schools in the Fort area. When my husband took Ashutosh to see the Cathedral School, he was shocked. After the spacious grounds and huge buildings of the schools in Lucknow and Delhi, this campus looked practically poverty-stricken. Of course, compact buildings are to be expected in the downtown business district of Bombay, the financial capital of India.

Sudha Aatya, Ashutosh's paternal aunt, was married to Sadanand (Anukaka) Varde who, at the time, was the education minister of Maharashtra. He had a word with the principal, Dr Jacob, who agreed to give Ashutosh an entrance test. The same thing happened as at Delhi Public School. They were happy to admit him even though two months of the term had elapsed. He would go on to study there for the next four years. DPS followed the Central Board of Secondary Education (CBSE); Cathedral followed the Indian Certificate of Secondary Education (ICSE). Thanks to the CBSE curriculum, Ashutosh was at an advanced level in mathematics and science. Sometimes the teacher would ask Ashutosh to solve mathematics problems on the board for the class. At home, too, he would spend hours on the phone, solving the 'doubts' his friends had in these subjects. All his friends were full of praise for 'Kotoo' as they had nicknamed him.

On the last Saturday of April, just before the summer vacation, Speech Day was held at the Birla Matoshree Sabhagriha, a large hall in South Mumbai. In the ninth, tenth and eleventh standards, Ashutosh won prizes in science, mathematics and general proficiency. When his name was announced and he went on stage, the entire hall resounded with applause, the thumping of feet and the chanting of 'Kotoo-Kotoo'.

Looking back now at the photographs of the Speech Days of those three years, I am rather impressed. In the first year, the chief guests were Mrs and Dr Homi Sethna (the then chairman of the Atomic Energy Commission); in the second year, it was Mrs Gursharan Kaur and Dr Manmohan Singh (the then governor of the Reserve Bank of India and later the finance minister and the Prime Minister of India); in the third year, it was Mrs and Dr Raja Ramanna (the then director of the Bhabha Atomic Research Centre [BARC]). Here is a young Ashutosh, his head bowed, as Mrs Sethna hands him an award with a look of affection on her face. Then comes another Ashutosh, with Mrs Gursharan Kaur, who has a serious look, and this time he is meeting her eyes. The third Ashutosh is with the delicate Mrs Raja Ramanna, and he is towering over her and has a 'couldn't care less' look as he accepts his prize.

At this remove, I have no idea whether the camera had captured the various shades of adolescent attitude or whether it was my imagination.

We came to Bombay in May 1979. It was going to take a while to get quarters at Badhwar Park in Colaba, so it was decided that we would stay with Vijayrao's parents in Dadar. Cathedral School was in South Bombay and Ashutosh would have to travel by local train or bus. It was my habit, when we arrived in a new city, to discover it by going around in local transport, regardless of the inconvenience. Ashutosh and I enjoyed these excursions into each new city. So I was not particularly concerned that he would have to take public transport.

Ashutosh had faced many transitions; he had to adjust to a new school's atmosphere each time his father got transferred. When he entered a new school in Lucknow, he was young and did not show any noticeable reaction. During the Lucknow-to-Delhi transition, I could see that he had felt somewhat out of place. In Lucknow, he had a whole gang of friends in the colony, we knew all their families, and they were all in government service. In comparison, the Delhi school was huge; the children came from different backgrounds and economic statuses. Most of them were from big business families. It was much more important for Ashutosh to do well in academics than it was for them. Every evening, for two or three hours, he would sit by my side on the lawn and work on mathematics and other subjects. He would fill book after book with revision. When this dedicated work brought good results in the semi-annual examinations, those very children began to befriend him. By the time we were ready to shift from Delhi to Bombay, he was older and capable of handling the change with remarkable maturity.

In Lucknow, my friend Mrs Chirmule (Sarayutai) had told me that Ashutosh would sit by the window of the classroom, gazing out with a lost look on his face. At Cathedral School in Bombay, my senior friend Meera Isaacs would often complain that Ashutosh was disrupting the class by making jokes sotto voce among his friends. Mrs Isaacs was an excellent English teacher who made Shakespeare come alive for her students. Teaching was her passion, and she had charisma. It bothered her that Ashutosh scored so well in other subjects but paid only scant attention to English literature. His essays seemed cursory. She expected him to bring his mind to bear here as well. She felt that he wrote very little but to my mind that was significant. She thought he should write in an expansive and literary style, but judging from his behaviour, it was not his cup of tea. Both of them had a great respect for each other, and he enjoyed her class, but his writing remained laconic.

Many years later, Ashutosh revealed that he actually enjoyed all the reading in the English classes, the Shakespeare and the short stories by the likes of Ernest Hemingway, William Faulkner, F. Scott Fitzgerald, James Thurber and Edward Hughes. He liked thinking about literature. The difficulty was that Ashutosh had severe writer's block. He dreaded the days when the teacher came to class and said, 'Today you all will write an essay.' It did not help that everyone else in class would start writing and filling pages, while Ashutosh would start panicking. Eventually, the teacher would say 'ten minutes left, time to start wrapping up' while Ashutosh had not yet written a word. Finally, to avoid getting a zero, he would quickly scribble a few paragraphs and get a 30 per cent grade. This went on throughout high school. At least after high school, he wouldn't have to deal with the phobia of writing—or so he thought.

He regretted that his English teachers got the wrong impression.

With His Grandparents

Ashutosh had a great time at home with his paternal grandfather. When he had some spare time from his homework and play, we would make up a four at bridge. Sometimes Sudha Aatya and Anu Kaka (who was an expert at bridge) or Dada Kaka–Meena Kaki (also experts at bridge) would join, and then the game would catch fire.

Mothe Baba loved travelling. He had travelled a great deal as a young man and then because his son Vijay was in the railways, he would express his desire to visit some tourist places he had wanted to see. In those days, cameras were not common; but still, he had a great collection of photographs. All these came to us. His favourite hobby was philately, and he had developed an extensive network of pen pals. His stamp collection was organized into albums that Ashutosh inherited. For a while, Ashutosh too shared this pastime.

When Ashutosh was in the ninth and tenth standard, Mothe Baba had developed a deep interest in nuclear fusion and fission; he would read about it and talk about it a great deal. He began to feel that his grandson should go to an American university like MIT for higher studies, and he expressed this feeling as well. Who knows since when Ashutosh's father had been thinking along these lines? Ashutosh certainly got positive support from his family for his scientific inclination through his growing years.

In March 1980, Ashutosh finished his ninth standard, and we shifted to Badhwar Park, Colaba, a residential community built for railway officers. I didn't even notice how his tenth standard came and went. There was no tension in the house, no feeling that this was a make-or-break year for him. It was also the year in which I took admission in a B Ed college. It was great fun.

At the same time other normal activities, including a steady stream of visitors to our house, continued. During this period, both of Ashutosh's grandmothers had some health problems, and they stayed with us for treatment.

During the Diwali and Christmas vacations, our schedules were jam-packed with festivities. Along with some relatives, we spent ten days of Christmas holidays in Matheran. Ashutosh took full part in all of this, the jokes, the mischief, the laughter. All of us went for long walks in the woods and visited all the scenic lookout points. We went to watch the sunset over the mountains, that kind of thing. In all my memories of these mountain visits, whether to the Himalayas or the Sahyadris, Ashutosh is always present.

His tenth-standard results were excellent. The staff felicitated him, and he received several scholarships. His name went up on the honour roll. He did not leave the school to go to junior college but continued at Cathedral.

Preparing for the Future

After his spectacular success in the ICSE board, he moved on to the eleventh standard. His father gave him a beautiful wristwatch and a pair of suede trousers. Now his aim was to get to the US after his twelfth standard, and the necessary research and preparation began.

He cleared the SAT exam between August and December 1981. He studied for his SATs at home, with his father helping him.

Ashutosh sat for his Test of English as a Foreign Language (TOEFL) and did extremely well there too.

After that, the process of seeking admission to universities began. This became a regular affair, which took over our dining table every day. At the same time, he was also preparing for the IIT entrance examinations.

The College Entrance Examination Board (CEEB), USA had published a tome to guide students seeking admission in American universities. Vijayrao had ordered this book. As it was very heavy, it was sent by sea mail. When a month passed, and it had not arrived, he informed them. The institution responded by sending the book immediately by air mail. (Naturally, the copy that had been sent by sea mail arrived soon after). After studying the book, which listed the specializations at which universities excelled, Ashutosh made his choice and sent out his applications.

In the eleventh standard, he sat for the National Talent Search Examination and did extremely well. He began to get a monthly scholarship of 200 rupees. In the twelfth standard, this became 300 rupees a month. All his books and educational expenses were covered by this money.

His scores in the TOEFL and the SATs were excellent: Mathematics: 800/800; Physics: 800/800; Chemistry: 790/800

Any university would have been happy to take him. The problem was money. We wanted a full scholarship, exemption from boarding and lodging charges and an Ivy League institution. It was not the practice of US universities to offer such scholarships and exemption to undergraduate students. We decided to try them all anyway but keep the IIT admission as Plan B.

All the Ivy League institutions are on the East Coast. They carry the impress of the British system of education and have a highbrow intellectual culture that they are proud of. They are all grand old institutions that hark back to the Old World. Their old stone walls are festooned with ivy from which they draw their name.

Ashutosh was going to Agrawal Classes in Dadar to prepare for the IIT entrance examinations. Classes were held every Sunday, but their question papers would come by post. These would have to be solved and returned to the class. All this, too, sat on our dining room table.

8

Passage to England

And so we come to 1982. Ashutosh's eleventh standard was coming to an end. In February, our Borivali flat was ready. As soon as we got possession, we found someone who wanted to rent it.

According to my cultural traditions, I very much wanted to have a Vastu Puja (housewarming ceremony). Vijayrao gave me ten days. We lived in Colaba and getting to Borivali took two-and-a-half hours. But I was adamant. I invited the entire family and our friends. I was determined that everything about this housewarming and puja should go perfectly. I had no one to help me. Added to that was my job at the school. At this time, Ashutosh stood four square behind me. Without an extra word, he helped to organize the necessary materials, to plan the ceremony and to follow through so that everything went according to plan. He also took charge of the hospitality, making sure all the guests were looked after. He saw to it that all four grandparents were not inconvenienced in any way. He thus made my dream come true.

At the end of April 1982, the first academic term of his twelfth standard was over. Speech Day happened and went well, and then unexpectedly, a fresh development emerged.

The Cathedral & John Connon School, founded by the Anglo-Scottish Education Society, was an elite school. The scions of business houses like Tata, Godrej and Ambani all studied here. Many expert educationists had served as principals. It was in touch with the best schools in the UK. There was an idea to start a student exchange programme with some of these British schools. Ten or twelve students were to spend six weeks in British homes. Ashutosh headed the list of those selected.

I heard the news but ignored it. Money was the issue. Our family's economy had no place for savings since Vijayrao had no belief in savings. But he decided that he was going to send Ashutosh to the UK. He did not worry himself about the money, but thought that the fledgling had received enough warmth in the nest and it was time for him to try out his wings.

The father in him was thinking of his son's future. He wanted Ashutosh to experience life abroad, or at least have a glimpse of what everyday life was like there. This was the reason he made this decision. When he had made a decision, he went about getting it done; in much the same manner, he began to work on making this happen. He took some money out of his salary and cut into Ashutosh's National Talent Search scholarship and made up the sum. The total expenses were to be about 9,000 rupees.

We began to buy all the necessary items. My eyes were, as always, fixed on the romantic horizon. I had always been fascinated by British history, impressed by the British spirit. I was delighted that my son was going to get to see Britain. At sixteen-and-a-half, Ashutosh was also in a state of high excitement. But he was also troubled by the expense his father was incurring on his behalf. His hi-fi friends, especially the girls, were dreaming of nightclubs and punk hairstyles. They already had family connections in the UK and so were not likely to experience any shortage of foreign currency. But Ashutosh had to manage with the limited pound sterling he could carry as per regulations. This must have disconcerted him. It wasn't only a question of money. These kids had already gone abroad on holidays. Being with these children for six weeks at a stretch, day and night, might be difficult for Ashutosh to take.

For a couple of days, he did seem to be disturbed. He initiated the conversation with: 'What do you expect from me, from this tour?' 'This will be an invaluable experience for you. A new environment, new people, new situations, no one can say now what lessons you will draw from all of this. Once you return and tell me everything that happened, that will be the time when we can make a correct estimate of the impact on you. But I do think that you will return mature and much enriched,' I said.

Return of the Native

Ashutosh was in England between 20 May 1982 and 2 July 1982. When he returned, the entire family came over to welcome him back and to hear of his experiences. When he was going, they were full of pride; he came home to a hero's welcome.

Each one in the family had their own perspective on this tour. At the time, there were very few telephones you could make international calls on. Letters took fifteen or twenty days to reach.

That meant we were going to find out about his experiences only on his return. He answered this barrage of eager questions in his own style.

When the dust settled, and the three of us were alone together, he began to talk. 'It seems like a dream,' he said. He then began to describe the greatness of London, the efficiency of the British lifestyle, the way historic spots from the medieval times onwards were recognized and protected, his solo treks in the British woods, the students he had met thanks to the exchange programme and their families, and the experiences he had had with them. He tried to summarize the conversations he'd had with them, but he was objective about their personalities and character traits. He spoke a lot about all this. He had visited Oxford and Cambridge and described student life at the great universities.

As Ashutosh described his experience of British people and Britain, his father looked very happy and satisfied with what his son had understood and felt that his son had got the best out of his trip. His pride in his son who had returned from a successful trip abroad was evident on his face. Father and son did not need to ask each other questions and receive answers. They knew each other's minds. There were very few question-and-answer conversations. His father did not tell him what he should be careful of in a foreign environment or what he should or should not do, or where he might stumble. Ashutosh figured out all this mostly by himself.

He knew exactly the kind of thing I was interested in and told me those stories and incidents. Some of these stories he told me himself; some I got to know about from a pocket diary that he gave me when he returned. There were very few notes. But you could get a good picture of what had happened from them. I visited places that I had long read about, seeing them through his eyes. I heard about the city of Bath for the first time from him. He loved the Roman ruins that he saw there.

He also made some like-minded new friends there. Vidur Sood and Anirudh Sahni were old friends from class. Vidur was the son of Kamini Kaushal, a popular Hindi film star of the 1940s to 1960s, and Anirudh was her step-grandson. Anirudh was a good, intelligent student. Sometimes Ashutosh wandered alone, sometimes the three of them roamed together. They played tennis and badminton, went swimming together. They went canoeing, ice-skating and rock-climbing, after some British students had taught them how. They watched plays at the Oxford theatre. There were social, educational and cultural programmes for all the Indian students. Perhaps out of a sense of discipline, he took part in all these.

Saloni, Gayatri, Mukeeta, Ayesha and Banoo were the names of some of the friends I found in his diary. For the Indian Night, these girls had dressed up in colourful costumes and performed the Garba. Ashutosh designed the lights for this performance. When the girls made biryani, he washed the vessels. He went sand-sledging with Ayesha, Banoo and Saloni. The sand was so dry that when the wind blew, it abraded everyone's faces. Climbing up the sand slopes was an ordeal.

They were also taken to farms to do some community service. The Cathedral students were divided into two groups. Ashutosh's group consisted mostly of girls. The other group had harvested the fields on the previous day. Ashutosh's group was to make bales and load them onto a trailer. The bales were good and heavy and hoisting them strained his back and neck. But it was a moment when he had to show his chivalry.

Computers were not common in those days. Naturally, the students were all attracted to them but didn't know much about them. Anirudh and Ashutosh tried to grasp what they were about. Everyone enjoyed playing the 'Invasion from Outer Space' video game. They presented an Indian cultural programme, but there was also an intellectual exchange. The Falklands War was a hot topic in those days. Ashutosh took part in this discussion and his interventions were much appreciated, or so his teacher Mr Elisha told me. We had both read Jacob Bronowski's bestselling book, *The Ascent of Man*. He used this book as the basis of his participation in the event.

Once, after breakfast, Ashutosh and Anirudh decided to go to Bridgend, Wales and caught the 9.23 a.m. bus. They arrived at 10.05 a.m. and went off to see the Brecon Beacons mountains and national park. This was already part of the programme, but at the last minute it had been dropped for some reason. Each of them had bought two-litre bottles of coke and some packets of biscuits. This was a very enjoyable trip. On the way, they passed pretty villages like Gilfach Goch, Williamstown, Penygraig, Tonypandy, Ferndale and Maerdy. At around 12.30 p.m., they arrived at Aberdare in Wales. They wandered about in the village a little and made some purchases: a rucksack, Rubik's cubes and sweaters. There was not much time so they had to rush to catch the 1.17 bus to Brecon Beacons. They lost track of each other, but fortunately, met on the bus. By this time, Anirudh was in a state and in all the confusion, they missed the stop for Brecon Beacons and ended up at another village altogether, reaching at 3.05 p.m. They immediately caught the 3.20 p.m. bus which dropped them at Libanus. They had to walk three miles through pouring rain until they reached the top of the hill. Their hands and feet were frozen. When they reached Brecon Beacons, there was another disappointment in store. This area was known as a nature reserve. Ashutosh was very keen to see it, but all they found was an information centre, some toilets and an English pub. It had a great view but was known mainly as a camping site, and the only way to enjoy it was to stay for a few days. After a little walking about, they bought some information brochures and then started off again.

Back at Libanus, they had to catch the 5.49 p.m. bus to Cardiff. They found they were late, so they cut a good ten minutes off the walk by running down the hill. They had to change buses twice and reached Cardiff only at 7.50 p.m. The next bus back was at 10.30 p.m. For two hours and forty minutes, they saw the sights of Cardiff—the riverside, the fort, the market, the museum, and the concert hall. The 10.30 p.m. bus dropped them off at an unknown village at 11.20 p.m. When they began to ask for directions to get home to St Donat's Castle, they met a British couple who gave them a lift in their Ford Cortina. This saved them a one-hour trudge. The car was very posh and well-sprung; it seemed to be floating in air. Finally, they got to bed at midnight.

We had not talked about what he should buy in England. There was only enough pocket money to allow him to travel a little and to eat well. But he still managed to find small appropriate gifts for everyone in the family. He bought me two Corning oven-proof casseroles. For his father, he bought a battery charger for the car. I was so proud of him.

While he was in England, he got to see an important person. He told me about it with great enthusiasm. He had spent four days with a family in Taunton, Somerset. The West Indian cricketer Vivian Richards was living next door. Ashutosh saw him a number of times. I had always thought of Ashutosh as my equal, but when he returned from his UK trip, I felt he had truly become an adult.

The fledgling was now ready to leave the nest and take its first flight in the open air, under the great blue sky.

Wedding photograph of Vijay and Manik, December 1961, Pune
Standing: Anukaka (Sadanand Varde), Vijay, Ashok, Shridhardada
Middle row: Sudha Varde with Abhijit, Manik, Mothebaba, Mothi Aai and Meena Vahini
Front row: Jhelum (Chingu), Gautam Sr., Leena

Ashutosh at five years, accepting first prize in art competition from Mrs Mathur, Railway Officers Club, Lucknow, 1971.

A visit to the Taj Mahal, Agra, September 1977. (L-R): Balasaheb, Indutai, Ashutosh, Manik and Vilasmama

Ashutosh accepting prizes for academic excellence:

Top: From Mrs Homi Sethna in Class 9, April 1980.

Middle: From Mrs Gursharan Kaur (wife of Dr Manmohan Singh) in Class 10, April 1981.

Bottom: From Mrs Raja Ramanna in Class 11, April 1982.

Cathedral and John Cannon School, Bombay

Ashutosh's farewell dinner before he set off for America, Badhwar Park Railway Colony residence, Bombay, August 1983. Front (L-R): Manik, Ashutosh and Vijay Kotwal. Back (L-R): Baba Chitnis, Shridhar Kaka, Dr Suma Chitnis and Meena Kaki

Being welcomed in State College, Pennsylvania, USA, September 1983. (L-R): Lalit Maoshi, Parimal, Ashutosh and Dr G.P. Patil

Ashutosh on a holiday with his Aai, Alibaug, July 1985

Ashutosh and Aai at the temple of Philae on the Nile at Aswan, Egypt, February 1990.

Ashutosh, Vijay Kotwal, Manik Kotwal and Jyotsna Maoshi Taggersay in Washington D.C., in front of the White House, March 1992

Ashutosh during his convocation ceremony at University of Pennsylvania, receiving dual degrees of Bachelor of Science (Electrical Engineering) and Bachelor of Science (Economics), 1988.

Inaugurating the Hadron Collider Physics Symposium (2006), organized and chaired by Ashutosh at Duke University.

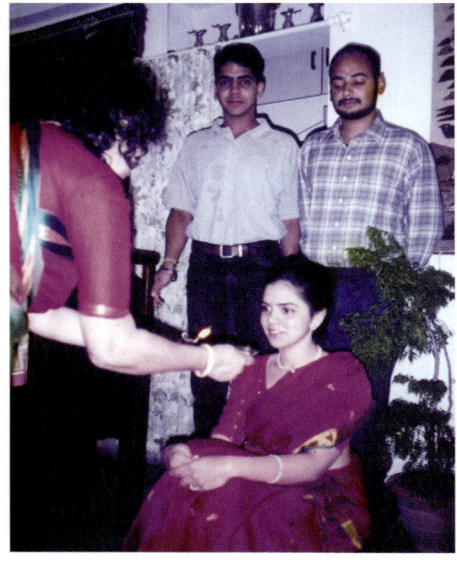

Ashwini's traditional felicitation at engagement. Back row, Ashwini's younger brother Rahul, and Ashutosh.

Ashutosh and Ashwini (centre) at their engagement ceremony in Mumbai, October 1996. With Deepak Phene and Vinaya Phene.

Ashutosh and Ashwini's wedding, 23 December 1996

Urmila mami, Aai, Ashutosh, Papa and Dilip mama at the wedding reception, December 1996.

Ashutosh and Ashwini at their new house in Durham, North Carolina, May 2000, waiting for the stork to deliver Gautam.

Ashwini and Ashutosh with little Gautam in the Duke University gardens.

A happy family. Standing: Ashutosh and Ashwini. Sitting: Vijay, Gautam at five and a half months and Manik. Durham, February 2001.

Ashwini, Gautam and Ashutosh at Gautam's thread ceremony. Pune, 3 July 2011.

Gautam reciting the scriptures for Lakshmi Pooja during the Diwali festival, with Mo (Manik) and Ashwini-Ashutosh in their Chicago home, 2014.

Gautam with Aao (Vijay), Mo (Manik) and Ashutosh on the steps of Shivneri Fort, Maharashtra, July 2011

9

Enterprise and Accomplishment

ONE NEEDS TO HAVE A PLAN FOR THE FUTURE THAT WILL TAKE into account the possibility of success. The credit for recognizing his son's qualities and setting him on the right career path goes to Ashutosh's father. He is a perceptive man, far-sighted, with wide intellectual horizons. He is aware of his limitations but also sure of his abilities. He has tremendous drive. Once he gets an idea into his head, he does not let go until it is accomplished. Obstacles do not deter him, and he does not allow himself to get discouraged by them. He had decided that his son would study in the US, and he was determined to make this happen.

In the beginning, I was a little confused. I could see that he would move away from us because of IIT. All the same it was always possible to visit him wherever he was within the country. That he would go abroad for postgraduate studies was a given. But that would be later; at present, he was too young.

However, the goal was clear to both father and son. Ashutosh was to get into an Ivy League university with a full scholarship and supporting bursaries, because it would not be possible for us to pay for it otherwise.

Ashutosh was going for undergraduate studies. We wanted him to benefit from the fundamental research that went on in these institutions, from their magnificent libraries, from their progressive methodologies of instruction, and from the company of and competition with other talented students. His uncle, my husband's younger brother, had been in the educational field for several years in the US and Canada, and it was he who first sowed the seeds of this dream. His grandfather had nurtured it and started dreaming about a bright future for his grandson. Then father and son had taken up the challenge and begun the work.

Looking at all this energy and enthusiasm, I controlled my disquiet. I did not want to be a wet blanket. The fledgling was beginning to test out his wings, making his first cautious forays out into the world. One of Sant Tukaram's abhangs (devotional songs) talks beautifully about how the kite will soar in the heavens but her heart will be with her fledglings, asleep in the warmth of the nest. She knows the sky into which her young ones will soon fly. She knows the limitless arch of the sky, she knows from experience the perils of the winds that sweep under it and the potential they have for driving a young bird off its course, the possibility of a sudden, unexpected attack …

Here, it was completely the opposite. The mother's world was limited to the nest.

She did know a little about the world into which her son was about to make his first flights, and she did feel the pull of it. Most of what she knew came from reading and from the stories she had heard from others, and it was to this world that her son was going. It was not a short tourist trip; he was going on a mission. He was going to attain an immensity of knowledge, to create his own identity, to find his feet there. He was leaving behind all the ties and bonds of our love.

I knew this was not going to be a walk in the park for him; there would be problems, questions would arise, he would have to choose when 'two roads diverged in a wood' and perhaps there would be more than just two roads. All these questions milled hazily about in my head. But I didn't even have the imagination to think what might happen. So what advice could I give him, what direction could I suggest?

Thus, I resolved not to let it bother me. I had faith in him and in the face of the determination shown by father and son, I slammed the door on my doubts.

Filling out forms for entrance to US universities is an ordeal. The forms that must be filled seek to understand the applicants in their entirety, not just their academic suitability but also their extracurricular interests and activities, their artistic and sporting interests ... in short, their fundamental personalities. A series of essays has to be written.

Academic references from teachers attesting to their attainments must be sought and secured. Each application requires a payment (in dollars) to accompany it.

The replies from the universities were all very encouraging and made us proud. 'Such a student can only be an asset to our university,' the universities echoed each other. But the question of obtaining a scholarship remained.

Most US universities did not give scholarships to undergraduate students; nor were they allowed to work. The University of

Pennsylvania offered a tuition waiver; we would have to pay for the rest. We could not accept this and had to turn down their offer. Immediately, we got a reply: 'We can offer a twelve-thousand-dollar yearly scholarship and hostel accommodation, which should sort out your economic problems. Just come on over.' We would have to arrange for $1,000 a year, they said.

UPenn had a certain educational advantage. The Wharton Business School, one of the top business schools in the world, is part of the university. In general, one does not get a scholarship for independent study, but since Ashutosh was going to study engineering, this could be made possible if he pursued both degrees simultaneously. He would have to major in finance and in electronic engineering in the next five years. It was also possible for him to spend a year at Edinburgh in Scotland during the course of this programme. Keeping this in mind, Ashutosh decided to accept the UPenn offer and informed them accordingly.

Now the question of that $1,000 arose. At the time, the Reserve Bank of India did not allow you to send money abroad for educational purposes. Vijayrao applied to forty-eight institutions for help. The Harris and Eliza Kempner Foundation agreed to give us $800 a year for the next five years. Vijayrao's brother Ashok Kaka gave $1,200 a year. When Ashutosh graduated from UPenn, he returned these funds to Ashok Kaka and the Kempner Foundation with gratitude.

Ashutosh needed a sponsor, but we had no family nor any friends in America. As it happened, Sudha Aatya knew an old functionary of the Rashtriya Seva Dal, Dr G.P. Patil, who was professor of statistics at Pennsylvania State University; we received a double serving of help from him. He invited Ashutosh to stay with him for the first eight days in the US. Parimal, his son, was the same age as

Ashutosh and they could share a room. Ashutosh had found a good place to stay.

We still had to organize the money for Ashutosh's ticket. This was when we discovered how big-hearted people can be. The Ichalkaranji Education Endowment Foundation did not generally fund undergraduate studies, but they made an exception in his case and gave him a scholarship, a first for them. J.J. Marshall and Nani Palkhivala, two great Parsis, also provided assistance.

I have a woman's outlook. While his father was dealing with the issues of the outside world, I was worried about his food and how he was going to deal with the cold weather. Since I knew that Indians cannot take the cold, I started knitting. Ashutosh's eating habits were simple. He was not fussy. I gave him his first lessons in cooking. On the first day, he outdid his teacher.

His departure for the US began to take shape. Friends and family all showered praise on him. Some also began to show concern. They wondered how we were sending our only son at such a tender age to such a far-off place. Others wondered how a shy boy would manage in North American society, full of go-getters and extroverts.

My mother became very sentimental. Balasaheb also began to feel pangs of anxiety, but he tried to take a philosophical approach. 'Everyone is born with their own destiny. No one can change someone else's destiny.' Of course, we also had our moments of anxiety when we thought about him going so far away, but we never allowed this fear to make a permanent home in our heads. Did we fear that because of his youth and being in an alien environment, he would become lonely and upset, get into bad company and develop bad habits, fail to cope with his studies and fall behind his class and be unable to communicate any of this? Never for a moment.

Preparation and Departure

Finally, March 1983 dawned. Ashutosh's twelfth-standard examinations came around. He had prepared for the IIT examinations, which he would take in May.

Welcome letters were arriving from America. It was now about 70 to 80 per cent sure that he would be going to America after the twelfth standard. His paternal grandfather was in seventh heaven at his grandson's success.

On 24 March 1983, I was teaching in class. A call came from the Dadar house, with the tragic news of Mothe Baba's death. I raced home to Colaba. It was Ashutosh who opened the door and said, 'Aai, I am going to Dadar.' I calmed him down a bit and we both went to Dadar. After we reached Mothe Baba's house, he began to sob. I had never seen him so distraught.

He had prepared thoroughly for the IIT entrance examination. The results were excellent. He got into IIT-Bombay for electronic engineering.

A moment in the entrance examination was like something out of a play. On the last day, the first paper was Mathematics. It was a difficult paper. I was going to St Xavier's College with his lunch when I heard the students lamenting. There was a whole bunch of Cathedral School students in the corner of one of the verandas. In the middle of them was Ashutosh, sitting in the pose of a hero from a romantic film who had lost everything. He saw me and said disconsolately, 'Aai, I'm not going to eat. And I'm not going to appear for the next paper either.'

I went off and began to read a book. The other students knew that they had no chance, but they could not bear to see their 'Kotoo' in such a state of despair. 'Kotoo, eat your lunch, man. You have to write the next paper,' they were all insisting. There were five to seven minutes left for the next paper when he came to me and said, 'Aai, give me something to eat.' He ate quickly and silently and went off to sit for the next paper.

Even before the IIT results were declared, the following American universities had sent Ashutosh letters of acceptance: UPenn, Caltech, Cornell, Princeton and MIT. And though we had not sent an application to the University of Texas in Austin, the authorities there asked if he would like to join, having seen his SAT scores. But since they would not offer any economic assistance, his father wrote and refused. Then another letter came from UPenn. Ashutosh was given an annual scholarship of $12,000.

Now that we were sure he would join UPenn in August 1983, we began to collect the relevant documents. Only the I-20 form remained, which was essential for the American visa. And so it seemed that he would have to start studying at IIT until the visa was in hand. Ashutosh spent the month of July 1983 at the IIT Bombay hostel in Powai. He never told us if he was ragged or how much he had to endure. When I asked him about the ragging and other matters, he simply said, 'I'm not going to tell you about all that.'

However, about his experience as a freshman in the US, he talked openly. 'There, new students are welcomed and looked after. Our culture drives some students to abandon their studies, and that is not right.'

In July, the I-20 form arrived and we started preparations in earnest. He had to reach UPenn by 1 September. We got the ticket for his flight on 28 August. It began to look like the visa might present a problem. The sponsorship letter written by Prof. G.P. Patil had, by mistake, mentioned the name Ashok (who lived in Canada) instead of Ashutosh. At that time, one could only use the post in order to send letters. There was no time to make the correction. Vijayrao decided to gather courage, go to the visa office and sort things out. We had heard that the visa officers were tough people, prone to finding fault, unwilling to make concessions. In this case, the officer at the window proved to be a godsend. She did not ask too many questions and signed the form. Instead, she said to Vijayrao, 'The university really wants him to come over. He has a strong case. Why are you worrying your head?'

Now the final stamp of approval had been secured for Ashutosh's trip to North America. As the date of his departure neared, the tempo of our preparations increased. The four or five days before he actually left seemed as if Diwali was approaching. Guests began to stream into the house. There were well-wishers galore. There were blessings to be called down from the gods, he had an auspicious bath and then we had festivities. We made his favourite dishes, like tel poli and kaanawale, and some non-vegetarian delicacies.

On the day he left for the airport, my mind was in a whirl. That he was going so far gave me anxiety but that he was going for further studies filled me with happiness and pride. And there was the certainty that he would achieve something great. These ideas spun inside my head like a pinwheel. And call it the will of God or call it destiny but suddenly it was as if a bright light was shining inside my head.

After so many years, it is still clear in my head: such a young man, with his boarding pass, his cabin luggage and his tennis racquet in hand ... *Tera Allah nigehbaan, tera Maula nigehbaan* ... (May God protect you, may He keep you safe) we thought, echoing Zia Sarhadi's beautiful words from the film *Elan* as we bade him farewell.

OUT OF THE NEST

May–June 1982. On the banks of the Thames during his first trip abroad.

Identity card for working in the dining hall of the University of Pennsylvania.

The Swissair flight to Zurich took off. From that moment, the next twelve years of his life that Ashutosh spent at universities were out of our vision. I have put together what happened during this time using his letters, our meetings every two years, and some conversations occasioned by the writing of this book. This is a collage of the outstanding events and opportunities that came his way.

10

New Horizons

The 1980s were a different time altogether. There were no computers, no email, never mind Skype, which we don't use even today. If you wanted to make a telephone call, you had to book a trunk call. We were on opposite sides of the globe; when it was night here, it was day there. And even if you booked a call, you had no idea when it would come through. Besides, my husband was very clear: we were not going to waste our son's time with ordinary chitchat, with questions like, 'How are you?' So phone calls were saved for truly urgent matters, or for Diwali or birthdays.

My standard questions arose out of maternal concern: 'How are you?', 'What do you eat on the weekends?', 'Are you very cold?' To which my son would reply, 'Aai, this is America; is anyone going to go hungry here?' And so I stopped asking those questions. I never got anything from him that might be considered to be of 'human interest'. Most of the conversation was about his work or allied matters and perhaps if he had travelled somewhere new.

Though it is true we knew no one in the US, there were always some godsent people to support him. Mohan Desai, the uncle of Nilesh, one of Ashutosh's close friends from Lucknow, came to the airport to welcome him and take him home. After a swim in their Long Island home's swimming pool and lunch, Mohan Desai dropped him off at LaGuardia Airport, where Ashutosh caught a flight to Harrisburg. At Harrisburg, G.P. Patil and his wife, Lalit Maushi, picked him up; Ashutosh found a loving home with them. This was the first time he stayed in someone's house without us being there. Though he had come so far and was now in a strange new environment, the Patil family, especially Parimal, Pawan and Parag, three boys of his age group, never allowed him to feel alone. Though he was often lost in his own thoughts, he did manage to keep a balance. The Patil family behaved as if he were family and did not go out of their way to treat him differently.

Parimal was also going to UPenn, where he and Ashutosh became roommates.

Ashutosh's Chingu Tai (his cousin, the noted Odissi dancer Jhelum Varde-Paranjape) had a friend, Reena Vankhudre, who lived in Philadelphia and whose husband, Prashant, was pursuing a PhD at Wharton. Here, too, Ashutosh found another loving home. Prashant offered him advice as an elder brother would.

The I-20 form had come late. Then we had faced the issue of the wrong name. Now another problem surfaced. On the form, the visa had been granted for thirty days. As soon as Ashutosh got to UPenn, he went to the International Students' Office and got this set right.

Another headache. UPenn had accepted Ashutosh as a Benjamin Franklin Scholar. The curriculum for such a student is pitched at a higher level. Ashutosh was keen on these honours classes but they were full. Professor Summers was reluctant to accept Ashutosh into the economics honours class. This happened with physics as well.

Ashutosh took his problem to the Benjamin Franklin Scholar programme office. There, a certain Mrs Durnham had the same mindset as Mrs Madan from Delhi. When she had a word with the professors, they relented and Ashutosh was admitted to both classes.

When faced with obstacles such as these, Ashutosh worked out who he had to meet, visited them, spoke politely and got things done but he had to move out of his comfort zone to do this. His behaviour was socially appropriate. He participated in class discussions, but since the conversation at the dining table was about girls, he rarely opened his mouth. He did not feel the need to interact with other people or to 'network'. He did not care to say things to please others although he was always willing to help someone who needed it. He liked being with people who offered him the stimulus of new ideas, of intellectual conversation. He would become friends with them. He stayed away from the emotionally needy. His nature has not changed even today.

When the first term started, he took a course in English literature. He had always had a mental block about writing so he may have been worried, since writing was an essential part of a literature course. But by some magic, he began to score high marks in English too. It might have been the new environment or the way of teaching or a different set of expectations that the teacher had. But Ashutosh thinks his English teachers in high school in India were as good as the teacher at UPenn. The real reason was most likely that there was some change in him, whose origin has remained a mystery. Regardless, this turnaround was a very pleasant development for him and, of course, incredibly exciting for us. His professor praised him highly for his composite essay on Thomas Pynchon's *The Crying of Lot 49* and T.S. Eliot's *The Wasteland*. He was recognized for his analytical abilities. Many years later, Ashutosh remarked that he wished he could figure out how his fear of writing went away; whether it evaporated on its own or he overcame it somehow.

Apart from the English course, he took mathematics, economics and computer programming. The computer programming course was in the Moore School building, near the hostel and taught the computer language PASCAL. Each week he had twenty-one hours of classroom instruction. He had to work at the dining hall for three hours a day, four days a week. He did this for four semesters. On one day, he might have to wash dishes, the next day it might be vacuuming, another time he might be clearing the garbage. He never took on the job of serving people because you would have to make contact with other people. Here, you had to do the work mechanically, which he could manage.

The used dishes would be put on a conveyor belt, which took them to a lift and then to the floor below. There, they were washed and put on another conveyor belt, which took them back to the dining hall above. The discipline with which this operation took place impressed him. The students ran the dining service, though the food was cooked by a contractor. This made it possible for the students to eat cheaply and to earn a little money. Besides studying and earning money, he also began to do other things. Five days a week, food was served in the hostel. There was a kitchenette for the students to cook on weekends. There was a fridge in which you could store things like eggs, milk, cornflakes, cheese, chicken pieces, all bought from the supermarket.

It was also important to stay in contact with the scholarship office and manage the bank work. All this time, he kept in touch with G.P. Kaka and Ashok Kaka too.

He got to see classic films like *Psycho*, *Excalibur*, *The Great Dictator* and *Sophie's Choice* at a concessional rate on the campus. He saw *Gone with the Wind*, his favourite, two or three times.

The Ivy League colleges on the East Coast have sports competitions too. UPenn had football matches on the Franklin Field every Saturday. UPenn and Princeton had a long-standing rivalry. American football is a hybrid game, drawing from England's rugby and France's soccer. Ashutosh did participate a little, but to him, the game seemed to lack drama. He found watching baseball on the television much more fun.

However, Ashutosh did enjoy playing cricket against Princeton, Haverford and other East Coast colleges and universities. America is not a cricketing nation. And so, when they did play cricket, it often drew a curious crowd of spectators. The UPenn team would hire a bus and drive to Princeton (New Jersey). They had to buy their own white trousers. And he did say that the sweaters I had knitted came in handy!

'Do you feel lonely?' I was asked once in a letter. When he told me he had used my name as a computer password, it was the icing on the cake.

Senior students had another responsibility, which they could take on if they chose. They could mentor a freshman. Elaine Friedman or 'Lainey' was a medical student and became a friend. She would sit with the freshmen, chatting and laughing, helping them solve problems, and sometimes even take them out for a meal to a nearby Mexican restaurant, and generally counselled them. In return, the mentors got to stay for free in the hostel.

It was a completely different experience from the one he had had at IIT-Bombay. The construction of the buildings, their establishment, the decoration, the impeccable cleanliness, the high-quality canteen, this was how he experienced UPenn. But most importantly, it was how they treated the new students that made all the difference. The tradition at IIT was: If you can take the ragging and bear with it, we can be friends. At UPenn, new students were treated gently, given help and made to feel safe.

There was little politics on campus. The universities of the East Coast were largely Democratic, or so it was said. However, there was also said to be a trend towards the Republican Party at UPenn. One of Ronald Reagan's senior statesmen made frequent trips to the campus. But there was no political propaganda.

There were many fraternity halls on campus. Each one had its own culture. Some were sports fraternities, others had an academic bent, while there were those that were famous only for their beer parties. Ashutosh had a select bunch of good friends. Mansoor Khan and Aurangzeb Mohammed, two Pakistani students, worked with him in the dining service. They were on the same wavelength. Gordon O'Brien was Ashutosh's squash and tennis partner and another close friend. They were nice boys, simple, open and jolly.

The fledgling had spread his wings and was beginning to test the currents of the air. His opinions were now getting stronger …

11

Prof. Fortune, a Remarkable 'Guru'

In 1984, Ashutosh had finished two terms at UPenn. He had done well, appearing on the Dean's List in pride of position. Then in 1985, he featured on the National Dean's List.

The three months of the 1984 summer vacation began. Most students, whether American or foreign, go home at this time; if not, they travel. But Ashutosh had to stay in the hostel and take a summer job. Some professors would take on the Benjamin Franklin Scholarship students as assistants. They advertised for these posts. They had projects on hand and needed assistance. They paid the students from their grants. If they didn't have a grant, then the students got credits.

To get a Bachelor of Science in Engineering, Ashutosh needed 40 course credits; for a Bachelor of Science in Economics, he needed 36 course credits. In 1984, when Ronald Reagan was President of the US, there was a sudden cut in the amount of funding available to college professors and universities; summer jobs also took a hit.

There were some in the life sciences, but only one in Physics. Prof. H. Terry (Terence) Fortune was a nuclear physicist. He was looking for a student who had some knowledge of computers.

Ashutosh had a good grasp of physics but he didn't have as much experience with computers as Prof. Fortune would have liked. All the same, Ashutosh applied. Prof. Fortune, in turn, called Ashutosh's physics teacher, Prof. David Balamuth, who said, 'Don't think twice, just go ahead and hire him.'

Prof. Fortune then took the trouble of calling Ashutosh. He set him to work at the Tandem Particle Accelerator behind the physics building. Instead of setting him on computer programming, he got him to work on analysis of the data and of making mathematical calculations based on it.

Ashutosh actually met Prof. Fortune only a few times that summer. Most of the time, he was travelling in pursuit of his research. His PhD students were in touch with him, and these students would assign Ashutosh his work.

In any research, there are jobs that you must do after turning off your mind or setting your brain aside because they are so boring and repetitive. But it is only after these jobs have been done that you get to do the jobs where you must use your mind.

Being the youngest member of the team, Ashutosh was given all the drudge work. But he still managed to make time to analyse data on the nucleus of Selenium-80, an isotope of the metal Selenium. He began to feel that he was starting on an exploration of some of nature's deepest secrets.

At the Tandem Accelerator Laboratory, he began to work on stripping reactions in nuclear physics with the help of a multi-angle spectrometer. These are reactions where a projectile nucleus grazes a target nucleus in such a manner that the target nucleus absorbs a part of the projectile. He began to do fresh research on the nuclear spectra of Selenium and Germanium. In the (d,p) reaction, the deuteron strikes the nucleus and a proton is released. In the (t,p) reaction, the triton strikes the target and a proton is released. When a proton and a neutron combine, they form the deuteron. When a proton and two neutrons combine, they form a triton. In (d,p) and (t,p) reactions, one or more neutrons are shifted from the projectile to the target nucleus.

Ashutosh met a number of the right people at the right moment in his life in the US and, of all of them, Prof. Fortune was one of the earliest and most important mentors for him.

Then the summer was over, the job ended and his sophomore year began. More new courses, more new subjects to study, more work at the dining service and some games. This was also the year he began to study finance. He was now a student of the world-famous Wharton School. The course was rigorous, with lots of reading and research. And so, through the year, he was too busy to get in touch with Prof. Fortune.

The summer of 1985. Once again, the search for a summer job. With some hesitation, Ashutosh called Prof. Fortune who replied with great frankness that he had been very impressed with Ashutosh's work in the previous year and offered him a summer job. Ashutosh's friend Gordon was delighted at this: a single call and a summer job fixed, wow!

Many years later when Ashutosh was applying for his green card, it was Prof. Fortune who wrote a recommendation letter in which he said:

> I have known Professor Kotwal since the mid 1980s when he was an undergraduate student at the University of Pennsylvania.

He came to work in our nuclear physics research group, and performed exceedingly well. We published two papers from his earliest work. I was so impressed with Kotwal that I invited him to join our research effort in intermediate-energy physics at Los Alamos, New Mexico. He made significant contributions to that work earning a co-author status on two more publications—still as an undergraduate.

Prof. Fortune was an impressive presence with a full white beard in the style of Rabindranath Tagore. He was from humble origins, his father had been a sharecropper. He had graduated with a PhD from Florida State University and had conducted post-doctoral research at the Argonne National Laboratory.

Ashutosh described his experience at Los Alamos in the summer of 1987. 'At the lunch table, we would all sit together. There would be a great deal of conversation.' There were two postdocs, three graduate students and, like Ashutosh, two more undergraduates. Prof. Fortune held court. He would talk about a variety of topics, offering his opinions on them; he never forgot his position and status.

Ashutosh recalls all of Prof. Fortune's advice. One of these recollections was, 'It is better that you are a good scientist and know your field fully albeit you may not be a nice person, than to be a nice person and a bad scientist.' Prof. Fortune was a nuclear physicist, while all along, Ashutosh had been drawn to electronics. Prof. Fortune thought Ashutosh might be suited to particle physics. It was he who planted the dream of becoming a professor and doing research in Ashutosh's head.

The Nobel Prize committee often sought Prof. Fortune's advice and some of the people he had recommended had even won. He had recommended Niels Bohr's highly regarded son Aage Bohr for the Nobel Prize.

Prof. Fortune was sure that Ashutosh had what it took to do research in particle physics. He would say, 'The kind of joy you get from fundamental physics you will never get from the applied sciences.' He added, 'In order to prove the theoretical aspects of the work you do in fundamental physics, you need to have a desire to experiment. You need instrumentation. And that's where applied physics and engineering comes in.' Prof. Fortune wanted Ashutosh to pursue fundamental physics rather than technology or the applied sciences. 'From applied physics you get some devices and methods that can be used in everyday life. Take a company like IBM. They make transistors, lasers, and display screens. The scientists who work there are into technology.'

Fundamental physics seemed to be an exciting adventure to Ashutosh. There are some limitations because of the instrumentation. However, there are no limits to the scientific imagination. Instead of using instruments, it is sometimes necessary to use the mind and the imagination. Thought experiments must be designed and conclusions must be sought based on them. One must expand and extend one's thinking. While talking about Ashutosh's work, he would say, 'The experimental physicist might be able to propound principles from his work but the theoretical physicist may not always be able to devise experiments.' He would also say, 'If you only study electronics, you will never be able to do physics; if you study physics, however, you will be able to design electronics and use it for new experiments in fundamental physics.'

He kept an eye on his favourite student, even later during Ashutosh's future research work. He commented on Ashutosh's precise measurement of the W boson mass, saying: 'Prof. Kotwal performed an extremely sophisticated analysis of the data, achieving a precision of 0.1 per cent. Such high precision is crucial if one is to reveal an inconsistency with the standard model.'

This was how he nurtured the attraction that Ashutosh felt for science.

12

Visiting India, Living in Scotland

During the 1985 summer vacation, Ashutosh had had another opportunity to work with Prof. Fortune and managed to save some money. And so, on 7 August 1985, Ashutosh went to India, his first visit after two years.

Though we were all there to greet him on his return, it took him ages to get out of Customs. All the others from his flight had left. When he came out, one-and-a-half hours later, he was still the same Ashutosh, young and simple. He had a big Panasonic two-in-one music player under one arm and this was the reason why he was plucked out of the line and made to wait. The Customs officials ignored him for a while and then they began to ask him a number of searching questions. He had only one answer to all these: 'My mother likes music and so I bought it.'

Something must have persuaded them to let him go. When they asked him where he was headed, he gave them his paternal grandfather's Dadar address. They decided he was 'one of us, a boy from a good family, studying alone in America', and becoming more supportive, they let him go.

Ashutosh was with us for seven weeks. We travelled around a lot together. Each weekend we went out of town: Alibag, Nava Sheva, Thal Vayshet, Bhimashankar, Karnala National Park and Pune to see his grandfather and grandmother. We went to Garhwal for fifteen days, staying in Mussoorie and visiting Kedarnath and Badrinath. During our two-day stay in Mussoorie, there was a thunderstorm; the rain fell so heavily, it became impossible to go out. We spent all our time in the hotel, wrapped up in blankets, eating hot aloo parathas and drinking Ovaltine, playing endless games of three-nought-four. Once again, Ashutosh enjoyed beating us at cards.

From Mussoorie, we went to Rishikesh and Devprayag, Rudraprayag and seven other 'Prayag' without neglecting a visit to Gaurikund; this was an unforgettable experience. How much we talked and how much we enjoyed nature's bounty. We were delighted at the sight of the starting point of so many of the beautiful and sanctified tributaries of the Ganga: the Bhagirathi, Mandakini, Alaknanda, Pindari and the Son.

From Gaurikund, it was an 18-km climb to Kedarnath; it was challenging and dangerous, but it was also from where you get the best views of the Himalayas. Vijayrao and I opted for a pony ride, but Ashutosh said he would hike. Gaurikund is at an altitude of 6,000 feet and Kedarnath Temple is at 11,660 feet, so it was quite a steep day hike. It was also raining, the cold rain of the mountains. Kedarnath Temple was near a glacier at the base of Kedarnath mountain. When we reached there in the evening, I was completely exhausted, but father and son began to romp about in the snow. And while we were having fun, a sad event also happened that very day. Fortunately, Ashutosh had met my mother before our trip, after an absence of two years. She had had the pleasure of seeing her grandson again. But while we were away, she fell ill and suddenly passed away. Ashutosh took this news with composure as against his reaction when Mothe Baba passed away.

◦∼◦

Scotland Sojourn

At the end of September, Ashutosh left India again and went to Scotland. When he had been given the scholarship at UPenn, one of the stipulations was that he had the choice to spend his third year in Scotland. He could have foregone this opportunity, as he had grown accustomed to the lifestyle and academic environment in America.

He had the security of a summer job with Prof. Fortune. Scotland represented a fresh challenge but also new opportunities, so he decided to go there. He would face a greater degree of cold than he was accustomed to in the US. But he made good use of his time, enjoying fresh vistas of nature, exploring new cities and trying his hand at new adventure sports. He took courses in engineering and devised a new testing circuit for which he got a patent.

The new term at the University of Edinburgh was to begin in September. The atmosphere was very different from that of America. It was deeply influenced by the British way of life. The architecture of the stone buildings on the campus was very beautiful. The Palace of Holyroodhouse was the historical home of Scottish royalty and the official residence of the British Royal Family in Scotland. Being very close to the Arctic Circle, summer days last long and there is bright sunlight until late in the evening, whereas in winter it gets dark at 3 p.m.

In Scotland they play a great deal of squash. That meant Ashutosh had to accept defeat often but he kept playing anyway. There were many sporting activities available. There was skiing, climbing, scuba diving, hot-air ballooning and he joined many of these clubs. He began to haunt the slopes every weekend to learn skiing. The love of skiing he developed there is with him still and is now shared by his son.

A Scottish friend, Angus Keddie, invited him to spend Christmas with his family. His home was in Arbroath on the east coast of Scotland, between Aberdeen and Edinburgh. Angus's father had a hospital. Ashutosh attended midnight mass with the Keddie family and took part in the carol singing as well. He went to greet the patients who were in hospital on Christmas. He even took part in the Scottish dancing at the midnight Christmas Eve party.

Later Angus's mother, Anne, wrote me a letter in which she expressed her delight at being able to host Ashutosh. She liked his quiet and pleasant character. She said she would always remember the Christmas that he had spent with them. He did not seem ill at ease in another culture and this pleased her greatly.

During this vacation, he also went to Glasgow. The snow covered everything, so even though he did not get to see any bushes, flowers or birds he spent a lot of time at the libraries and art galleries. Pollok Park had a historic museum set in the middle of its spacious grounds. It was well worth a visit. He also visited Loch Lomond, a lake close to Glasgow. This was a picturesque spot, replete with the beauties of nature.

He took the West Highland Railway Line to see Fort William. On the way, he passed through the lonely and beautiful Rannoch Moor and still remembers its forbidding splendour. From there he took an evening bus to Glencoe village.

Edinburgh has a rich performing-arts tradition. Ashutosh got to see Shakespeare's plays, a French ballet, *Cinderella* and Ibsen's plays as directed by Ingmar Bergman. The Russian Orchestra performing *Fiddle-Faddle* impressed him deeply. No one would miss the Military Tattoo at Edinburgh Castle. And the fireworks that followed were simply amazing. Over the walls of the battlements, the fireworks flowed, like a waterfall. And from the gardens below the hilltop castle, the heavenly music of Beethoven, Strauss and Haydn fell beautifully upon the ears.

In the north of Scotland, he got to go skiing and mountain climbing, while touring the world-famous glens and lochs of the area. He developed a liking for skiing after learning it in Scotland. There are many fine slopes in the states of Pennsylvania, Vermont and Utah. He could really ski to his heart's content and got in a lot of practice.

Skiing is a strenuous sport. After you have learnt a few manoeuvres, the chances of falling are reduced. At first the slopes seem frightening, but after a while, one begins to feel that one has gained complete control. The next steps are to learn how to gracefully swerve and change course.

One has to stay in log cabins on a skiing trip. Loch Tay, a huge lake, is about two hours from Edinburgh. It was a full moon night when he went. The sky was cloudless. The night was a poem in silver, the day a golden one. The air was so free of pollution that the moon shone even brighter. After one got used to the darkness, the snow-covered mountains and the frozen lake were bathed in this silver light.

A Daring Experiment and Academic Success

As if this were not enough, Ashutosh took it into his head that he must go parachute jumping. The instructor accredited by the university offered nine hours of instruction. Ashutosh joined the club. The nine hours consisted of some lectures and some practicals. Then one Saturday, ten of them went to the town of Branton in Northumberland, to the south of Edinburgh. The weather was good that day but the wind was strong. They had to wait in a very cold shed for the weather to improve.

The instructor familiarized them with the terrain. He pointed out the buildings, trees, meadows, railway lines and the British air-defence radar set-up. The drop point was fixed. The plane was a single-engine Cessna 207. It would carry the pilot, the instructor and six jumpers, some of whom were novices and some old hands. The ripcord of the parachute was attached to a stout nail.

It did not seem that the weather was going to change. They had to sleep there. But in the morning, when they saw that the wind had dropped, they all ran to the airfield.

They quickly climbed into overalls, leather overshoes and helmets. Each carried a reserve parachute tied to their stomach. They were to jump from a height of 2,000 feet. The free fall would last for four seconds. The first parachute would be deployed after five seconds; and if that failed, then the second ripcord would have to be pulled after seven seconds. A huge orange mark had been made on the snow beneath them. With one eye on the wind drift indicator, the instructor would decide the place where they would jump. Since visibility was poor, the morning was wasted.

In the afternoon, they got their chance. The aircraft took off and at 300 feet, all of them got ready. Everyone had their eyes fixed on their altimeters, which were attached to their chests. At 2,000 feet, the aircraft began to turn, the engine was turned off and the aircraft began to sway. The instructor began his announcements.

'Everyone to the door.'

'Put one foot out.'

'Squat on your left leg.'

'Hold on to the top of the door.'

'Left hand on the threshold.'

'Look up at sixty degrees.'

'Look at zero.'

'Don't look down.'

'Bend backwards.'

'Spread your arms and legs.'

Ashutosh followed these instructions to the letter and made his jump. Now was the time to count the seconds. Thoughts flashed through his head: 'Where am I? What am I doing? Where is that plane going?' He began to hear a flapping sound. A very sweet flapping. Above his head, the parachute had opened. He caught hold of the parachute handles and began to enjoy the bird's eye view he had of the world. He was only aware of himself, nothing else mattered. For a few short but blissful moments, he had escaped the limitations of his human form, achieved a level of transcendence.

He now had two minutes to bring his body, his knees, his feet and his ankles into the correct posture for landing. He had to keep his eyes fixed on the landing spot to get his feet back on terra firma. If he made a mistake now, he could hurt himself badly.

But once again, he followed instructions to the letter. Although he had enjoyed drifting and gliding through the air, he was still in his senses; he made his first landing perfectly.

He took courage and made another jump that day, once again storing up the memories of that experience. And then he returned to Edinburgh.

When we read about these exploits in a letter, our breaths stopped. It was only his descriptions of the event that had us breathing again.

For the rest of the summer, he spent seven days in Paris and seven days in London. He explored those cities inside out. He estimated that he walked about 150 km and lost 5 kg in weight!

Throughout his year in Scotland, he enjoyed the open air and took advantage of the magnificent playing fields. He also travelled a lot and enjoyed the famous Edinburgh Arts Festival. He got a chance to see the libraries and art galleries of London, Paris and Glasgow.

But he was also paying attention to his studies. He got As in microelectronics, analogue communication and digital circuits. He topped the class in high-energy physics and electromagnetism. During this time, he also wrote a paper with the title 'Submicron MOSFET features using X-ray lithography'.

And so the year in Scotland came to an end. Once again, it was summer, and once again, he had to look for a summer job. The Scottish visa did not allow him to take a campus job. But he had heard that one of the professors had started his own circuit design company. Two graduates of the University of Edinburgh were working with him. The project manager, Clive Robinson, became Ashutosh's mentor. The professor's name was Roger Walmsley. He recognized Ashutosh's talent and gave him a job. In a month, Ashutosh designed a circuit. No one was sure whether it would work or not. Ashutosh was sure; and the circuit did work. Not only that, it was sold to a client.

The circuit was of great importance. It was used to test other devices. Since it was the summer vacation, Dr Walmsley had gone out of town with his wife and children. In his absence, people from other companies would approach this company if they had problems.

Much time, effort, and expenditure would be saved because of the circuit Ashutosh had designed. Later, he heard that Dr Walmsley took out a patent on that circuit.

He worked at Walmsley's company for two-and-a-half months before his time in Scotland came to an end and he headed back to UPenn for the next two years of study.

13

Los Alamos and Harvard

The fourth academic year began at UPenn. Ashutosh took courses in psychology and French. He wrote an essay for the psychology course. He had studied French in school for four years in India. The academic standard was much higher at UPenn. The emphasis here was on the writing of essays and on conversational skills.

The Christmas vacation of 1986 began. He had spent the Christmas vacations of 1983 and 1984 at the hostel. He had planned to do the same that year. A good example of how well the university looked after him was that they funded his trips to India in 1986 and of 1987. We were overjoyed.

In 1986, he got to celebrate his twenty-first birthday with the Kotwal–Pradhan family at home. Mothi Aai was now getting on in years; her heart was ailing; her feet were swollen. We felt the absence of Mothe Baba and Indutai (my mother). Ashutosh brought Mothi Aai soft warm slippers and a huge teddy bear from America.

As she took tentative steps in her new footwear, her face filled with happiness. We were in Nagpur at the time. French and psychology were subjects I loved and which I could understand. Thus, this time around, Ashutosh and I were sharing a lot and his father was listening

As was our tradition, we took these two bonus vacations and stayed at the Tadoba Tiger Sanctuary. We saw many animals but no tiger. We also went for a short trip to Goa where, about 16 km south of Madgaon, was the beautiful Cavelossim beach. The Dalmia Company had built a beautiful resort called The Old Anchor right by the beach. In 1983, Vijayrao had bought a timeshare scheme that allowed us to go and spend a week there.

When Ashutosh came in 1987, we took him to Cavelossim. He was delighted with it; the Zuari River was on one side, the beach on the other. The stress of getting there and the heat exhausted me. I just wanted to sit down and rest, maybe drink a glass of cool water. Ashutosh said, 'Aai, what is hunger and thirst in front of this beauty?' And he rushed off for a swim.

In the summer of 1987, Prof. Fortune asked Ashutosh to join him at Los Alamos in New Mexico, to participate in a research project on intermediate-energy nuclear physics. He would be conducting experiments at the Los Alamos Meson Physics Facility, a division of the Los Alamos National Laboratory. This was where the Manhattan Project, led by J. Robert Oppenheimer, had been developed—the one that gave birth to the atomic bomb used in the Second World War. Ashutosh had to get security clearance to enter the premises of the Los Alamos National Laboratory and operate the experiments using an apparatus called the Energetic Pion Channel and Spectrometer.

At Los Alamos, Ashutosh had to deal with mathematics and measurements at the quantum level. He had not studied any of this in class. But by this time he had made great strides in his understanding of computer software. He figured out the kind of program he needed to make the relevant calculations and wrote it himself. He and Prof. Fortune published a paper based on these nuclear-physics calculations.

Ashutosh stayed at Los Alamos for two-and-a-half months. He got to attend a conference on the muon-nucleon and the pion-nucleon interactions. Nobel Prize-winning scientist Hans Bethe presented a paper on neutrinos and astrophysics. Prof. Fortune was also a good bridge player. He would get Ashutosh to play as his partner. He even took part in the duplicate bridge tournament in the club. In New Mexico, there was a settlement of Pueblo Indians, the original inhabitants of the area. There was a deep influence of the Spanish on their way of life. Ashutosh went to watch their rodeos. He also enjoyed their dancing.

But in his opinion, the major attraction of the area was its mind-boggling natural beauty. As in Scotland, he took some long walks over the mesas, often in the early morning in order to take photographs of the sunrise. He enjoyed taking pictures of storms too, of the purple lightning crackling amidst the dramatic cloudscapes.

The laboratory had to close for ten days because the mechanism that emitted the beam needed repairs. The rest of the staff went home. As always, Ashutosh remained alone, which was precisely what he wanted. He visited the archaeological site where 700-year-old Indian homes were still preserved; he also visited the Bandelier National Monument; he hired a car to tour the Jemez mountains, where he saw a million-year-old volcano that had once spat fire and lava and ash. To the west, formed by this ancient lava flow, lies the Pajarito mountain range (a word that means little bird in Spanish). The water that flowed down carved mesas and canyons out of the ground. This was the beginning of the city of Los Alamos. In this hellish landscape, he also saw rivers of brimstone.

When the job at Los Alamos ended, Ashutosh returned to UPenn in Philadelphia; his fifth and final year had begun. Ashutosh got to visit Louisville, Kentucky. There is a society of engineers in America, which admits only the elite of the community. Its name is Tau Beta Pi. At the end of the fourth year, Ashutosh was chosen as the secretary of the UPenn chapter of the society. The society had a meeting in Louisville during the fall of 1987.

In the final year, engineering students at UPenn develop and execute an advanced design project. Ashutosh proposed to his professor, Dr Van der Spiegel, that he would design and develop a complete silicon chip using very large-scale integration (VLSI) techniques. The experience of circuit design in Edinburgh stood him in good stead. He came up with an idea that would be useful to the chip design industry, and Prof. Van der Spiegel agreed. Over the year, the elaborate design steadily took shape. Finally, after passing all checks, the circuit was sent for fabrication. When the fabricated chip came back from the foundry, Ashutosh connected it to the power supply for final testing.

Would it work as designed? The moment of truth ... it worked! Ashutosh and Prof. Van der Spiegel were both very happy. Ashutosh has still preserved a poster-sized printout of that integrated circuit layout.

At this point, Ashutosh was fairly sure that he was going to pursue postgraduate studies in physics. Having conducted research in both fundamental physics and electronics, he was confident in this decision. Prof. Fortune's advice rang true. He had to study his options carefully and make some decisions about his plan of action. He gave the Graduate Record Examination in English, physics and mathematics. The PhD programme applications required him to write a statement of purpose. His educational and research record at

UPenn was impeccable. And so, every university to which he applied accepted him with full financial support: Harvard, MIT, Princeton, UPenn, Caltech, Stanford and the University of Chicago.

∽

The Choice of University—the Criteria and the Decision

Although he shows no external sign of it, each decision Ashutosh takes is done with due consideration, after weighing the pros and cons. In those days, he was trying to make up his mind about which field of physics he should specialize in; which in turn would determine his choice of university.

His attitude was: 'I knew that I would have to make up my mind for myself, without paying attention to other people's opinions, for this was going to be my life's work. If I were unclear about my own goals and my own desires, how was it possible for someone else to tell me? And so, what was the point of asking other people?' He spent many days investigating the universities and their specializations.

Cornell was a leader in the field of condensed matter. Harvard was equally good in this field but it also excelled in theory, as did Princeton. In particle physics, Harvard, Chicago, MIT, Caltech and Stanford were the top choices. Experiments in high energy physics were being conducted at Fermilab, which was close to Chicago. Stanford had the Stanford Linear Accelerator Centre (SLAC). In addition, Fermilab and CERN (Conseil Européen pour la Recherche Nucléaire or the European Centre for Nuclear Research, in Switzerland, near Geneva) were giving SLAC a run for its money. With SLAC, he would mostly meet other students of Stanford and Berkeley. At Fermilab and CERN, there were larger international projects.

As a physics school, Caltech was famous; its professors and students had a great dialogue going. Caltech was also known for research in astronomy and nuclear physics. While walking around the Caltech campus, Ashutosh happened to be waiting for a lift. When it arrived, the doors opened, and a wheelchair emerged. Lost in thought, Ashutosh walked into the lift when suddenly it was as if he were struck by lightning. It was Stephen Hawking in that wheelchair! The lift doors were about to shut; he forced them open and jumped out. He took the opportunity to gaze upon his hero.

Meanwhile, Harvard wrote that they had accepted him with financial support. He received a letter from the dean saying that he had been accepted into the PhD programme of September 1988–1989. They were going to give him a scholarship: $12,715 towards fees and $450 as medical expenses. In addition, he would receive a yearly grant of $22,255 for food and accommodation. And he would be given a teaching fellowship. The fellows are expected to deliver some lectures, direct students in their laboratory work, and conduct small tests.

Prof. Pipkin, chair of the physics department, welcomed him with these words, 'I am sure that many other famous universities have also offered you PhD positions. This is the result of the hard work you have put in over the last few years and I offer you my congratulations. I welcome you to our laboratory.'

Similar letters of invitation and congratulations came from other universities.

Many of them had written at length about the facilities he would enjoy and the laboratories in which he would get to work. They had remarked upon his fine academic career and on the letters of recommendation that he had received from his teachers. Each one tried to persuade him to join their university.

Caltech invited him to tour their campus. He was to meet all the professors and he would be told about their research projects. There was lunch at one of the professors' homes and he was introduced to many of them there. Similar invitations came from Stanford, MIT, Princeton and Chicago.

Princeton expressed the opinion that any university that accepted him would benefit from his work in their laboratories, in view of his work so far. Princeton would be able to provide the right setting and facilities for him to grow and develop as a physicist.

Chicago, Stanford, UPenn and MIT were all eager for him to enrol. They were all willing to give him scholarships. They told him of the facilities that they would be able to provide. The universities there have developed a tradition of welcoming new students and acknowledging their academic excellence and capabilities. During the month of March 1988, Ashutosh visited Harvard, MIT, Stanford, Princeton and Caltech. He walked through the campuses, met faculty members and had discussions with them.

Now he had made up his mind; it would be Harvard. He was eager to join. In that time, he also had to do an important job for the Kotwal family. His cousin Bansie was getting married to Ashok Vaswani, a love marriage, on 22 January 1988. Meena Kaki had gone from India to attend the wedding. Dada Kaka was busy and could not.

Ashutosh was their favourite. Meena Kaki enjoyed celebrating the Ganapati festival at her place and she would have Ashutosh perform the puja. Even now she wanted him to perform the Kanyadaan ceremony. The wedding was to take place in a temple in the borough of Queens in New York City, followed by lunch at a grand restaurant in Manhattan.

In May 1988, Ashutosh was awarded a Bachelor of Science (or BS degree) in Electrical Engineering from the Moore School and a Bachelor of Science in Economics from UPenn's Wharton School.

Both degrees were conferred on him with special Latin words of honour, 'Summa Cum Laude', indicating that he had graduated with the highest distinction.

VNIVERSITAS
PENNSYLVANIENSIS
OMNIBVS HAS LITTERAS LECTVRIS SALVTEM DICIT

Cum academiis antiquus mos sit scientiis litterisve humanioribus excultos titulo iusto condecorare nos igitur auctoritate Curatorum nobis commissa ASHUTOSH VIJAY KOTWAL ob studia a Professoribus approbata ad gradum BACHELOR OF SCIENCE IN ECONOMICS admisimus eique omnia iura honores privilegia ad hunc gradum pertinentia libenter concessimus Cuius rei testimonio nomina nostra die mensis Maii XVI Anno Salutis MCMLXXXVIII et Vniversitatis conditae CCXLVIII Philadelphiae subscripsimus
HIC GRADVS CONLATVS EST SVMMA CVM LAVDE

Mary Flynn Meyers
Sigilli Custos

Shelden Hackney
PRAESES

Russell E. Palmer
DECANVS

The Wharton School
of the University of Pennsylvania
Founded 1881 by Joseph Wharton
congratulates you
on the successful completion of your
Baccalaureate Degree
With All Rights and Privileges Pertaining Thereto
Given in the City of Philadelphia, Commonwealth of Pennsylvania
May 15, 1988

Marion L. Oliver, Vice Dean and Director
Wharton Undergraduate Division

Russell E. Palmer, Dean
The Wharton School

Undergraduate Awards and Honours

When he joined UPenn, Ashutosh had already been awarded the Benjamin Franklin Scholarship, which made him eligible for Honours courses.

America has an organization called the National Dean's List, members of which are drawn from the American Association for Higher Education. They keep track of the best students across the country and create the list as an encouragement to greater achievement. This organization sent a letter congratulating Ashutosh. He found out that he was on the National Dean's List which they announced:

> You have been selected by the above-named faculty member [David P. Pope] to receive honorary award recognition by having your biography published in the eighth annual edition of THE NATIONAL DEAN'S LIST 1984-85.

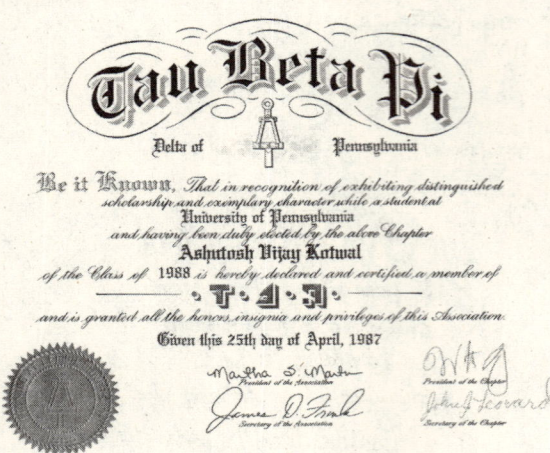

THE NATIONAL DEAN'S LIST is the largest, most prestigious publication in the country recognizing academically gifted students selected by their college dean or comparable faculty representative. Each year 2,500 of our nation's finest colleges and universities use the publication as a special award to recognize their most outstanding students. Only one half of one per cent of our nation's college students receive this award. We commend you for your accomplishments. As a National Dean's List student, you are eligible to compete for $25,000 in scholarship awards and to use the Student Referral Service, a valuable reference service for students applying to graduate school or seeking employment.

Four organizations in America, which track the best and brightest of the student community, made him a member:

- Tau Beta Pi: An elite national engineering honours society. On 25 April 1987, Ashutosh was elected as a representative of Tau Beta Pi's Pennsylvania chapter and was appointed the secretary. This national engineering organization felicitated Ashutosh with a full membership and an award certificate.
- Pi Mu Epsilon: An elite national mathematics honours society. Ashutosh was s elected as an honorary member of this body for the aptitude he had shown for mathematics.
- Beta Gamma Sigma: An exclusive national business honour society. On 19 April 1988, Ashutosh was elected an honorary member of the society.
- Eta Kappa Nu: The honor society of IEEE (the Institute of Electrical and Electronics Engineers), the world's largest technical professional organization for the advancement of technology.

At this time, we were in Iraq. Rail India Technical and Economic Service (RITES) had secured a contract to maintain and operate the railway lines from Baghdad to Husaybah, where the Euphrates crossed the Iraq–Syria border. Vijarao was the head of the Electrical Department.

14

Summer Job at IBM

In the summer of 1988, Prof. Fortune asked whether Ashutosh would return to Los Alamos, but Ashutosh wanted to see how research in physics was used in industry. He decided to work at IBM.

He had a half-hour interview on the telephone. IBM's Thomas J. Watson Research Centre is in New York State, 25 miles from Manhattan. As it is the main research facility, 2,300 people work there. There are other smaller facilities in Cambridge, Albany, Zurich, Tokyo and Silicon Valley.

IBM is known all over the world for its high-speed computers, its storage discs and its mainframe computers. Ashutosh worked on the high-definition flat-panel television screen. He devised mathematical models for amorphous silicon transistors. He wrote the equations that would help put these transistors on to computer screens. He checked whether they were the right fit and had the appropriate characteristics. These transistors are still used in liquid crystal displays (LCD).

IBM was then working on these liquid crystal display (LCD) screens. They were used first in computers and then to replace the cathode ray tube in television sets. Each pixel in an image on the screen is matched to an amorphous silicon transistor that controls the voltage on it. It was Ashutosh's job to measure and analyse the conduction properties of these transistors. The integrated circuits would be inscribed on a sheet of glass; a television screen of this kind would be only an inch thick and could be hung on the wall like a painting. It was a novel idea when Ashutosh worked on it.

The silicon transistors are placed on the screen at low temperatures. At higher temperatures, this did not work because the glass melts. At low temperatures, the amorphous silicon transistors had different characteristics from the crystalline silicon transistors that were commonly used. These characteristics had to be measured. IBM had the best instruments for this and Ashutosh made precise measurements of the transistors' voltage-current functions.

Then he found that these measurements could not be explained by existing calculations. Ashutosh decided to study the physics equations of amorphous silicon and wrote his own equations for these transistors. He then wrote a detailed computer program to calculate the solutions of these equations. He would work on the computer all night long and obtain the desired results by the next morning. He devised many computer models to match the measurements and the results of the monitoring experiments.

In the beginning, the computer he used was a small desktop. As the complexity of his calculations increased, the need for a faster computer was felt. He asked for a high-speed computer. He could then calculate multiple characteristics at the same time.

He worked at IBM in this manner for two months. He had to make a presentation of this work. He wrote a paper as well. Many people sought out the paper. There was a large audience at his presentation. His boss's boss was also present. There was a long discussion. Many heads nodded in approval and assent. There were also some naysayers. There were many PhDs present. Ashutosh had not even started his PhD and this made them defensive. The discussion went on for an hour and a half.

The paper he wrote titled 'A device model for the amorphous silicon staggered electrode thin film transistor' was published in a special issue of the journal of the Institute of Electrical and Electronics Engineers. He co-authored the paper with his supervisor, Dr R.R. Troutman. These amorphous silicon thin-film transistors are now used for all active-matrix liquid crystal displays, such as computer and laptop screens, and flat-screen televisions.

In the summer of 1989, Troutman invited him to come back to IBM but by this time he was working on his PhD at Harvard in particle physics and it was not possible for him to return.

In July 1988, we were in Iraq when we heard of my father's death. By this time, Ashutosh had spent five years in the US. Seeing how good he was at his studies, Balasaheb had dreamt of his grandson as an IAS officer. He felt bad that Ashutosh had abandoned IIT, had left the National Talent Scholarship behind and gone abroad to study, but he had hidden his feelings. For him, Harvard had a certain glamour attached to it because it was John F. Kennedy's alma mater. So he was very happy when Ashutosh announced that he would be doing his PhD there.

Ashutosh was alone in the US when he heard about his grandfather's death. I have no way to understand what his responses were, how he dealt with this bereavement. When we told him over the telephone, he said, 'Haan', but later, in a letter, he said, 'One era is over. My childhood has come to an end.'

While he was working at IBM, he was living in New York. His studies at UPenn were over. He had moved his stuff to a friend's house as he had to vacate the hostel. In New York, he managed to find some time to play tennis despite the demands of his job.

After two-and-a-half months of work at IBM, in September 1988, he left New York to stay in Boston. He stayed in Boston for two years and then moved to a town called Geneva near Chicago because he wanted to do his PhD on the E665 experiment which was being conducted at the Fermi National Accelerator Laboratory located nearby at Batavia, Illinois. He rented a small house in Geneva along with two housemates, Tom, an American, and Fotis, a Greek, both his friends from Harvard.

15

Iraq–Jordan–Egypt

In 1988, my husband and I went to live in Iraq. In February 1990, Ashutosh came to visit us there. This was quite a gamble because Iraq and the US did not have very good diplomatic relations at the time. His friends had warned him that if the immigration authorities saw an Iraq stamp on his passport, they might not let him back into the country. But he came anyway.

When he arrived, we toured Iraq extensively and visited Jordan and Egypt as well. Ashutosh loves visiting museums and enjoys taking others to them. He had a great interest in different building styles. It always surprises me how much he knows about a place even before he has visited it. Who knows when he gets the time to do all that reading? We had already been in Iraq for two-and-a-half years when he arrived. The two of us had already seen Baghdad, Samarra, Najaf and Karbala; but visiting them with Ashutosh gave them an entirely new meaning. We drove through the desert to visit the ancient Parthian city of Hatra in northern Iraq, a first-century site that was still very well-preserved. He had done some deep research on the ancient architecture of Babylon and had understood it thoroughly.

On our trip around Iraq, Jordan and Egypt, he was our guide, our historian and our resident gourmet. We did not use a travel company, nor did we ever have a tour guide with us. Jamil, our Iraqi driver, was with us during our tour in Iraq. We took a taxi to Amman, the capital of Jordan, from Baghdad. This was an overnight drive through the desert of western Iraq and eastern Jordan. For each lap of the journey, we hired another taxi. The whole enterprise was built around Ashutosh's energy and his enthusiasm.

After touring Amman, we went to see the Dead Sea. Ashutosh and his father went for a swim. This sea is 1,410 feet below sea level and has a maximum depth of 997 feet. Its salinity is very high, at 34 per cent, making it about ten times as salty as ordinary seawater. Animal and vegetable life cannot survive in it. The density of the water is 1.25 kg/litre. And so, if you try to swim in it, you float on the surface. There are photos of Ashutosh and his father floating on the surface of the Dead Sea.

On the western edge of the desert in Jordan, overlooking the point where the Jordan River meets the Dead Sea, rises Mount Nebo. When Moses led the Jews out of captivity from Egypt, parting the Red Sea, he was granted a view of the Promised Land from this mountain. We saw all these places. There are some exquisite examples of mosaic art in Jordan, dating back to the Byzantine empire. In the Memorial Church of Moses on Mount Nebo, the floors and walls are covered with beautiful mosaics depicting flora, fauna and scenes of natural beauty; there are also some portraits and other things. In the nearby Byzantine town of Madaba, on the floor of Saint George's Church, is a huge map of the Promised Land, made of two million individual stones. From Mount Nebo, we could see the Jordan flowing by and beyond its western bank, we could see the skyline of Jerusalem.

Jordan was also where we saw a hugely romantic site, which we would have missed had Ashutosh not insisted we go there. And if we had not gone, we would have missed the experience of a lifetime. In the south of Jordan, there are huge sandstone mountains. In the ravines of these mountains that were created by water, the ancient city of Petra was carved into the rock. The name, meaning 'rock', has its origins in a mix of Greek and Arabic. It is also known as the 'Red Rose City' because of the pink colour of the stone.

In 1985, UNESCO named Petra a World Heritage Site, calling it 'one of the most precious properties of man's cultural heritage'. The Western world had no idea of its existence until 1812, when Johann Ludwig Burckhardt, a Swiss explorer, discovered it. Its geographical location had kept this archaeological jewel from being discovered: it is surrounded by mountains in the Wadi Araba.

A wadi is a space in the desert that is habitable. This wadi stretches from the Bay of Aqaba to the Dead Sea. There is a route to it that winds its narrow way around the Jabal Haroun Mountain, where Moses' brother Aaron is said to be buried.

One can scarcely believe one's eyes when one looks at the ancient buildings here. Half of it seems built and half of it seems carved underground in rock. There are places of worship, grave memorials, homes, public halls and the like. One can see various influences at work: Greek, Egyptian, Arab, Syrian and Roman. Many places show signs of the barrage that must have been mounted by the Bedouin raiders. This ancient city and its beautiful art have been preserved meticulously. The original inhabitants were experts at water conservation; one sees signs of this everywhere; in the underwater storage caverns and wells. In the arid desert, this city must have seemed like an oasis. The nickname for it was Al-Khazneh, or the national treasure house, which also refers to its most magnificent temple and facade.

The Arab king Aretas of the Nabatean dynasty reigned between 9 BC and 40 AD. Petra was his capital. In the Christian era, Cornelius Palma was the Roman governor of Syria, who conquered the Nabatean kingdom. Then the Persian dynasty of the Sassanids took over. From that point onwards, Petra began to fade in importance. Even though it was once an important staging point on the trade route from Palmyra to Asia, it started to slip into insignificance, once Palmyra in Syria started gaining importance as the trade capital of West Asia.

In the modern era, once again, important historical events began to happen in Petra. In 1917, after the third battle of the Gaza Strip, T.E. Lawrence (Lawrence of Arabia) led the British and Palestinian forces on an attack on the Ottoman Army. Lawrence led the uprising himself. The wife of Sheikh Khalil led a women's battalion, and they defeated the Ottomans easily. Lawrence's ploy worked.

That we went and saw Petra and understood its history was all thanks to Ashutosh. As we travelled by boat to Egypt via the Bay of Aqaba, he brought another geographic wonder to our attention. You can see the borders of four countries from this bay: Egypt, Israel, Jordan and Saudi Arabia!

In the cold night air of the Sinai Desert, we disembarked and took the bus to Cairo. There are many moments I cannot forget: the Suez Canal, the grand buildings of Cairo, the sudden sight of the Pyramids at the edge of the city and Ashutosh's excitement at seeing all of this.

When we were at the Cairo Museum, he displayed a profound knowledge of the Egyptian civilization. The ancient Egyptians had an interesting view of life after death; it would largely resemble our life here on earth and this belief was reflected in their death ceremonies. Many of the items that were meant for use in the afterlife were on display in the museum. They had developed much of the technology needed for this. This was very exciting for Ashutosh.

We visited Luxor, the Temple of Abu Simbel with its magnificent statues, the mosques of the mediaeval period of Cairo, and the Coptic churches and ancient cistern that were built around the same time. We went deep into the sanctum sanctorum of the pyramids to see the graves there. As archaeological investigations conducted by many countries were still happening, it was possible to see only those things that would not disturb their research.

During this kind of journey, the one who is determined to see as much as possible has to have patience and fortitude when dealing with the externalities; it is a test of one's patience. I will never forget our trip from Cairo to Aswan.

The Cairo railway station was grand but the rail journey after that harked back to ancient times. There were no other travellers in our compartment. There were no arrangements for food and drink on the train. There was no drinking water available either. The train stopped when it stopped and started when it started. There was no one to ask where we were and there was the language barrier as well. The toilets were a disaster.

We somehow made it through this three-day journey, whose scheduled time was one day. I was in a state but Ashutosh didn't seem fazed. Once more I learnt from my son how to keep one's mind fresh, how to keep one's eyes and ears open, how to drive one's body to its limits.

16

... And America

By the time Ashutosh had spent nine years in America, we had met four times. In 1985, he came back for seven weeks; in 1986 for two weeks; in 1987 again for two weeks; and in 1990, we had three weeks together in Iraq, Jordan and Egypt! We did not have much idea of how he lived in America. In February 1992, we went to stay with him. At the end of April, Vijayrao's leave ended and so he returned to India. I stayed on for another month. For two-and-a-half months, we toured America extensively in his second-hand Nissan, which often clocked 450 to 500 miles a day.

We saw the casinos of Las Vegas. We visited the grand metropolises of America: Chicago, New York, San Francisco, Los Angeles, San Diego, Las Vegas, Atlanta, Washington DC, Philadelphia and Boston. We also toured many of the world-class universities: Harvard, Princeton, MIT, Caltech, Berkeley, Stanford and of course, his first university, UPenn which he showed us with great enthusiasm. We had also planned a trip to Hawaii. I had always wanted to see Hollywood, Universal Studios, Sunset Boulevard and Disneyland. I loved the San Diego Zoo.

The other places on our must-see list were the Yosemite National Park and the ancient giant sequoia trees. A story from our trip there. It was afternoon, around 3.30 or 4 p.m. It suddenly began to grow dark, a wind sprang up and the rain came pouring down. The windscreen wipers on the hired car failed. We could see nothing in front of us. It was on the highway so we could not stop. Ashutosh drove the car off the highway onto a leafy detour. The sound of the wind and the battering of the rain were unbelievable. But Ashutosh got out of the car. He repaired the wipers. He outfaced the storm for at least fifteen to twenty minutes. And then he drove through the storm, through the dark, over the rough roads of the Yosemite National Park. Neither father nor son paid any attention to my pleas that we should get out of there as soon as possible. Some of the granite cliffs we saw in that park were truly extraordinary. What did it matter that we had to fight our way through a storm?

From San Francisco, we flew to the islands of Hawaii, in the middle of the Pacific Ocean. The city of Honolulu is on the island of Oahu. There are thousands of duplex apartments built for tourists by the sea. We stayed in one of them. We spent days on the beach. The water was clean and blue. It was not very deep, about 3–4 feet.

Beautiful multicoloured tropical fish swam around in it. Ashutosh and his father did a lot of snorkelling at the Hanauma Bay beach and saw many fish and took photographs. I would sit by the edge of the sea and watch. After much persuasion from Ashutosh, I agreed to give it a go but as soon as my head went under water, my snorkelling apparatus seemed to malfunction and water went into my nose and mouth. I began to gasp and choke. I surfaced and began to shriek a bit. Ashutosh came running up. I clasped my arms around his neck and with great difficulty, he brought me ashore and then said, 'I had no idea that a person could drown in 1.5 feet of water.'

We visited the historic site of the Pearl Harbour bombing in the Second World War. Ashutosh knew a great deal about the war between Japan and America. He went on his own one day to see the big island of Hawaii, which has an active volcano on it. It is still possible to see red-hot lava swirling about inside it. Hawaii is known for its vibrant and vivid varieties of hibiscus, and for its pelicans, among other things.

The airport in Honolulu is huge. One has to walk a lot there. We were flying Continental Airlines. We had to catch our flight at gate number 24. Viijayrao had been suffering from gout for a long time. He had an attack of gout and was walking very slowly. No wheelchairs seemed available. Ashutosh went ahead to the boarding gate to ask them to wait but Vijayrao was walking so slowly that by the time we reached, the gate had been closed. The next flight was early the following morning and so, rather than risk more walking, we spent the night at the airport.

During our stay in America, we also visited Vijayrao's younger brother in Canada for fifteen days. We boarded a bus at Seattle, on the northwestern border of the US, from where Vancouver is four hours away. Most of the road passes through a dark, deep forest. When we crossed the border, it was raining and temperatures had dropped. Vancouver is a fun city. Truus, Ashok's wife, took us around the city. The three of us also wandered around a lot. Victoria Island and Canada Place were memorable places. The University of British Columbia campus where Ashok Kaka worked was very beautiful. He had a splendid office. In front, the sea, and beyond it, the looming mountains. Ashok got his undergraduate degree from IIT and then went to America where he acquired a master's degree in engineering.

Then he earned a doctorate in economics and became a professor of economics. He was the head of the department at the University of British Columbia. He would often come to India to do research on agricultural and developmental economics. He was a lover of literature and studied it carefully.

Ashutosh wanted to ski on Whistler Mountain. All three of us went to the ski resort. It was very cold and the two of us bowed out, but Ashutosh went skiing alone. He came back after four or five hours, his clothes soaked, because he had taken a few spills on the slopes.

While we were travelling in the US, Ashutosh took us to those places that had meaning and value for him: Chicago, New York, San Francisco, Washington DC ... and in each of these places we visited the fine arts museums, the libraries and places of scientific interest.

We had read a lot about the American Civil War and so we went to many of the sites that were close by in North Carolina. As in the UK, historic sites were preserved with great care and love. In South Carolina, we visited the 300-year-old city of Charleston; this was a beautiful city full of exquisite houses, well-designed streets and gardens full of trees and flowers.

We also saw the sandy hills of Kitty Hawk, the site at which the Wright Brothers demonstrated the first heavier-than-air flight; it was a place that commemorated the American spirit. That flight lasted twelve seconds. The Wright brothers had visited this lonely windswept place for many years, living in a simple house, working on their experiments, camping in the middle of nowhere. They would bring their equipment all the way from Ohio, more than 1,000 km away. There was a museum with archival documents and photographs that told the story of the development of air travel. And all around us, there was a limitless expanse of sky. All this added up to a memorable experience. There was a monument in the form of a sculpture rising to the sky glorifying human imagination and creativity. We were touched by the serious and respectful way in which American families visited this place.

Ashutosh's enthusiasm in showing us these places added immeasurably to the depth of our experience. He was then twenty-six years old. We began to think about a suitable life partner for him. Mrs Sudha Gokhale of Atlanta suggested some suitable young Indian women. She even organized some meetings. Although he obediently went to these meetings, it was clear Ashutosh's priority was his PhD, so we did not force the issue.

This was a rather expensive trip, but Ashutosh bore all the costs. He used some of the money that he had saved from his scholarship, but the most important thing was that he took time off from his PhD to be with us.

17

The Immersive Education Experience

During his five years at UPenn, Ashutosh had studied electronics, finance and economics. But because of the flexibility of the American education system, he could also study English literature, the French language and psychology.

Thomas Pynchon's novel *The Crying of Lot 49* and T.S. Eliot's famous poem *The Waste Land* were prescribed texts. Ashutosh wrote a detailed essay comparing the themes of the two. He did an analysis of the collapse of modern society depicted in these books using the example of science, his favourite subject. The professor was all praise for his deft analysis and the depth of his research. One gets a good example of how he could connect with important issues in his essay for the English literature class.

He used the notion of entropy to explain the two books. In any closed system, the amount of disorder always increases. This is entropy, a concept scientists began to use when they were trying to improve the efficacy of thermal engines in the eighteenth century. Entropy began to be widely used by other scientists as well. Many basic tenets of physics are based on the idea of entropy.

The second law of thermodynamics is seen as one of the most important laws of physics. It is possible to state this law in terms of entropy. It can be stated as the tendency of entropy to always increase. If the measure of entropy in one section of a system decreases, it will only be because there has been a corresponding increase in another section of the system.

Different parts of the universe are always interacting spontaneously. And so the measure of entropy in the universe is always increasing. At a certain time, it will reach the maximum point of disorder. At this point, it is impossible for energy to transform itself. Then the process of metamorphosis stops.

It is possible to use the concept of entropy to understand the work of both Pynchon and Eliot, who reflect on the state of society in their times. These days, relationships between human beings are agenda-based. Intellectual and emotional exchanges have reached their lowest point.

Thomas Pynchon uses the device of Maxwell's Demon to suggest a way back for a society gone horribly wrong. This has its origins in the theoretical construct James Maxwell Clerk devised to challenge the second law of thermodynamics. But in reality, such a construct is impossible. Pynchon wants to say that some people in society can be alert and alive, and it is through the existence of such people that the world may be saved.

Eliot's contention, Ashutosh says, is that *The Waste Land* can be brought to fresh life again. He has suggested the importance of a moral internal life. His poem ends with 'Shantih, shantih, shantih'.

At the point when the universe returns to oneness with God, the transformations between matter and energy will also end because they will also achieve a similar unity. Eliot dreams of a time when all human souls achieve peace. Ashutosh must have absorbed the principles of Advaita Hindu philosophy at some point in the past. This was the background against which he read and appreciated Eliot's epic poem. The scientific research he was going to do was also going to aim at this ultimate peace. The poem arrived at the right time, planting seeds that would sprout in the future.

Ashutosh's professor really liked the essay. She made appreciative comments and gave it an A grade. An extract from her remarks is offered here: 'This is a fascinating essay—clear, original and well-supported. You merge religion and science with great facility, and in ways that even Pynchon's critics haven't fully connected. Your connections to Eliot are also consistently excellent.'

It was at UPenn that he must have developed the habit of working on really different subjects and producing papers one after the other. In December 1987, he wrote an essay: 'On the parallel distributed processing (PDP) model for the brain'! Here is an abstract of the remarks by his professor who gave him an A grade: 'This paper was first-rate, and fun to read. In the immediate future, most tests of the PDP approach will not involve direct brain research, but computer modeling of human performance and non-intrusive cognitive experiments.'

Artificial intelligence was also one of their subjects. Ashutosh wrote an essay comparing the working of the human brain with that of the computer, pointing out the similarities and differences. It was thought-provoking and interesting. Then the professors wrote comments and remarks that were also very readable.

As he had studied economics at Wharton, his understanding of the subject was also thorough. To understand the state of the world's economy and to understand America's place in that economy, it was necessary to study a wide and eclectic range of subjects. The increasing importance of management in the modern world was underlined in many of the books that he read at the time.

At one point in time, the American car industry had been second to none. This was no longer the case. Ashutosh read Brock Yates's *The Decline and Fall of the American Automobile Industry* and wrote a commentary on it. In March 1987, he wrote an essay that showed his understanding of the subject. He explained Brock Yates's basic hypothesis as follows:

Countries like Japan studied the problems that arose periodically in the car industry and focused on finding remedies. This research was generally conducted by the private sector. On the other hand, research in the car industry in the US tended to be on the level of ideas and dealt with issues on a large canvas. The result was that Japanese research was industry-driven and the results of their research could be applied directly and quickly to production; hence the country could be seen to be racing ahead.

Taking this discussion further, Yates said, the main reason for the decline of American research is the lack of focus on technology. The car industry is dominated by bean counters. In their drive to maximize short-term profits, they ignore the long-term implications on quality.

Here, Yates offers the examples of pioneering industrialists like Henry Ford and Alfred Sloan. Henry Ford had the dream of creating a car for the people. Sloan was weak on technology. His General Motors Company ran on a hierarchical power structure and financial controls, which became a paradigm of corporate management. It is not difficult to see that in such corporations, financial men are in power. The development of technology is relegated to the background. In one phase of the industry, Sloan invented the slogan 'Make money, not cars', which became the industry's mantra. General Motors and Ford began to decline. Smaller nations like Japan, France and Germany pressed down on the accelerator and surged ahead of America. Technology and industry are locked in a struggle, Yates maintained, and America would have to find a way to reclaim Ford's dream.

Ashutosh said that Yates felt such a turnaround would be fundamental to any change in the status of the American car industry. Yates maintained that it is necessary to pay more attention to technology, and Ashutosh agrees that he is right. But his discussion of this area seemed to fall a bit short. It needs to be extended and amplified. The internal conflicts in the administration of large companies are deep-rooted.

At the beginning of the twentieth century, this happened in America first. When you are involved in a big industry, planning of work and power needs some level of decentralization and bureaucratization. When you want to control the various hierarchical levels of the bureaucracy, you have to take into account the varying abilities of the people involved; when the industrial organization is huge, then the higher and lower administrative levels do not communicate and the issues cannot be identified easily and controlled. The production line is taken care of by the lower level of administration while the policymakers are at a higher level. This was what happened in Sloan's huge establishment. This ramping up of the bureaucracy meant that profit became the primary motive and priority. No one paid attention to technology and its importance began to fade.

As time passed, technology became an integral part of human life. Other nations began to take the lead in car technology. The demand for well-designed cars was increasing. At this point, the bureaucracy that governed the American giant motor companies began to look outdated and absurd. The dialogue between the different levels lost its flexibility; the habit of creating balanced and well-thought-out compromise ended; the ability to judge the new winds of change flowing through the marketplace had also ended. It became impossible for these companies to build modern cars.

Ashutosh felt that in the age of technology, big companies like General Motors had bureaucracies that were stagnant and unwieldy. American industry needs to be more inventive and more aggressive. If this does not happen, it will not be possible to rectify all that is wrong with American production. Nissan and Toyota were actually rather small companies compared to GM and Ford. These big companies need to formulate a policy for the world market. They would need to compete in several markets including the family car, the sports car and the luxury car. Taking advantage of these shortcomings in the American car industry, the smaller companies built their niches in the world market and began to focus on them. They devoted themselves to satisfying the needs of their consumers. This was how they were successful in introducing modern engineering technology into their products. Having to compete on these varying fronts, the American companies kept on losing ground.

Furthermore, Yates says that it is not the cost of American labour versus Japanese labour that makes the difference between the price of the respective cars. The difference between an American car and cars made by other nations was only about $1,500, of which only $500 is contributed by the higher labour cost. The remainder is due to lower labour productivity in America. Ashutosh says that Yates neglects to mention that the average American worker in an American car plant was older than the Japanese worker, which could be responsible for the lower productivity. Further, if American workers were laid off, the older, perhaps less efficient workers stayed because of their seniority.

Yates criticized the car that Sloan's GM produced, a pale imitation of the popular Honda Accord. Ashutosh did not agree. Technology has a long tradition of borrowing and lending across nations. Japan, for instance, benefited a great deal from this tradition. To him, it is the American ego that prevented the American car industry from being able to learn something from the popularity of the products of a company like Honda. Thus, America fell behind in the small car segment. This was the reason why the American car industry ended up in second place.

Ashutosh felt that since Yates had failed to analyse the deep-rooted causes for the decline of the American car industry, it would not be possible to find solutions on the basis of his work. Yates felt that if some 'hungry lions'—individuals who were both aggressive and inventive—take over Detroit, then this decline can be arrested and reversed. Ashutosh feels that in a time of rapidly developing technology, big car companies are past their optimal size. They need to be smaller, nimble and with ears close to the ground. This is the important point that Yates had missed.

Ashutosh's experiences at Wharton and in the field of industry built his understanding and his self-confidence. For a while, he did dream of a Wall Street job at which he would make millions. But this was only a passing fancy. As such, in his heart, he still craved for the depths of basic and fundamental issues, which in a way was the Kingdom of God, whose ramparts the superficial waves of money and glory could not disturb. His mind was still drawn to the limitless expanse of particle physics.

18

Ashutosh's PhD Thesis—and World Fame

In 1988, Ashutosh graduated summa cum laude from UPenn. He had decided to pursue research in particle physics and was going to do his PhD at Harvard. He would conduct research at the Fermi National Accelerator Laboratory at Batavia near Chicago.

Named after the famous Italian physicist Enrico Fermi, this laboratory brings together fine minds from across the world's scientific institutions for the purpose of research and experimentation. When Ashutosh joined Harvard, an experiment on muon scattering with the code name E665 was being conducted at Fermilab. Scientists working on this experiment wanted Ashutosh to be part of it. Professor Richard B. Nickerson and Professor Richard Wilson took a special interest in Ashutosh. Professor Francis Pipkin took him on as a research assistant and gave him a project in electronics. In addition to being part of his curriculum, he had also worked on electronics in his summer jobs.

Professor Pipkin would often discuss the progress of the experiment with him. Unfortunately, in 1992, Prof. Francis Pipkin passed away.

The proton and neutron are the fundamental particles that make up the nucleus. To investigate their structure at E665, scientists used a beam of muons of 470 GeV (billion or giga electron-Volts) energy. Since a target of free neutrons cannot be made, a deuterium target (whose nuclei are deuterons, which contain a proton and a neutron) is used. The muons scattered off the nucleons and their incoming and outgoing energies and directions were accurately measured. This meticulous job needed infinite patience. It was necessary to come up with some new and novel ideas to deal with the complicated problems that had surfaced at that point.

This was an opportunity for Ashutosh to use the new designs in electronics that he had devised. His designs were compatible with the specific requirements of E665.

Analysis of the experimental data needed the information produced by his electronic devices. Ashutosh also created a novel trigger system that ended up delivering physics results that the senior scientists had not anticipated. No one else in the E665 team could do this.

Prof. Nickerson was Ashutosh's first mentor on the E665 experiment. He was very supportive of Ashutosh's ideas. When Ashutosh joined this experiment in 1989 as a summer student, he had not yet learnt how to drive. Prof. Nickerson often gave him a ride and this gave them the opportunity to discuss physics at length. Ashutosh learnt a lot from these discussions.

The Importance of E665

Collisions between fundamental particles are the central and basic procedure with which research in particle physics proceeds. In order to be able to do this, particle beams of high energy have to be created. The proton has a substructure; this has been established beyond doubt; we know that it is made up of quarks and gluons. The scientific world wants to know whether electrons, muons and neutrinos are actually 'elementary' particles or whether they have substructures too.

The muon is the electron's doppelganger. In the twentieth century, the muon was discovered while looking at cosmic rays. The neutrino is an extremely light particle, also like an electron but with a neutral charge. The neutrino is produced when there is a weak interaction (such as the one causing beta radiation) involving the electron or the muon.

The Tevatron accelerator at Fermilab would use two alternate modes for accelerating particles: the proton-antiproton collider and the fixed-target mode. In the fixed-target mode, the proton beam was used to make other particle beams. The muon beam of 470 GeV energy was used in the E665 experiment. In 1987, 1990 and 1991 important measurements were made using this beam.

When the high-energy muons hit protons and neutrons, the latter break apart and quarks are released. The quarks create a spray of high-energy particles. It is very important to measure their energy as accurately as possible. It is a delicate and intricate operation. This was Ashutosh's task on the E665 experiment.

Making a 470 GeV muon beam is a huge technical project. Fermilab had made the highest-energy muon beam in the world. Thus, the experiment was unlikely to be repeated in the near future. This experience would prove very useful to Ashutosh when he was later studying proton–proton collisions at the Large Hadron Collider and the proton–antiproton collisions at the Tevatron.

After Professor Pipkin's death, Professor Richard Wilson became Ashutosh's guide. The Fermilab accelerator's run had ended. Having obtained as much data as possible, the other students had left. There were a few, like Arijit Banerjee and Panagiotis Spentzouris, who were also finishing their PhDs, who offered moral support. Banerjee took on the role of a sounding board for Ashutosh. Spentzouris and Ashutosh collaborated on two projects and worked very well together. Their collaborative spirit was noted and appreciated by seniors in E665, particularly Prof. Heidi Schellman and Dr Hugh Montgomery. Both Prof. Schellman and Dr Montgomery were proud of Ashutosh and Spentzouris for their professional camaraderie which benefited the experiment greatly and they gave their example to other students.

During this period, Professor Wilson was very supportive of Ashutosh's PhD topic to measure the proton and deuteron structure. He knew from experience how challenging a task this was. But he had faith in Ashutosh's capabilities and dedication, and knew that if anyone could do it, it was Ashutosh. He was also very generous. He sent Ashutosh to France and Russia to discuss the proton and deuteron structure and the results of the E665 experiment. Prof. Schellman and Dr Montgomery were also very supportive and engaged with Ashutosh in many discussions as he explained his solutions to thorny problems. Schellman was the leader of the E665 experiment when Ashutosh published his measurements and she was delighted with the quality and impact of his work.

Ashutosh's effort in bringing out, practically single-handedly, unprecedented results from E665, was unique in the annals of Fermilab. The scientific community was all praise for his work. Professor Nickerson moved on to Queen's College, University of

Oxford, but he kept an eye on Ashutosh's progress. In 1999, he explained his student's contribution to the world's understanding of particle physics as part of his letter of support for Ashutosh's permanent residency application:

> Perhaps his most important efforts have been in pioneering work in understanding forward particle production and detection. The investigation of the W boson is vital because of its role in the electroweak symmetry breaking mechanism, which underpins our whole way of understanding fundamental physics. The W particle mass measurement is one of the most important in particle physics and it is difficult to do accurately. The key to reducing the theoretical uncertainty in the measurement lies in understanding forward W production. Professor Kotwal developed a very sophisticated analysis which led to a precision of 0.1 %. Such precise measurements can lead to breakthroughs by allowing very small inconsistencies with current theoretical models to be detected.
>
> Another area of particular note is Professor Kotwal's work on the search for substructure in the particles that we currently consider to be fundamental. He created interest amongst the international community in particle physics with his work in this area. It was recently presented in the largest particle physics conference, ICHEP (at Vancouver) and will shortly be published in the most prestigious journal, PRL. Currently, the results provide the best limits on possible substructure when compared with certain theories.
>
> These ground-breaking areas of research followed a Ph.D. thesis in which the same was true. Professor Kotwal explored new kinematic regimes in proton and deuteron structure functions, producing a unique measurement with the highest energy muon beams ever produced. These measurements

remain the best in their kinematic area and are regularly used by physicists at DESY in Germany where a team of 800 work on analysing data of a comparable sort.

Northwestern University Professor Heidi Schellman, who led E665 between 1991 and 1996, said:

Ashutosh joined E665 as a graduate student and was very important to the 1990/91 data runs. He designed and installed the beam spill monitoring system (a very sophisticated electronic design which is a product of his training as an electrical engineer). He also designed and installed a calorimeter-based trigger which was originally intended for trigger studies but ended up being used for quasi-real photo-production measurements. After the run ended, he single-handedly did the offline calibration for the calorimeter. All of this work was done carefully and well and has contributed a great deal to the success of the experiment.

His thesis topic was very ambitious, determination of the proton structure function F_2. F_2 measures the distribution of charges within the proton and is one of the major confirmations of the quark model. This is a difficult measurement which requires precise knowledge of the detector and trigger acceptance, efficiency and resolution. Ashutosh performed a systematic study of the trigger and tracking acceptance of the detector. Using this information, he wrote enhanced computer simulations in order to properly reproduce the details of our triggers and acceptance. This is a step which the competing experiment was unable to do, despite having a much larger group working on a similar project.

Ashutosh's thesis work was the premier result from the experiment and was published in 1996. His work now appears on all summary plots of structure functions. Let me emphasize that Ashutosh was the driving force in this work. He has received advice from more senior people when needed but he did the work and provided most of the ideas. Such work is usually done by teams of 10-20 people, Ashutosh as a student, did it essentially single-handedly.

[...]

In my opinion, which was shared by most of my colleagues on E665, Ashutosh was the best of the 30 students on the experiment ... Intellectually, I would rank him at the top of all experimental high-energy physicists in his age group, both for his technical skills and his ability to formulate and carry out top-flight physics projects.

Professor Richard Wilson of Harvard, who was his PhD guide, said that his thesis was first-rate and added:

Kotwal presented his PhD thesis to Harvard University in 1995 on precise measurements of the cross-section for scattering of mu mesons by protons at low momentum transfer. This work is a very valuable addition to our understanding of the proton structure. It is currently the best result to be compared with theories of particle substructure. This was performed with the highest-energy muon beam ever and explored a new kinematic regime that had never been measured before. This still unique measurement has never been superseded. The HERA accelerator in Germany, with a total of 800 physicists working on two experiments, compares their results with this measurement.

Professor Kotwal is now considered an expert in this area. He has a deep and detailed understanding of quantum chromodynamics, proton structure and photon-hadron interactions, and has been invited to present his results at many international conferences. He personally devised one strategy for structure-function measurement used for the first time in the experiment. He wrote and published the measurement in the prestigious *Physical Review D* journal of the American Physical Society. The measurements are internationally acclaimed and cited in the 'Review of Particle Properties' which is the compilation of cutting-edge measurements. All of Professor Kotwal's work has therefore been cited many times in international journals and conferences.

Since he finished his PhD (and therefore stopped working with me) he worked at Columbia University. While working at Columbia he carried out two main lines of research. He made an important measurement of the mass of the W particle. This is one of the most important precision measurements in particle physics. It is a constraint on the electroweak symmetry breaking mechanism which is the most important unsolved question in particle physics today. The theory of the 'Standard Model' needs the Higgs particle to be consistent. Kotwal carried out a very sophisticated analysis and measured the W mass with precision of 0.1%. Kotwal measured the forward W production, previously uncharted, which is the key to reducing theoretical uncertainty in the mass measurement. This was the pioneering work in understanding forward W production and detection and can reveal an inconsistency with the Standard Model, which would be the biggest breakthrough in the field in a decade.

[...]

Professor Kotwal is not only a skilled builder of apparatus and a skilled analyst but a leader. In the field of experimental high energy physics, the need for international collaboration is great. He has already assumed numerous leadership positions such as chairperson of conveners on DØ, overseeing research activities of over 100 physicists, organized public presentations and publications of several results, convener of calorimeter upgrade meetings, and coordinator of calorimeter upgrade work at Fermilab.

In summary, Professor Ashutosh Kotwal has already demonstrated that he is an outstanding scientist with outstanding leadership qualities which will be of great benefit to the whole world and to the USA in particular.

Harvard University recognized this cutting-edge work and awarded him his PhD.

The international particle physics community has a database for monitoring numerous research papers. Stanford University's Linear Accelerator Centre began this work of gathering important particle physics publications. Ashutosh's thesis had been cited 255 times by 2012. By 2021, the number of citations had gone up to 378. A paper that receives 250 citations is known as a 'famous paper'; one that has more than 500 citations acquires 'renowned paper' status. Some of Ashutosh's papers are well on their way to acquiring this status.

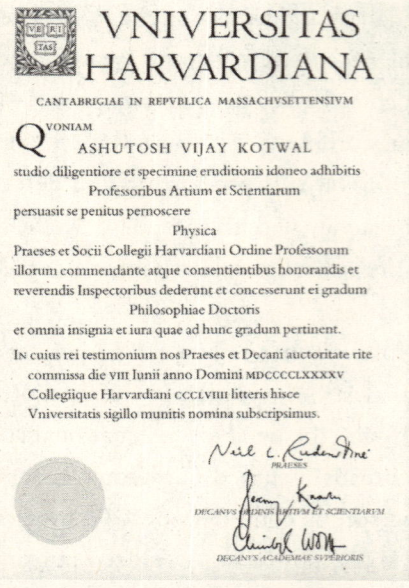

The PhD certificate in Latin awarded by Harvard University to Ashutosh.

SPREADING WINGS

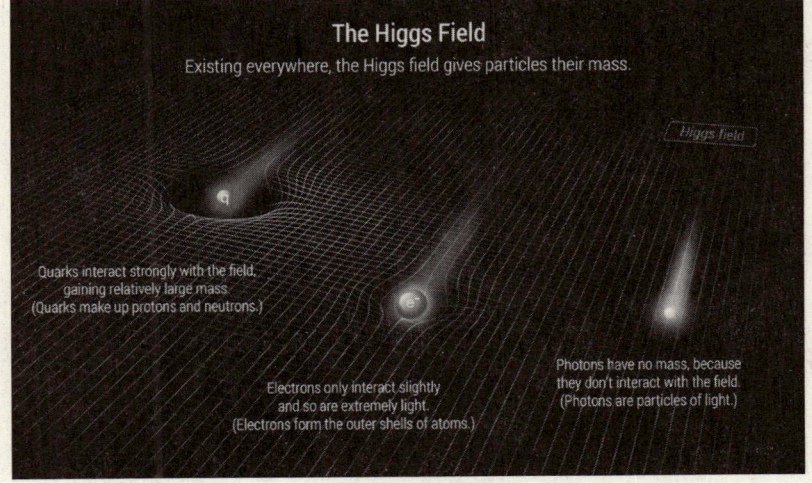

4 July 2012, Geneva. Higgs Boson discovered
Image credits: Edupedia Publications Pvt. Ltd. and Pen2Print

The title 'Spreading Wings' signifies the tremendous and rapid growth of fundamental science and Ashutosh's contribution to it. Beginning in the twentieth century, scientific knowledge grew in geometrical progression. This is a limitless flight, an unbounded flight, and one that shows no sign of ending. Ashutosh is one of a flock of independent-minded and creative scientists who have soared together.

I felt it was necessary to explain a little of the science behind all this to my readers. Technology and science are now an inseparable part of our lives, dedicated to making them smoother and easier. I admired the intense and limitless curiosity about the world and its functioning that I saw in the quest for science. The rational approach that gets exhibited in this quest made a strong impact on my mind. In the way that everyone forgets personal and political differences and comes together with all their heart and mind and nerve and sinew, to try and discover the truth—that for me seems to come close to the divine.

19

The Science of Particle Physics

ARISTOTLE, THE GREEK PHILOSOPHER, SUGGESTED THAT THE entire world and all that was in it, was made of four basic elements: fire, earth, water and air. We have come a long way since then. But even today our knowledge of the composition of some chemical substances remains at the level of knowing the elements that compose them. The basic unit of most substances is a molecule. The molecule has all the chemical qualities of the substance itself. The molecule, in turn, is made up of atoms. Atoms are the fundamental component of every element.

If the atom is dissected further, you find at the centre a heavy nucleus and, surrounding it, a cloud of electrons. The nucleus, in turn, is made of protons and neutrons, snugly fitted together. In the 1960s and 1970s, it was discovered that the protons and neutrons were also composed of other smaller elementary particles. These were called quarks, the name taken from James Joyce's novel *Finnegans Wake*. Bombarding them with a great deal of energy, it was discovered that these quarks can have an independent existence for a very short time. Since then, the quarks have been the subject of intensive study.

In the scientific world, atoms are known as building blocks of nature, of the world, of the universe. An atom is created when these smaller particles come together. The study of the subatomic world, of the particles that make up the atom and their interaction with each other, is known as particle physics.

A New Paradigm

When the twentieth century dawned, a new revolution took place in the world of physics. Albert Einstein's theory of relativity and Max Planck's quantum physics helped establish the new discipline of particle physics. To understand the subatomic world, a new paradigm was needed and quantum theory brought that to birth. Our understanding of space and time was rewritten by the theory of relativity. These two components of our reality which had seemed distinct were now braided into one. Using the basic theories of quantum mechanics and relativity, renowned scientists were beginning to predict the connections between matter and the forces of electromagnetism. A new theoretical framework called relativistic quantum field theory began to emerge and from it, the significance of the proton and the neutron, the forces between them and the forces that generated them and other particles such as quarks and neutrinos also emerged. The existence of these particles has been experimentally verified.

To understand the limitless universe around us, it is necessary to understand the minute particles that exist at the subatomic level. The ancient Greeks envisaged the idea of the atom, the word itself means 'indivisible' in Greek.

To use an analogy: every language has a great wealth of words. But these words are all made of the same letters, which generally amount to a handful. These are used in different permutations and combinations and out of these, words arise. In the same way, atoms come together to form different substances. The billions of things we see around us are all made of a handful of these particles. Particle physicists concern themselves with identifying and understanding these particles.

The Greeks saw the atom as indivisible. That the atom is divisible, that it can indeed be split, was demonstrated in the twentieth century. Between 1909 and 1932, scientists like J.J. Thompson, Ernest Rutherford, Niels Bohr and James Chadwick offered us an atomic replica of the solar system. They showed that the atom is not the final indivisible component of all nature, but it has a nucleus consisting of protons and neutrons and a cloud of electrons around it.

In Search of the Quark

At this point in the story, scientists believed that the protons, neutrons and electrons were the ultimate building blocks of all matter. But in experiments conducted at the Stanford Linear Accelerator Centre during 1967–1973, scientists got a chance to 'look into' the interior of a nucleus. This was when they discovered that protons and neutrons were both made up of smaller particles. They gave them the quirky name of quarks.

Once again, it was thought that there were two kinds of quarks. They were named, with admirable simplicity, 'up quark' and 'down quark'. The proton has two up quarks and one down quark; the neutron has one up and two down quarks. So at this point, all of the matter we experience was thought to be made of electrons, up and down quarks. No finer or smaller constituent particles had been discovered.

But there was also proof that other smaller particles exist. In 1956, Frederick Reines and Clyde Cowan found experimental proof at a nuclear reactor and the neutrino, the fourth kind of particle, was discovered. In the 1930s, Wolfgang Pauli had predicted that this particle should exist. It was difficult to prove its existence because the neutrino is nearly massless and weakly interacting. It can travel for millions of miles through rock without losing energy. Every day, trillions of these neutrinos pour in from the universe and pass through the Earth. They pass through our bodies and emerge without us noticing.

The Electron Family

In the 1930s, scientists discovered a close relative of the electron. This particle had about 200 times the mass of the electron. It was named the muon. These particles also pass through the Earth every day, emanating from the interactions of cosmic protons in the upper atmosphere. This particle was so unexpected by scientists that the Nobel laureate Isidor Isaac Rabi's exclamation has taken on a legendary quality: 'Who ordered that?' he asked.

With greater opportunities to investigate the subatomic sphere and with higher levels of energy available, scientists began to dissect the atomic nucleus further. Scientists began to wonder whether it was possible to create a smaller version of the Big Bang with which the universe had started off, in the laboratory. In the debris of this explosion, surely new subatomic particles would be found?

They began to succeed at this attempt. They found two more quarks other than up and down: charm and strange. Another heavier relative of the electron also emerged: it was named tau. Two close relatives of the originally discovered neutrino were also found: what had been called the neutrino now became the electron-neutrino. The new neutrinos were named the muon-neutrino and the tau-neutrino, because each of the neutrinos was associated by the weak interaction with the electron, the muon or the tau, respectively.

These new particles are not to be found in any familiar object nor can they be called building blocks. The charm and strange quarks are created only in very high-energy collisions and exist for only a very brief moment in time before transforming to the other particles. The same is true for the tau and the muon. The neutrinos, though stable, are too weakly interacting to build anything.

The story does not end there. Each of these particles has its anti-particles, which are like the particles in all respects except that their electrical charge is the opposite. For example, the electron has a negative charge; the positively charged anti-electron is the positron. They are alike in all other respects but their electric charges are -1 and +1 respectively. Their mass is the same and when they combine, they destroy each other, and energy is released. And of course, energy can be converted back to matter and antimatter.

The prediction of antimatter was made in 1928 by the brilliant theoretical physicist Paul Dirac, when he combined the mathematics of quantum mechanics and special relativity. A few years later, in 1932, Carl Anderson discovered the positron in cosmic rays, the first particle of antimatter to be discovered.

The Family of Particles

These subatomic particles have been divided into three groups. They are called families. Each family has two types of quarks, one electron (or a close relative) and a neutrino (or a close relative). These families can be shown in a table given below. The masses of the particles are presented as ratios to the proton mass. The exact value of the mass of the lightest neutrino is not experimentally known, but the differences in their masses are known.

If you look at the table, you can see that similar particles have been placed together. From family to family, the masses grow larger. But the table also presents some questions. The first: If the electron, the up quark, and the down quark are enough to constitute all familiar objects around us made of mass, why do we need the others? This question has a logical answer by starting at the other end; there are multiple families to begin with. The heavier particles are naturally able to transform into the lighter ones by releasing energy, since mass and energy are related by $E = mc^2$. Thus, the stable particles that can build the world around us are automatically the lightest ones from the first family.

The next question: But then, why are there three families? Why not one or four or any other number? Another question: Are the differences in mass between particles governed by any law? For example, the tau mass is 3,477 times the mass of the electron. Why is the top quark mass 80,000 times the mass of an up quark? Superficially, these numbers look like they are random, but is there a scientific rule that governs their relationships? Finding this out is one of the jobs of the particle physicist.

Table: Quark and Lepton Families

	FAMILY - 1			FAMILY - 2			FAMILY - 3		
particle	mass	electric charge	particle	mass	electric charge	particle	mass	electric charge
electron	0.00054	-1	muon	0.113	-1	tau	1.89	-1
electron neutrino	$< 2 \times 10^{-9}$	0	muon neutrino	< 0.0002	0	tau neutrino	<0.02	0
up quark	0.0023	2/3	charm quark	1.35	2/3	top quark	184	2/3
down quark	0.0050	$-1/3$	strange quark	0.10	$-1/3$	bottom quark	4.46	$-1/3$

The Forces of Nature

There are some forces at work in nature. If these are examined, they give rise to other questions. All around us we see clear examples of the law of cause and effect.

In the game of tipcat, for instance, you hit the small stick with the big stick. The bungee jumper throws herself off a high ledge, plunging towards the earth. High-speed magnetic levitation trains are kept fixed to the track by magnets. When an object is pushed, pulled or shaken, its state of rest or motion changes. We also see changes in substances when they are beaten, thrown, ejected, dried, twisted, crushed, cooled, heated or burnt. There are four forces working in nature: gravity, electromagnetism, the weak and the strong force.

We are all familiar with the force of gravity. It is what keeps the earth revolving around the sun and keeps us attached to the earth. Weight is the force on a mass when gravity is acting on it. Electromagnetic force is also familiar: the telephone, radio, television, motor and computer all run on electromagnetism. The crackle of lightning and the glowing candle flame are both examples of electromagnetism. Electromagnetic force is like gravity of the subatomic world; it is what holds the atom together. In other words, the relationship between the electromagnetic force and electric charge of a particle is akin to the relationship between gravity and mass, except that there is no repulsive gravity. The weak and strong forces are mostly not part of our everyday experience. They have their effect only at the tiny distances and fleeting time spans within the atom. They are, thus, subatomic forces. The strong force holds the quarks together and keeps the protons and neutrons together in the nucleus. The weak force causes radioactive beta rays to be emitted from substances like uranium and radium.

Each force is associated with a particle at the subatomic level. That particle can be said to be the smallest quantum, or packet, of the force. For example, the photon is the smallest packet of the electromagnetic force. Similarly, the W and Z bosons and the gluons are the smallest bundles of the weak and strong force interactions respectively. In 1979 and 1983, respectively, the gluon and the W and Z bosons were discovered and described. The existence of the graviton (G)—which should be the smallest bundle of the gravitational force—has not been experimentally demonstrated yet.

Gravity is the weakest of all the forces. That is why the graviton is so difficult to detect. The electromagnetic force is a billion-billion-billion-billion times stronger. (In mathematical terms that is 10^{36} times stronger.) The strong force is a hundred times as strong as the electromagnetic force and millions of times stronger than the weak force.

If the characteristics of these forces were to change, the nature of our universe would be very different. The protons in the nucleus would be impelled to move apart since they have the same electric charge; but the strong force overcomes their electromagnetic repulsion and keeps them in place. If that were the case, the nucleus would blow apart and no elements heavier than hydrogen would have formed. The nature of our universe is , therefore, dependent on the characteristics of these forces and these subatomic particles. Particle physicists want to understand these characteristics.

Before the arrival of quantum physics, it was believed that when two particles interacted with each other they did so through the void of space without any intermediary, by the so-called 'action at a distance'. Newton saw this as a flaw in his gravitational theory. After we began to take a quantum look at these interactions, the explanation became a lot more appealing to logic. Now, it is understood that when two particles interact, they do so with the exchange of the force-mediating particles. The troubling notion of 'action at a distance' has disappeared from our perspective; in quantum theory, interactions are described by emission and absorption of force-mediating particles by the matter particles.

So if we are to try and translate electromagnetic forces into quantum language, it would be tantamount to saying that the electromagnetically charged particles (the electron and the proton, for instance) create an electromagnetic field around themselves. The quantum particles that transmit forces and build up this electromagnetic field are known as photons.

Categorizing the Particles

Let us try and define the particles that come up again and again in particle physics:

- Fermions: Particles that constitute matter and interact with each other are called fermions.
- Bosons: Particles that enable the interaction of fermions are called bosons. Bosons are transmitter particles that mediate forces.
- Baryons: Fermions that are made up of quarks and interact by the strong force are called baryons.
- Mesons: Bosons that are made up of quarks and antiquarks and transmit the strong force are called mesons. And since the quarks also experience the electromagnetic and weak forces, so do the baryons and mesons.

- Hadrons: Originating from the Greek word 'hadros'—strong, heavy, and impressive in appearance—hadrons are subatomic composite particles made up of two or more quarks held together by the strong force. The proton and the neutron contribute most of the mass you see around you and are examples of baryons. Baryons and mesons together make up the set of hadrons, which are all the strongly-interacting composite particles made up of quarks and/or antiquarks.
- Leptons: This set of particles comprises electrons, muons, tau, their corresponding neutrinos, and their anti-particles, which are all fermions. They interact through the electromagnetic and/or the weak force. These particles do not participate in the strong interactions.

We have said that gluons mediate the strong force and we have also said that mesons mediate the strong force. So it is important to understand the difference between gluons and mesons.

At low-energy levels, the quarks in a neutron, proton or meson are tightly bound together. Protons and neutrons have three quarks each. Mesons have one quark and an antiquark. At low energy levels, it is the mesons that enable interaction between a proton and/or a neutron, and between baryons in general. This is because at low energy levels, quarks and gluons have no independent existence. They are all bound inside baryons and mesons. At this level, therefore, while talking about particles and forces, we talk about the proton, the neutron and the meson.

At high-energy levels, by the principles of quantum mechanics, it is possible to study the interactions at infinitesimal distances, deep inside the hadrons. At these small distances, the quarks and gluons appear to be freely moving, and so their footprints can be observed and measured directly. Their binding effects only show up at the larger distances corresponding to the size of the hadrons, which is about 10^{-15} m (a femtometer). Hence, the collisions between quarks or between quarks and gluons can be observed directly at small distances, i.e., high energies, and the gluons are the carriers of the strong force in this regime.

Table: Interactions of Matter Via Forces

No.	Force/Field	Particle family	Interacting particles (fermions)	Force carriers (bosons)
1	Gravity	Matter & fields	All particles	Graviton (G)
2	Electro-magnetism	Charged particles	Quarks & charged leptons	Photon (γ)
3	Strong force	Hadrons	Quarks & baryons	Gluons (g) & mesons
4	Weak force	Hadrons & leptons	Quarks, baryons, electron, muon, tau & the three neutrinos	W & Z bosons

There are two kinds of fermions, quarks and leptons from which matter is composed. The quark group consists of up (u), down (d), charm (c), strange (s), top (t), and bottom (b) quarks. The lepton group consists of the electron (e), muon (μ), and tau(τ), and the neutrinos (νe), ($\nu\mu$), ($\nu\tau$). Leptons can wander around independently, while quarks are bound inside hadrons at low energies (long distances).

The interaction between particles takes place with the help of force-carrier particles. W and Z bosons mediate the weak force, the photon mediates the electromagnetic force and the gluon mediates the strong force. A special property of the W and Z bosons and the gluons is that they can also interact with each other, by the same force they are mediating; in the quantum picture, a W boson can emit or absorb another W or Z boson, and a gluon can emit or absorb another gluon.

Standard Model of Particles

Before the discovery of the Higgs boson, its entry in the table of elementary particles was vacant. With the discovery of this particle in 2012 at CERN, this last missing entry in the Standard Model was filled.

Standard model theory was developed during the 1960s and 1970s. Till now, it has been the basis for all scientific investigation in particle physics. With advances in research, this theory is falling short in some regards. New approaches and ideas are being tried now.

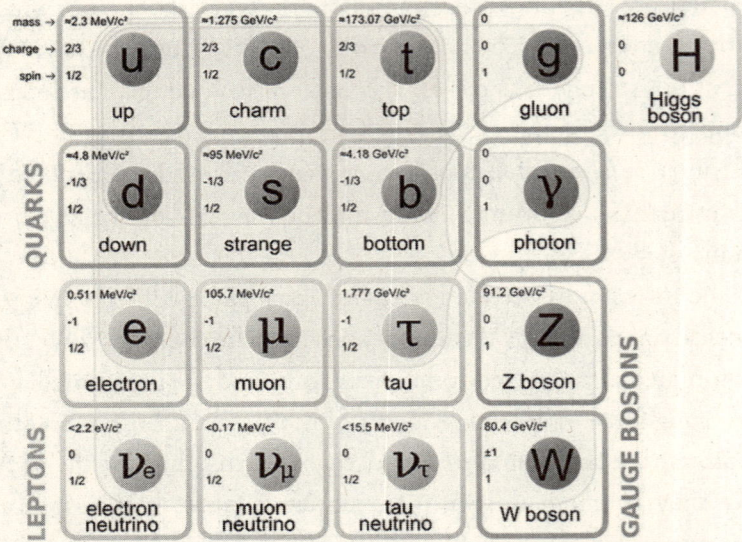

Elementary particles of the Standard Model, and their mass, electric charge and intrinsic angular momentum (i.e. spin). Per Einstein's special relativity equation m = E/c^2, mass units are energy (in millions or billions of electron-Volts, MeV and GeV respectively) over c^2, where c denotes the speed of light. The unit of spin is $h/(2\pi)$ where h is Planck's constant. The proton's charge is +1 in the particle physics convention. (Credit: Wikipedia)

20

In the Beginning

The study of particle physics is the study of the fundamental laws of nature. Fundamental particles play a dynamic and vital role in the cosmogony or the beginning of the universe; they control the nature and functioning of the world. The mechanism of the universe and its functioning is controlled by these natural laws. Therefore, it seems natural that the study of the beginning of the universe and its development would be of interest to the particle physicist.

The rishis of ancient India had considered the origin of the universe and propounded some theories. In the Rig Veda, one finds mention of these ideas, but they could not divine the connection between space and time, which modern science has understood. For most of our intellectual history, we had not developed the necessary ideation to develop hypotheses around the origin of the universe. There was no question of experimental verification as the kind of equipment that was needed could not be manufactured.

Many Cosmogonies

A revolution in the field of physics began with the dawn of the twentieth century. Albert Einstein's theory of relativity changed many fundamental assumptions. Astronomy and physics developed at the same pace. Using the theory of relativity, in 1927, for the first time, a theory of an expanding universe was suggested by the Belgian catholic priest and scientist Georges LeMaître. In 1931, he proposed the first version of the Big Bang theory for the beginning of the universe.

This was the primaeval atom, a single immensely intense concentrated point in which all of the universe's energy, space and time was bound up. When this point exploded, the universe as we know it came into being. George Gamow and Ralph Alpher were among the early advocates and developers of this theory. The British astrophysicist Fred Hoyle invented the popular name 'Big Bang'. This name, which used the common language of the people, helped make this scientific theory accessible.

But Prof. Hoyle himself had another theory in mind. This was the Steady State hypothesis. This stated that the universe is infinite. It has no beginning and no end. The universe was always there and will always be there. It is expanding constantly but maintaining a constant average density. Mass and energy are constantly being created and so the concentration remains the same. Prof. Jayant Narlikar has worked on the Steady State hypothesis with Prof. Hoyle, who was Prof. Narlikar's advisor at the University of Cambridge.

The Big Bang theory and the Steady State hypothesis have both been worked on by different scientists. The Big Bang theory is receiving more experimental proof in its support. The characteristics of the world as we know it agree with the Big Bang theory, and not with the Steady State hypothesis.

～

The Changing Face of the Universe

In 1924, Edwin Hubble discovered the presence of other galaxies using a 100-inch-diameter telescope on Mount Wilson. He said that these fuzzy nebulae that he had seen were galaxies just like the Milky Way to which we belong. And so the size of the known universe suddenly expanded a hundredfold. In 1929, he proved that these galaxies were hurtling away from each other through space. This created an identifiable pattern called red shift, an increase in the wavelength of light received due to the movement of the source of the light wave away from the detector. Using measurements of red shifts and distances, he showed that other galaxies were receding from us with speeds proportional to their distance from us. Using this Hubble Law, it was possible to deduce that the galaxies were all hurtling away from each other and therefore the universe was expanding. As the measurements became more refined, it was calculated that the Big Bang occurred 13.8 billion years ago.

Perhaps it is useful to explain the term red shift that has been used above. When Hubble and the astronomer Vesto Slipher studied the light coming from other galaxies, they noticed that the light seemed stretched, as if it had been 'shifted' towards the red end of the spectrum. (Red is the longest wavelength in the visible spectrum, violet is the shortest.) This meant that the light from these galaxies had its wavelength stretched or lengthened. Using the rules of special relativity, it was deduced that the galaxies were moving away from us. If a galaxy is coming towards the detector, then there is a blue shift; the light is 'shifted' towards the violet end of the spectrum, the wavelength having been shortened according to special relativity. A similar phenomenon applies to sound waves. This is called the Doppler Effect. As the source approaches the detector, the frequency of sound waves increases and the sound becomes shriller. As the source recedes from the detector, the frequency of sound decreases.

The general theory of relativity has an explanation for these findings. As light travels through the immense emptiness of space, which is itself constantly expanding, it gets acted upon by gravity and is stretched; thus, its energy decreases. And as it travels through the universe, its frequency reduces, and this accounts for the Hubble effect.

Before the dawn of general relativity, the universe was a simple place. It was a place without beginning and without end. From the observational perspective, there was a single galaxy to deal with. There were billions of stars in it, and these could be seen.

Today, the universe—with a hundred billion galaxies—has become a lot more complex, but we are beginning to understand it better.

∽

The Cosmological Timetable

To understand what happened, we have to wind the clock back 13.8 billion years to come to the 'first' moment in time as we know it. The universe was then concentrated into a single point of unimaginable density. It also had an unimaginable amount of energy and temperature. This was an unstable point since the tightly curved space and time would expand according to Einstein's equation of general relativity. This was what led to the Big Bang, the huge explosion that brought the universe with space and time into being. Energy came bursting forth, making its way through the fabric of space and time. This is still going on and is predicted to continue until the end of time.

'The universe is expanding,' it is often said. This does not mean that a lot of space was empty and filling it was the job of the mass and energy contained in that first primeval point. It means that the fabric of space and time itself is expanding, like the surface area of a balloon as it is filled, and the galaxies are flowing outwards with it like dots on the balloon's surface.

In the first few seconds after the Big Bang, the universe began to take shape. But it was in the first second, in a fraction of the first second—in 10^{-32} of a second, in fact—that the universe went from minuscule to magnificent, when cosmic inflation happened. For the rest of that nanosecond, the universe was so hot and so compressed that it was only a swirling plasma of quarks, gluons, leptons, W and Z bosons and photons. This plasma continued to expand, at a slower rate, and began to cool. At a microsecond, the universe was a soup of quarks and gluons. By three minutes, protons and helium nuclei had formed, and atoms formed 400,000 years later. Ultimately, more than a hundred billion galaxies flickered into existence. In each of these galaxies, a hundred billion stars and perhaps as many planets came into being.

This is the beginning of our universe's history: a soup of quarks, leptons and elementary force-mediating bosons. And so over billions of years of evolution, our universe, our world and even life have all come into being from a simple particle soup to a complex lived reality. How all this happened and what were the causes of all this formation are of special interest to the physicist and the particle physicist.

When we travel backwards in time to that first moment, we can see the entire history of the universe unfold. Let us assume that an imaginary clock begins ticking at the moment of the Big Bang. After the first 10^{-10} seconds are over, we know a lot about that early time.

Going back even further, into that period of cosmic inflation, theoretical physicists have a number of ideas about what could have happened. However, no proof of any of these ideas has been found yet. And trying to imagine what happened even before that is a matter of speculation.

A hundred seconds in, the temperature dropped below 10 billion degrees Celsius. Three minutes later, nucleosynthesis occurred. Protons and neutrons that would form the nuclei of helium and hydrogen had been created. Seven times as many protons as neutrons were created. Neutrons and protons combined to form deuterons and subsequently helium nuclei. Since many protons were left over, the most common element, hydrogen, has the simplest nucleus, a single proton. It took three minutes before the first helium nuclei were formed. The first elements to be formed after the Big Bang were thus hydrogen, helium and a little bit of lithium.

Four hundred thousand years after the Big Bang, temperatures came down considerably. The average temperature fell below 3,000 degrees Celsius. Going below this temperature was important because now electrons and nuclei could be drawn to each other, and the first atoms could come into existence. The attraction between electrons and the nucleus gave the atom a neutral charge, and the first stream of photons began to emerge.

Echoes of the Big Bang

And so it came to pass that radiation and matter decoupled from each other and the universe became transparent to light. In the process, an echo of light was generated from the surface of the last scattering, when the gases were still ionized. This light echo travels through space to get to us. This is known as cosmic microwave background radiation, discovered by accident in 1964. This is evidence of the Big Bang because it is radiation that fills the dark spaces of the universe almost uniformly in all directions and can be perceived through a sensitive radio telescope.

Physicists Arno Penzias and Robert Wilson were working in the Bell Telephone Laboratories. They decided to use a microwave antenna as a radio telescope. This antenna was built for a satellite communication system but was no longer needed for this purpose. In whatever direction they turned this radio telescope, they got the same microwave signal of 7-cm wavelength. At first, they thought it was some electronic disturbance in the antenna. But the telescope was highly sensitive and free of noise. They even wondered if it might not be pigeon poop producing this disturbance.

Even after cleaning everything thoroughly, the signal remained, undisturbed and invariant. And when they ran out of every other option, they came to the conclusion that the signal must be coming from outer space. The intensity of it was uniform in all directions, which meant it could not be coming from one fixed point. And that in turn meant it was coming from everywhere. The only phenomenon that could be producing such a signal would be the relics of radiation—the radiation generated by the Big Bang. It is the light echo that had been red-shifted to become microwave radiation since its emission 13.8 billion years ago.

When radio astronomers conducted further investigations into the microwave radiation coming from outer space, they placed their stamp of approval on this hypothesis. This was evidence of the expansion of the universe from the Big Bang. The extremely sensitive new instruments of the twenty-first century, placed on satellites, made very precise measurements of this radiation. The tools available to astronomers and particle physicists having improved dramatically, they were now able to prepare a detailed report of those first few seconds.

At Brookhaven National Laboratory in the US and at CERN, it was possible to recreate a quark-and-gluon plasma. As the plasma expanded and cooled, it was found that mesons, protons and neutrons were indeed generated from the plasma, as quarks and gluons do not have an independent existence at low temperatures. It became clear that the world was formed because of all four interactions of gravitation, the weak force, the strong force and electromagnetism! Since gravity and electromagnetism have infinite range, the scattered particles were drawn together, atoms, galaxies and stars began to form and the universe began to take the shape we see today.

That the galaxies are speeding away from each other due to the expanding universe is because of Einstein's equation of gravity. In this equation, that mysterious substance known as dark matter also plays a crucial role. Dark energy is supposed to be responsible for increasing the speed of the expansion of the universe. But this, too, is a mystery at the moment. Dark energy causes a repulsion that combats the attractive gravity of matter and dark matter.

Fierce War

As the evidence for the Big Bang theory began to grow, the Russian scientist and human rights activist Andrei Sakharov posited a theory, uniting particle physics and cosmology. At the level of the known equations of particle physics, there is almost no bias towards either matter or antimatter. The equations are almost symmetric between matter and antimatter. And yet, we observe matter but almost no antimatter. In the turmoil of the Big Bang, Sakharov said, the symmetry between matter and antimatter must have been broken. Otherwise, in the first nanosecond an equal amount of matter and antimatter would have been generated. The two should have cancelled each other out and returned to being energy. But some special and yet unknown laws of nature deflected their actions towards matter. One might say they chose matter over antimatter. In this fierce war, a few particles were saved from annihilation, out of crores of warriors and those formed the visible universe as we know it.

This story of creation seems far-fetched, at times. And the question surfaces again and again: who was the prime mover? Religion and science have both tried to answer this question which has produced dialogue and dissent between the two for centuries. There are those who insist that there must be a Creator who started it all. There are others who say that there is no role for a Creator or a prime mover; this concept is superfluous to the theory. But one must also accept that there are some limits to the theories and analyses of science.

What happened in the first 10^{-43} seconds of the Big Bang remains a mystery. This infinitesimal time span is referred to as the 'Planck Era'. Neither the laws of general relativity nor those of quantum physics seem to apply to this time. Quantum theory maintains that the rules of behaviour at extremely small distances must be universal but as long as they cannot explain the functioning of gravity, the Holy Grail of explaining the moment of the origin of the universe is still far off.

21

Standard Model Theory

In the first trillionth of a second after the Big Bang, there were no protons and neutrons in existence. All of creation was a plasma soup in which the particles that were to make up the world, such as quarks and leptons, and those that transmit forces, such as gluons, photons, W and Z bosons, were all present. This seems to be proven beyond doubt. These particles have been generated in experiments at accelerators for short periods of time.

To understand what exactly happened in this epoch and its timelines, a combination of astrophysics and particle physics has been used. This is the Standard Model theory which was developed sixty years ago. The theory seeks to explain how the various particles came together to form the universe that we know today and has thrown up some deeply interesting and unforeseen relationships both at the subatomic and the macroscopic level.

At the end of the nineteenth century, physics rested on Newton's laws of gravitation and motion and Maxwell's theory of electromagnetism, and such knowledge as was available about the atom and its behaviour. It was also felt that our understanding of the world was complete. X-rays and radioactivity had not yet been identified. It was also not understood that in order to further the boundaries of our understanding it might be necessary to change some of the fundamental assumptions we had made about nature. It was felt that the existing theories of science sufficed.

But new ideas were also beginning to emerge. The theory of relativity and quantum theory, the discovery of atomic structure and further subatomic particles gave physics a new direction and started it off down the road to the Standard Model theory. This would be a way to understand the entire universe and all that had happened since the beginning.

The Development of the Model

The Standard Model seeks to explain the interaction between the subatomic particles. The model came into being in the second half of the twentieth century, based on contributions from scientists from all over the world. In the 1970s, the existence of quarks and gluons was proved. In 1983, the W and Z bosons were discovered. In 1995, the top quark's existence was proved, completing the quark sector. In the year 2000, the tau neutrino followed, completing the lepton sector. The Higgs boson was found in 2012, completing the model. These results proved what the model had theoretically foretold. It began to be known as 'The Theory of Almost Everything'.

It was in 1961 that the first bricks of the theory were laid down. Sheldon Glashow postulated a relationship between the weak force and the electromagnetic force. In 1967, Abdus Salam and Steven

Weinberg added the Higgs mechanism to the Standard Model, so that the fermions and the W and Z bosons could be massive and still preserve other important properties of the theory.

In 1973 at CERN, experiments using neutrino beams detected the interaction of the Z boson. This evidence gave the electroweak theory a big boost. In 1983, the W and Z bosons were discovered and their characteristics seemed to match with those predicted by the Standard Model theory.

During this time, many scientists came together to work on the strong force. It was also experimentally proven that quarks were partially charged, thus giving further proof of the quark sector of the Standard Model.

From the interactions between these particles that have been discovered, it is also possible to understand the relationship between matter and energy, and prove one of the famous equations from special relativity, $E = mc^2$.

All that we know about the elementary particle behaviour has gone into the making of the Standard Model theory. To particle physicists, the next step is finding the common ground, the Theory of Everything. At the time of writing, the Standard Model theory has withstood all tests. It helps explain the characteristics of the subatomic particles with a great degree of accuracy. Its axiomatic simplicity has attracted much praise from the scientific community. Light rays, X-rays and radio waves can be explained by the model in terms of quantum theory; the reason is because photons are devoid of mass but only have momentum and energy; their quanta of energy help describe electromagnetic radiation.

Some Flaws

When the quantum theory of electromagnetism was applied to explain the weak force, some conceptual problems showed up. The weak force acts at the subatomic level via the W and Z bosons, which are massive particles. It is not possible to understand, using just the logic of the electromagnetic force, how the weak force could act via massive particles. The electromagnetic force acts via the massless photon, which is in perfect agreement with observations. So the W and Z bosons should also be massless, which they are most definitely not. The concept of the Higgs field was invented to resolve this and similar conundrums, and the electroweak Standard Model theory was born. When the search for the Higgs boson concluded successfully, these conundrums were resolved.

Research in the field of astrophysics and cosmology lent credence to the Standard Model. Calculations of the amounts of primordial hydrogen, helium and lithium formed after the Big Bang agreed with observations.

There are still some phenomena that cannot be explained by the Standard Model theory. The existence of dark matter has been proven from astrophysical and cosmological observations, but we know very little else about dark matter. Does it consist of particles? If so, these particles cannot be described by the Standard Model theory.

There could be an entirely new and different family of particles and forces at work there. Some theoretical investigations do support such an idea. New experimental evidence is being actively sought to test the 'new particle' hypothesis of dark matter.

Much has been discovered, but scientists now understand that even more is left to be uncovered. New questions have been raised about the nature of matter and forces, including gravity. Once again, physicists will have to reorient themselves to study quantum physics and relativity.

The Standard Model theory is inadequate because:

- The model does not explain gravity. The principles of quantum physics, on the basis of which the Standard Model is built, are at odds with the principles of general relativity, i.e., gravity. So, a theory that combines and extends both sets of principles is not easy. The search for such a theory is motivated by considerations of the Planck Era of the Big Bang and of the core of black holes. Supersymmetric string theory is a candidate for such a theory.
- The Standard Model does not explain the rate of expansion of the universe. The explanation is offered by incorporating dark energy in Einstein's equation of general relativity. However, the observed amount of dark energy is deeply in conflict with the Standard Model calculation of dark energy. The calculated value of dark energy is much, much larger than the observed value. This puzzle of dark energy remains unresolved.
- As mentioned above, observations of dark matter do not fit into the Standard Model. In other words, the theory does not contain any explanation for the existence of dark matter. Beyond the Standard Model, supersymmetric particles may constitute the dark matter. More elaborate versions of the Higgs boson theory may also explain dark matter.
- The Standard Model does not have a good explanation of neutrinos having insignificant mass compared to other particles. In fact, the huge range of masses spanned by the leptons and the quarks, from the very light neutrinos to the very heavy top quark, is an unsolved puzzle in the Standard

Model. Theoretical ideas beyond the Standard Model have been proposed and their experimental verification is being pursued.

- As mentioned earlier, the excess of matter over antimatter in the universe does not fit with the Standard Model. Again, new theoretical explanations beyond the Standard Model have been proposed, and their experimental signatures are being pursued. Some of these ideas are based on more elaborate models of Higgs bosons, compared to the simplest version incorporated into the Standard Model.

22

Post-Doctoral Work

After a brief background to the subject, we are back with Ashutosh and his career.

Particle physics was Ashutosh's chosen field of study and research. In 1995, after getting his doctorate, Ashutosh joined Columbia University as a post-doctoral research associate. At that time the DØ experiment was operating at the Fermilab accelerator, near Chicago. This accelerator (called the Tevatron) was making beams of the highest energy particles in the world. Fermilab was the leader in high-energy physics research. DØ and Collider Detector at Fermilab (CDF) were its two biggest experiments. Fermilab's experimental results were seen as definitive across the world.

Taking Part in DØ

Professor Paul Grannis was the lead scientist on this experiment. He was a well-known and well-respected scientist. DØ was a collaboration between 450 scientists from many countries: US, Russia, France, Brazil, India, Colombia, South Korea, Mexico, Argentina, among others. The 5,500 tonne DØ detector had been built to explore the signals indicative of new subnuclear particles and the forces operating on them.

At the beginning of 1995, Fermilab had announced the discovery of the top quark, the end of a quest for this ultimate quark that completed the families of quarks in the Standard Model. Ashutosh started work on the experiment and his contribution was immediately appreciated. He proved experimentally that the electron, at a size of 1 billionth billionth of a centimetre, did not have any subsidiary or component particles. No other experiment had proved this with such stringent accuracy. His paper was published in the prestigious *Physical Review Letters*. The world of physics was electrified by this.

Perhaps one might pause here to recount a surprising incident. One billionth billionth of a centimetre means 10^{-18} of a centimetre. It is an unimaginably small number, 100,000 times smaller than a proton. If one were to take the inverse value, 10^{18} centimetres, the length would stretch one light year, way past our solar system. In comparison, the nearest star system, Alpha Centauri, is 4.4 light years away. This is what particle physics does; it deals with the unimaginably small. But there was one scientist who could imagine the unimaginable and measure it too: Ashutosh.

The research at DØ was on top quarks, W and Z bosons and searches for other new particles and forces. Everyone knew that if the behaviour and characteristics of top quarks and W and Z bosons were studied and calculated accurately, these results would be important in the quest for the Higgs boson. Only when the measurement and calculations are of the highest level of accuracy, can a way forward be found. To achieve such levels of accuracy, a huge amount of data must be gathered. The analysis of this data needs advanced mathematical computing, using appropriate software for its interpretation. The analysis must also be made at a similar level of intelligence and intuition. Ashutosh was selected as the leader of a group of a hundred scientists, all studying the W boson.

They could see his skill at dealing with such machinery and equipment. As an engineering student, he had studied analogue and digital circuit design. He was an expert in the subject. DØ's Run 2 calorimeter electronics was set up by him. This project cost $1.5 million. The leaders of the project had full faith in Ashutosh. He was also chosen as the editor of the report on upgrading the performance of the DØ calorimeter. He also contributed a great deal to the design of the essential software for the detector simulation. And of course, his knowledge of hardware was indispensable to the team. The calorimeter is one of the most important devices in particle physics research. It measures the energies and positions of all particles except muons and neutrinos. The majority of the particles pass through this device.

As Ashutosh's post-doctoral mentor, Tuts's guidance and advice were invaluable. He was in charge of the entire DØ upgrade project. He had delegated the calorimeter upgrade to Ashutosh. Whenever Ashutosh came up with a circuit design study or update, he would run it past Tuts and another scientist, Dean Schamberger. They had many interesting discussions. It was a hectic but exciting time. Ashutosh got to interact with electronics manufacturers and observed how Tuts negotiated contracts with the manufacturers' representatives. A situation arose where the electronics specifications set by Ashutosh were not being understood by the engineers of the manufacturing company in South Korea. The communication through their representatives based in Chicago was proving to be inadequate and direct contact was required. Ashutosh and Tuts took the help of a colleague on DØ who was fluent in Korean. Because of the time difference, a weekly conference call was booked at 9 p.m. between Ashutosh, Fermilab engineers and the engineers in Korea. Ashutosh's friend translated the conversation from the opposite sides of the Earth and over a couple of months, the communication gap was closed.

Particle physics is indeed an international enterprise at all levels!

Those were the days before electronic projectors, but Ashutosh told us that he was not even using software to make presentations. He would write slides by hand on plastic transparencies. Tuts showed him the benefits of using software like PowerPoint. So, at the next big workshop where Ashutosh was to present the progress of the calorimeter upgrade, he decided to make Powerpoint slides. The workshop was at Indiana University and Ashutosh could not find a printer to print his slides. Of course, he had never encountered such a situation when using handwritten slides. Tuts came to the rescue. He pulled out a portable slide printer from his bag, connected it to his laptop and printed Ashutosh's slides for him. The presentation went without a hitch and all of DØ was impressed with the progress. Close call!

When Ashutosh was leaving DØ and Columbia to join CDF as an assistant professor from Duke, Tuts organized a big send-off party and many friends and colleagues got together. Tuts even suggested in jest that, instead of leaving DØ, Ashutosh and the Duke group could join DØ. Of course, that could not be, since Prof. Al Goshaw of Duke was the CDF co-leader at the time. Ashutosh has fond memories of his time on the DØ experiment.

Three-Fold Knowledge

In the future this work would prove instructive. It would require $40 million to reconfigure DØ. The calorimeter was the major detector system in DØ. One could say it was the heart of the experiment. Without the calorimeter, most of the research would not have been possible. Sixty thousand electronic channels had to be redesigned inside the calorimeter. It was necessary to understand both digital and analogue electronics as well as to have a deep insight into the relevant theoretical realm of science. Ashutosh turned out to be the only person who could create computer models to run simulations of the calorimeter experiments. He had trained in electronics engineering; to his in-depth knowledge of physics, he brought his knowledge of computer coding.

Ashutosh developed electronics that worked twenty-five times faster than those in the previous calorimeter. This brought about a revolution in electronics as well. Along with many other analyses, the faster electronics was of great help in measuring the mass of the W boson more accurately. He became the convener of the group responsible for studying the W boson in the DØ Collaboration. This offered a set of new challenges and drew attention to him. He initiated many more discussions in the team. Within two years of starting post-doctoral work, to become a convener was a matter of some pride.

Ashutosh's post-doctoral years defined a career path that he has followed for the last twenty-five years. It was on the DØ experiment that he realized the importance of making even more precise measurements of the W boson's mass, because this was a sensitive measure of the properties of the Higgs boson and could reveal unexpected secrets of nature. There was data collected by the experiment that nobody had used to measure the W boson mass, because the requisite understanding of the data was considered to be too challenging. However, the data had unique characteristics that enabled a more precise measurement of the W boson mass. Ashutosh demonstrated this possibility to his senior colleagues Grannis, Montgomery, Tuts, Harry Weerts and Mark Strovink, who were convinced by Ashutosh's arguments. Then Ashutosh began the painstaking and detailed analysis and published the measurement in the prestigious journal *Physical Review Letters*. It was the first measurement of the W boson mass ever made, using data from the forward detectors of an experiment. This experience set him on the long-term trajectory of achieving world leadership in this arena over the next two-and-a-half decades.

The work done on the W boson under Ashutosh's leadership was noticed. In July 1998, during the International Conference of High-Energy Physics held in Vancouver, Canada, the largest ever to be held up to that point, Ashutosh presented their findings and these were met with acceptance and their novelty was recognized.

23

A Heavy Particle

The work for which Ashutosh is internationally famous is the accurate measurement of the mass of the W boson. I present here the image I have of this accomplishment.

On stage, every actor tries to present their best performance. In a play, the main roles are essayed by the lead actors. But the strings of all these 'puppets' are in the hands of the person behind the curtains—the sutradhar. The sutradhar at the subatomic level is the W boson.

When Ashutosh began his post-doctoral work (1995–1998), it was the W boson that drew his attention. He had studied it scientifically and had also taken part in group projects, many of which he had led, and these had produced good results.

From January 1999, he began teaching at Duke University and would travel twice a month from Durham, North Carolina where he lived to Batavia, near Chicago where Fermilab is located, in order to conduct his research. This meant that for twenty years as a professor, he managed a teaching career, other professional responsibilities, research at Fermilab and CERN, and still managed to conduct research into the mass of the W boson.

So what was it that kept him at it? Was it that important? What was to be gained by finding out its mass to a great degree of accuracy? To answer these questions, we will have to take a look at the history of the W boson and the goals of his research.

The idea of bosons was first proposed by the famous Indian scientist Professor Satyendranath Bose. All bosonic particles are named after him. Force-mediating particles must be bosons. The W and Z bosons are the weak bosons, also called intermediate vector bosons, because they mediate the weak force between particles.

W bosons can have a positive or negative charge: W^+ and W^- bosons. The Z boson being electrically neutral is its own antiparticle. These three particles have the same intrinsic angular momentum (i.e., spin) value, which corresponds to a vector in algebra, hence the name vector boson. They are short-lived particles; their lifespan is about 3×10^{-25} seconds. When the existence of these particles was proven, a very important part of the Standard Model theory was once again vindicated. Since the W boson mediates the weak force, it is so named—W for weak. The theory of the weak force proposed by Sheldon Glashow needed another mediator, hence the Z boson, also called Z^0 because it has no electrical charge.

The W boson mediates the absorption and emission of the neutrino, the electron and the positron from nuclei. This makes nuclear transmutation possible—the process in which neutrons become protons and vice versa. This process was the first indicator of the importance of the W boson and one of the reasons why it has been the focus of so much attention for so long.

The W and Z bosons are heavy particles, about eighty-five times as heavy as a proton. The large mass of these bosons makes the weak force a very short-range force at low energies, a range much smaller than the size of a proton.

The range of strong force is also extremely limited, to about the size of a proton. Inside the nucleus, this force keeps the protons and neutrons together, and its effect is limited to adjacent nucleons.

On the other hand, the ambit of the electromagnetic force is infinite because its transmitting particle, the photon, has no mass at all. This would also be true for the graviton, which is still only a theoretical construct.

Table: Relative Strengths of the Four Forces of Nature

No.	Force	Relative strength	Range of force
1	Gravity	1	infinite
2	Electromagnetic force	10^{36}	infinite
3	Strong force	10^{38}	10^{-15} metres
4	Weak force	$10^{29} - 10^{32}$	10^{-18} metres

At this point, it seems fitting to change the subject and address another issue because it is instructive and entertaining.

Neutrons and protons are held together in the nucleus because of the strong force, as we have seen above. As neutrons have no charge, they do not feel the mutual electric repulsion that protons do. Because of this, neutrons are responsible for balancing the repulsion between protons. This is the reason that if the nucleus has to remain stable, there must be neutrons in it. In large nuclei with higher atomic numbers, there is preponderance of neutrons to lend stability to the nucleus. Bismuth is an element, a metal with an atomic number of 83. This means it has 83 protons in its nucleus, and typically 126 neutrons. Elements with higher atomic numbers than Bismuth tend to be unstable and decompose spontaneously into elements with smaller nuclei. Uranium has an atomic number of 92, with typically 146 neutrons. Elements with larger atomic numbers are so unstable that, as a rule, they are rare in nature. Plutonium 94 is an element that mostly has an artificial existence, produced in nuclear reactors and separated for use in an atomic bomb. Nature understands that it is not a good idea to produce plutonium, but mankind does not agree.

The Higgs Mechanism

That the photon is without mass is a natural consequence of the fundamental theory of forces. The same logic applied to the weak force predicted that the W and Z bosons should be massless too. The fact that the W and Z bosons have such a large mass was a major stumbling block in the Standard Model theory. In 1964, papers on 'Spontaneous Symmetry Breaking' were published, suggesting the so-called Higgs mechanism as a way around this stumbling block. In this mechanism, a completely new and fundamental 'substance' called the Higgs field, fills all of space. The W and Z bosons, as well as the quarks and leptons, feel the presence of this space-filling stuff and this imparts the property of mass to all of them. Thus, the Higgs field is responsible for generating mass for all elementary particles. The Higgs boson is understood as a quantum or packet of energy in a wave travelling in this Higgs field, just as a photon is a packet of energy in an electromagnetic wave. And so, the speculation about the existence of the Higgs boson began.

Taken together, the Higgs mechanism and the electroweak force would fit into the Standard Model theory. This was a very valuable proposition. When all the other pieces of the Standard Model fell into place following their experimental discoveries, this proposition helped to boost research into the Higgs boson.

The Higgs mechanism and its boson remained a theoretical proposition for almost fifty years. There were two possible ways, different but complementary, in which this might be proved. Quantum theory offered the uncertainty principle as one of the possible ways. In quantum theory, all fundamental particles fluctuate in and out of the vacuum spontaneously, everywhere and all the time. Where does the energy come from to create particles out of nothing? The answer is the uncertainty principle, which permits energy to not be conserved, as long as the violation occurs over a very short time interval. The larger the amount of borrowed energy, the shorter the time period of this loan must be. The product of these amounts is the all-important Planck's constant of quantum mechanics.

If the Higgs boson exists, it must also take part in these vacuum fluctuations.

These fluctuations have an impact on the mass of the W boson. This effect is small, but it can be quantified precisely in the theory. In order to be able to measure this impact, it was necessary to measure the mass of the W boson with as high a degree of accuracy as possible. This had to be within the range of +/- 0.05 per cent or better. Then, by comparing the calculated and the measured masses of the W boson, the existence of the Higgs boson could be inferred. Even better, if the accuracies were high enough, the mass of the Higgs boson itself could also be inferred. This was the very ambitious plan that Ashutosh embarked on.

In the 1950s, the weak force began to be studied. By 1967, it was possible to postulate a link between electromagnetism and the weak force and their combination was given the new name of electroweak force. For this work, Sheldon Glashow, Steven Weinberg and Abdus Salam were awarded the Nobel Prize in physics. In this theory, for beta decay to occur, it was necessary to postulate the existence of the W boson. The beta decay is a form of nuclear transmutation in which a neutron turns into a proton with the emission of an electron and an electron-neutrino. It is a form of radioactivity in which the beta particles are the emitted electrons.

Decay is the process of breakdown of a particle into other particles. In an accelerator-based experiment, the high-energy collisions produce heavy exotic particles by turning energy into mass. These massive particles exist for a very brief period of time and decay into lighter particles such as electrons, neutrinos, up and down quarks.

When the search for the W boson began, a huge accelerator called the Super Proton Synchrotron was built at CERN, motivated by the physicist Carlo Rubbia. Its engineering was figured out by Simon Van der Meer. The CERN laboratory succeeded magnificently, and Rubbia and Van der Meer were awarded the Nobel Prize for the discovery of the W and Z bosons. The W boson is such a massive particle that it could be produced artificially at only two laboratories: CERN and Fermilab.

Electroweak Symmetry Breaking (EWSB)

In 1896, Antoine-Henri Becquerel discovered that uranium produced a new kind of penetrating radiation, which was later shown to consist of alpha, (α) beta (β) and gamma (γ) rays. This natural radioactivity causes a change at the nuclear level and such elements are called naturally radioactive substances. Further research proved that the alpha (α) particles were the nuclei of helium and the beta (β) rays were electrons.

The weak force works between a pair of quarks or between a pair of leptons. The electromagnetic force works between quarks and leptons in a similar way. The electromagnetic force is transmitted by the photon, which has no mass and so the range of the force is infinite; the range of the weak force is extremely limited as it is transmitted by the vector bosons, which have a large mass. Weinberg and Salam theorized that at energies beyond 100 GeV the large mass of the weak vector bosons does not suppress the weak force. The behaviour of weak vector bosons becomes similar to photons. The weak force begins to act like the electromagnetic force and the two forces can be partly combined. At extremely high energy, the electromagnetic force and the weak force appear unified while at low energy, the two forces appear to work independently of each other.

The process by which they are divided is called Electroweak Symmetry Breaking (EWSB).

The question that confronted physicists was how do the elementary particles acquire mass? All particles are naturally massless according to the theoretical principles. To provide a theoretical answer to the question of the observed masses, the EWSB model was propounded. The Higgs mechanism provides the EWSB. It postulated the idea of the Higgs Field, a quantum field that permeates all of space according to the Standard Model. This field is neutral and without electric charge, it does not interact with the photon which can continue to be a massless particle. However, the weak vector bosons do interact with the Higgs field and appear as massive particles. Thus, the Higgs field disrupts the original symmetry between the weak and the electromagnetic force.

Understanding the behaviour and characteristics of the W boson is central to understanding the origins of our universe. Of the basic principles that physicists use to describe the beginning of the universe, the W boson is one of the most important and understanding it and its behaviour is central to particle physics. Even today, the existence of the world as we know it is dependent on the W boson having a large mass. For example, the nuclear fusion of four protons into a helium nucleus is the reaction that powers the sun. This reaction requires the conversion of protons to neutrons by the weak force at just the right rate, which is possible because the W boson has a large mass. Thus, it is one of the most important aspects of the universe for our own existence. It is important to investigate and understand it thoroughly. Knowing it well would prove useful in a host of other investigations in nuclear physics and in astrophysics.

New Theories, New Ways

As mentioned above, there are phenomena that the Standard Model does not explain. In order to accommodate them, extra clauses have to be added to the Standard Model theory. They are called extensions of the Standard Model. One possible extension incorporates the theoretical principles of supersymmetry.

The theory of supersymmetric particles was not only of interest to particle physics; it had relevance in cosmology as well. In the last few decades, while examining various galaxies, the orbits of stars have been studied. It was observed that near the outskirts of the galaxies, the stars' orbit velocities were too large compared to the predictions of conventional calculations based on the mass of gas and stars and the gravitational attraction that these exerted. The orbit velocities were consistent with the presence of additional matter. Slowly, more evidence began to accumulate that there was a lot more matter in the galaxies and clusters of galaxies, much of it invisible. This is now called dark matter, and there is about five times as much dark matter as known matter in the form of protons and neutrons. We know that dark matter exists because it exerts the force of gravity on the galactic and cosmological scales. Dark matter explains many of the observations of astrophysics and cosmology. In fact, it is now understood that dark matter played a crucial role in the formation of galaxies. Calculations show that the gravitational attraction of normal matter would not have been enough to form galaxies in the early universe. It was the significantly higher attractive gravity of the dark matter that caused galaxies to form. So, we owe our existence to dark matter.

It is well known that none of the Standard Model particles can make up the dark matter. However, in the supersymmetric extension of the Standard Model, additional particles are predicted and some of these new particles have properties consistent with dark matter. This is one of the reasons that the search for supersymmetric particles has been going on for a few decades.

Just as Standard Model calculations can be done all the way back to tiny fractions of a second after the Big Bang, such calculations can also be done using the supersymmetric and other extensions of the Standard Model. According to these calculations, these new particles would have an important role to play in the evolution of the universe.

To establish new physics like supersymmetry it was necessary to measure the mass of the W boson with as high a degree of accuracy as possible. The value of the W boson mass in nature is influenced by the existence of new particles through quantum vacuum fluctuations, just like the vacuum fluctuations involving Higgs bosons. If supersymmetric particles exist, they will also participate in these fluctuations and make an additional small change to the W boson mass. With the conjecture of supersymmetric particles, the predicted mass of the W boson increases by up to 100 MeV relative to the Standard Model theory prediction, depending on the properties of the new particles. Similar calculations have been performed assuming the existence of additional Higgs-like bosons, which also change the W boson mass by a similar amount. These examples illustrate how the predicted value of the W boson mass changes from theory to theory. The power of the W boson mass measurement arises from its ability to adjudicate between these different hypotheses—to pass judgement and select the one closer to the truth, so to speak. The more accurate the measurement, the closer to the truth one can hone in.

Thus, establishing the mass of the W boson with utmost accuracy and comparing it with predicted values from different theories will be instrumental in going beyond the SM theory and treading the path of new physics. It would offer proof for or against the theories built around the interactions of particles and forces at the sub-nuclear level. The Standard Model theory is up for verification or augmentation.

24

Duke University and Collider Detector at Fermilab (CDF)

As a research scientist at Columbia University, Ashutosh had worked on the DØ experiment. At the end of 1998, his post-doctoral research came to an end. In 1999, he began as assistant professor at Duke University and went to live in the city of Durham, North Carolina. He began research on the CDF experiment. He had to re-establish himself at CDF.

CDF was a huge experiment with 700 scientists from sixty-one institutions and thirteen countries. In 1995, CDF and DØ were both focussed on the hunt for the top quark. This was a particle predicted by the Standard Model theory; it was supposed to be the most massive quark. At the beginning of his stint at CDF, Ashutosh did not get a good role on the project. There was a group of rather self-important scientists there. For a while, Ashutosh wandered from group to group. But this too was a kind of education for him. He was not being given the kind of project he would like to work on.

In some groups, he would be given software design work. He was not very enthusiastic about this initially, but despite that, he accepted the work.

He maximized all the opportunities presented to him. His ability was now coming to everyone's notice. He designed and built a calibration system for the electronics of the CDF detector that made the most accurate measurements of charged-particle momenta. He then took over the development of the sophisticated software that produced these measurements from the raw data of this detector. Eventually, he was asked to lead the electroweak physics group in which all W and Z boson analyses were conducted by a hundred scientists and students. He brought a new vision and gave this group a new thrust. He began to be known as the kind of person who knew exactly what was needed and who could be relied on to make sound decisions.

Between 1992 and 1995, the Tevatron completed its first run at Fermilab. Its second run started in 2001. During its second run at CDF, Ashutosh handled all aspects of the analysis relating to the measurement of the mass of the W boson. He devised a new protocol to analyse the W and Z boson data in a consistent manner, leading to a higher accuracy in the mass measurement.

Leading the Offline Software and Computing

There was an internal offline software and computing project that was part of the CDF experiment. Ashutosh was the co-leader of this project for two-and-a-half years, from July 2004 to December 2006. This was one of the seven most important positions to be held among those 700 scientists.

The online operations leader had the responsibility of operating the detector. The detector would record all the information generated by the collisions of the beam particles, for later analysis.

The offline leader had the following responsibilities:

- Providing all software tools needed for running scientific analyses of all the data.
- Keeping the calibrations of the detector ready.
- Getting the software code for all data processing written.
- Getting the simulation software written.
- Studying the outcome of the simulated collisions.
- Managing computer systems and modalities of data storage and access.

The purpose of the offline project was to ensure that the experiment's data analysis worked at its maximum capacity and fulfilled the scientific potential of all 700-plus collaborators. It was therefore necessary to ensure that the scientists had what they needed in terms of the most advanced software, analysis tools and computing technology capable of making extremely fine analyses, in order to publish the largest number of high-quality papers. The co-leaders of the CDF Collaboration, Professor Young-Kee Kim of the University of Chicago and Dr Robert Roser of Fermilab, had faith in Ashutosh's vision and supported his endeavours. They shared the goal of making the CDF experiment as productive a research enterprise as possible.

The amount of data generated during Ashutosh's tenure as co-leader of the offline project was four times the amount that had been generated in the history of CDF. Keeping in touch with all those working on the project and making sure they were all aligned required a high degree of diplomatic skill. As in the corporate world, there were many knotty problems of personality clashes. There were several moving parts. Getting everything to work harmoniously was a difficult job. It was a high-wire walk, deciding who had to know what, what decision might offend someone, whose advice might be the most useful or, in some cases, the least harmful to the project. In such an atmosphere, Ashutosh also discovered the need for and importance of allies and friends whom one could trust.

The co-leader of the offline software and computing project was Dr Pavel Murat alias Pasha, a close friend of Ashutosh. Many years later, in 2014, Ashutosh was deputed to Fermilab again as the Future Facilities Group Leader. By then, Ashutosh's son Gautam was a teenager. Every week, Pavel and Ashutosh would be joined by Gautam and Pavel's daughter who was about the same age as Gautam, to play badminton at the Fermilab Club.

༄

Once Again, the W Boson

In order to ascertain the mass of the W boson to a high degree of accuracy, one needs highly advanced and sensitive scientific equipment as much as the ability to analyse data with insight and understanding. The mass of the W boson had been measured at four different experiments already at CERN. The accelerator at CERN collided beams of electrons and positrons and was called the Large Electron-Positron (LEP) collider. The average of the four results was $80,376 \pm 33$ MeV/c^2 with a degree of error of 0.04 per cent. At the level of each experiment, the degree of error in each independent measurement was about 0.06 per cent. In 2001, this result from CERN was announced.

The W boson mass had also been measured at the first run of the Tevatron by the CDF and DØ experiments. Ashutosh's first measurement at DØ during his post-doctoral research was a big contributor to the Fermilab measurements. These measurements taken together had a degree of error of 0.074 per cent. So, at this time, the CERN measurement had almost twice the accuracy of the Fermilab measurement.

After this, work on the W boson mass measurement began at the CDF and DØ experiments at the second Tevatron run. The Tevatron accelerator collided proton and antiproton beams. The detectors at the Tevatron were as large as a three-storey house and weighed thousands of tonnes. Each had an estimated one million electronic sensors.

When particles are produced at high energies, these sensors must detect the faint and evanescent traces of their presence. The detectors must encircle the point where the collision takes place and register all the particles that come from it in terms of energy, direction and electrical charge.

In September 2003, Ashutosh became the co-founder and co-convener of the Tevatron Electroweak Working Group. He was already in an important leadership position at CDF as co-convener of the CDF Electroweak Physics group. The Fermilab experiments were set up so that their findings would be made available to scientists all over the world. The Tevatron Electroweak Working Group was tasked with understanding all W and Z boson measurements and studying the relationship between W and Z bosons, top quarks and the Higgs boson. Twenty scientists worked together in this study group.

Since the CERN LEP accelerator had stopped operating, the Tevatron Run 2 was the only place in the world where the W and Z bosons were being produced. Thus, it was the place where the W boson's mass would be measured for many more years, and where the 'god particle', as the Higgs boson was now being referred to, could be found. Therefore, the W boson's importance could not be understated.

Protons and antiprotons are twinned particles; they are composed of quarks. When they collide, it would be a mistake to take anything for granted. One cannot afford the slightest negligence. Each measurement, each calculation must be sweated over.

At the Tevatron, the protons and antiprotons hurtle at each other with 2 trillion electron-Volts (2 TeV) of combined energy. You would need a trillion batteries, mounted on each other, to generate that kind of energy. In a single second, 5 million collisions take place. In one out of 2.5 million such strikes between protons and antiprotons, a quark and antiquark annihilate to produce a W boson.

When the W boson decays, it is transformed into a quark–antiquark pair, or one electron/muon/tau and a corresponding neutrino. The same thing happens in beta decay when the W boson is emitted by a neutron as it turns into a proton. The first task of the detector is to identify those rare events in which a W boson is produced. It is extremely difficult to separate out the collision events in which the W bosons decay to quark–antiquark pairs, because there are too many other events that also contain quarks and antiquarks produced in the collisions. The reason is that protons and antiprotons each contain many quarks, antiquarks and gluons. They have a much higher probability of undergoing the strong interaction than the electroweak interaction. Therefore, the total rate of quark–antiquark production is much larger than the rate of W boson production. The rare W boson signal is lost in the large rate of background events.

However, all is not lost. It is possible to trace the decay of W bosons into electrons or muons, and also to measure their energy accurately. Electrons and muons have very distinctive signatures in the detector. These leptonic decays of W bosons are clearly identified. Like electrons, muons are very well understood. Muons are present in cosmic rays and bombard the Earth's surface from the atmosphere. About 200 muons pass through our bodies every second.

The next step is to measure all the particle energies in W boson events very accurately. This part of the research was very complicated. To resolve it would take many years.

After the discovery of the W boson in 1983, there were only two places in the world where they could be produced. Both of these were proton–antiproton accelerators. They had the capacity to generate extremely high collision energies. One was at CERN and the other was the Tevatron at Fermilab. In 1990, CERN commissioned the Large Electron-Positron Collider (LEP) and starting in 1995, its beam energy was doubled. This became the third site where W bosons could be produced and its mass measured.

Now this lepton collider was seen as state-of-the-art, and the Tevatron at Fermilab began to look a little outdated. The beams that were being used in the lepton collider, the electron and the positron, were indivisible. They could produce many W bosons without the debris that all the quarks and gluons in the protons produce. To find the W bosons in the middle of all the quarks and gluons emitted by a proton–antiproton collision was like finding the proverbial needle in a haystack. The lepton collider made this easier. The scientific world began to believe that the best measurement of the W boson mass would be made at LEP.

But Ashutosh kept faith in the Tevatron. He continued to believe that they would crack the problem of finding an accurate value for the mass of the W boson with the Fermilab data. He had been associated with the CDF experiment at Fermilab since 1999. Actually, this was no easy task. Three CDF colleagues were assigned to review all aspects of the data analysis led by Ashutosh.

A look at Ashutosh's logbook for 15 July 2004, reveals the list of mathematical problems he put down for the W boson analysis for that day. He knew for sure that he would not be able to solve the problem of measuring an accurate value for the mass of the W boson without resolving these and many other such issues. His senior colleagues were also beginning to put pressure on him to produce results that could be presented to the world. One of them was Professor Nigel Lockyer.

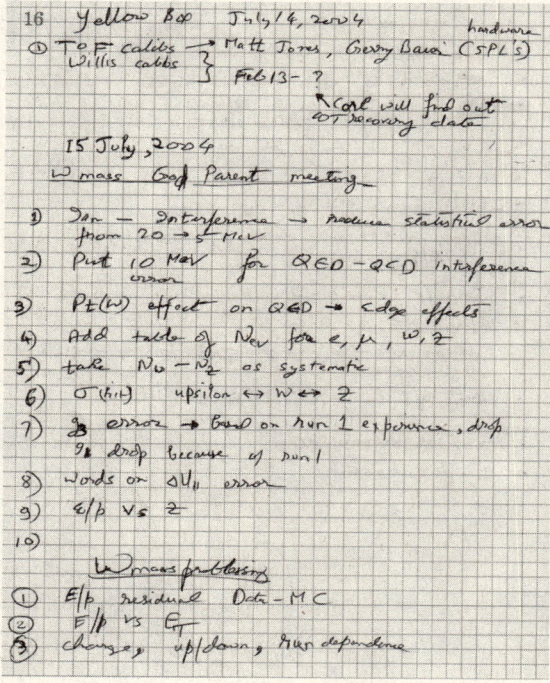

A page from Ashutosh's logbook documenting a discussion with the review committee which scrutinized his team's W boson mass analysis that was published in 2007.

The problems were knotty. The way forward was a subject of much dispute. Deep and intense thinking and the analysis of the data continued. Two-and-a-half years passed in this manner.

Ashutosh and the scientists working in his team at CDF knew that the scientific validity of their measurements was of paramount importance. A crucial aspect of scientific research is that scientists should be very careful not to introduce any human or psychological bias into the analysis procedure. Ashutosh's team used a special technique called 'blind procedure' in which the result of the analysis was kept hidden from everyone, including the analysts. Thus, the analysis could be made more and more sophisticated on the basis of scientific logic alone, without any psychological influence from prior knowledge of the W boson mass. The 'blind procedure' requires strict discipline; the analysis must be scrutinized, validated and finalized and only then is the result of the analysis revealed. This result is not to be changed by further analysis, without full disclosure to the entire scientific community.

On 14 December 2006, Ashutosh presented the measurement of the mass of the W boson at Fermilab.

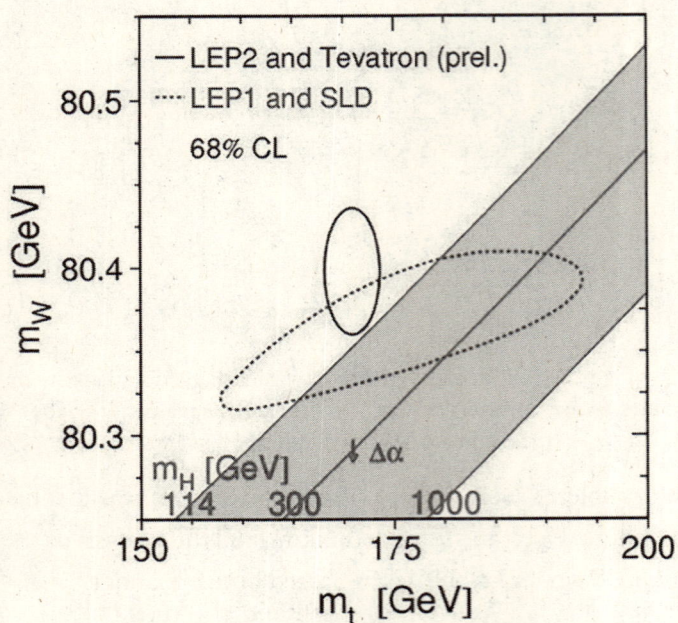

According to the Standard Model theory, the masses of the W boson, the Higgs boson and the top quark are related to each other. If two of them are known accurately, the third can be deduced. The diagram above illustrates that the mass of the Higgs boson is a function of the masses of the other two. The reason for this connection between the masses is the quantum vacuum fluctuations affecting the mass of the W boson. The top quark and the Higgs boson participate in these fluctuations. The size of the W boson mass shift induced by these fluctuations depends on the masses of the top quark and the Higgs boson. These vacuum fluctuations can be calculated in the Standard Model, which is a quantum theory.

The shaded diagonal band indicates all the possible masses of the Higgs boson, which had not been discovered yet. The range of possible masses is between 114 and 1000 GeV/c^2. For each possible Higgs boson mass value, a corresponding line can be drawn, such as the dotted diagonal line for 300 GeV/c^2. The range of possible values is based on theoretical deductions to be less than 1000 GeV/c^2, and on empirical evidence from the LEP experiments to be greater than 114 GeV/c^2.

Ashutosh presented the new measured value of the W boson mass: it was 80,413 ± 48 MeV/c^2. In the diagram, it is represented by the dotted vertical oval. The earlier calculations are shown in the horizontal oval in the diagram. These calculations were based on the assumption that the Standard Model is correct. The new measurement from Ashutosh does not make this assumption and is therefore an independent test of the Standard Model. No one had succeeded in measuring the W boson mass with such accuracy.

The new measurement showed the W boson to be heavier than previously recorded. The mass of the top quark was already measured. According to the new measurement of the W boson mass, the Higgs boson would be lighter than previously anticipated. The intersection of the vertical oval and the diagonal shaded bands showed where the Higgs boson's mass was expected to lie.

Ashutosh's measurement of the W boson mass with its ±0.06 per cent accuracy was accepted by the scientific community. This was the most accurate estimate of its mass in a single experimental setting.

It was also accepted that the Higgs boson could be lighter than previously thought. As such, it appeared that the elusive Higgs boson could possibly be detected at the Tevatron collision energy, and was not in the domain of the LHC alone.

The attitude of the world's scientists towards the capabilities of the Tevatron also changed; it was no longer looking so yesterday. That it should be the site of the most accurate measurement of the W boson mass was a game changer. Ashutosh and all the scientists who worked under his leadership were individually credited with this success.

One thing became clear—the progress of the CDF and DØ experiments at Fermilab was apparent to the world community. The excitement was palpable; the elusive Higgs boson seemed just that much closer. Their pursuit of the signatures of dark matter and extra dimensions was also ramping up.

'This new precision determination of the W boson mass by CDF is one of the most challenging and most important measurements from the Tevatron,' said the then Associate Director for High Energy Physics at the US Department of Energy's Office of Science, Dr Robin Staffin. 'Together, the W boson and top-quark masses allow us to triangulate the location of the elusive Higgs boson.'

Fermilab Director Dr Piermaria Oddone, praising this achievement by Ashutosh's team, said, 'Our experimenters are now in a position to look for some of the rarest and most amazing phenomena that theorists have predicted, as well as to find the completely unexpected. This is a very exciting time.'

In March 2007, the Large Hadron Collider, which was being set up at CERN, was the cynosure of all eyes. CERN was expected to be the site of Herculean achievements. But because of Ashutosh's successful measurement of the W boson mass, new shoots sprang up on the vine of American science. Since the W boson turned out to be heavier than anticipated, it was now predicted that the Higgs boson would be lighter than it was earlier believed. Thus, there was a greater chance that it might be found in a lower energy setting. Again, the Tevatron looked like it might be the site of the discovery of the Higgs boson. This hope gave a new scientific dimension to the economic cold war between Europe and America.

25

A Herculean Effort

The search for the 'god particle', the Higgs boson, had preoccupied the scientific world for more than forty years. Ashutosh was part of this race, but he would not give up on the challenge presented by the W boson.

On 14 December 2006, he presented the research he had done on the W boson and received international acceptance for his work. His measurement of the mass was 80,413 ± 48 MeV/c^2 with an accuracy of 0.06 per cent. He had already decided that he was going to try and reduce the margin of error. When he started work on the mass of the W boson at CDF, he only had a 100,000 bosons to work with. He had decided to step it up and use new data with a million bosons, ten times the previous number, to improve the accuracy by a factor of three. Over the next six years, he led a group of scientists from the Canadian national laboratory for particle physics (TRIUMF), University College London and Oxford University to get this done.

The 23 February 2012 Announcement

The US government's Department of Energy (DOE) was supporting the ongoing CDF and DØ experiments. In both experiments, the mass of the W boson was being studied. Finally, on 23 February 2012, the two institutions made the following announcement:

> The world's most precise measurement of the mass of the W boson, one of nature's elementary particles, has been achieved by scientists from the CDF and DØ collaborations at the Department of Energy's Fermi National Accelerator Laboratory. The new measurement is an important, independent constraint of the mass of the theorized Higgs boson. It also provides a rigorous test of the Standard Model that serves as the blueprint for our world, detailing the properties of the building blocks of matter and how they interact.

Working under Ashutosh's leadership, the group of scientists at CDF came to the conclusion that the W boson had a mass of $80,387 \pm 19$ MeV/c^2. Using all the Tevatron data that had been gathered earlier, including the data from the DØ experiment, the combined measurement was $80,387 \pm 16$ MeV/c^2, which was accepted as having a precision of 0.02 per cent.

When, on 23 February 2012, Ashutosh made this announcement, the eyes of the world's scientists were on him. Dr Bodhitha Jayatilaka, one of the post-doctoral researchers Ashutosh was guiding, relayed the announcement at an international conference in Italy. Three of India's greatest scientists, Dr Raghunath Mashelkar, Dr Jayant Narlikar and Dr Anil Kakodkar, sent congratulatory emails.

This W boson mass value helped the team led by Ashutosh to predict the mass of the Higgs boson. It was 90 GeV/c^2 with a 30 per cent margin of error. This helped narrow the range of possible Higgs boson masses compared to previous estimates.

'This measurement illustrates the great contributions that the Tevatron has made and continues to make with further analysis of its accumulated data,' said Fermilab Director Pier Oddone. 'The precision of the measurement is unprecedented and allows rigorous tests of our underlying theory of how the universe works.'

The Whereabouts of the Higgs Boson

The increased accuracy of the measurement of the mass of the W boson and the top quark helped with the triangulation of the whereabouts of the Higgs boson. It was predicted that the Higgs boson would have a mass less than 152 GeV/c^2 with a high degree of certainty.

The experiments being conducted at CERN's LHC had already excluded Higgs boson masses between 127 and 600 GeV/c^2. These findings agreed with each other. The mass of a particle is always given in terms of a particular energy level because of Einstein's famous formulation $E = mc^2$ (where 'c' represents the fixed speed of light), which means that mass is a form of energy.

The relationship between the masses of the W boson, the top quark and the Higgs boson can be made clear with the following diagram:

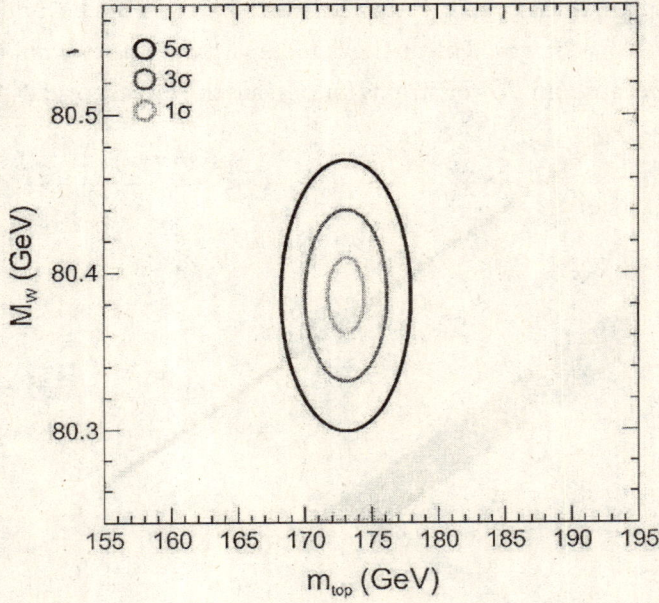

- The y-axis represents the mass of the W boson.
- The x-axis represents the mass of the top quark.
- The smallest oval indicates that the probability of the actual masses being outside it is 32 per cent.
- The intermediate oval indicates that the probability of the actual masses being outside it is 0.3 per cent.
- The largest oval indicates that the probability of the actual masses being outside it is 1/3,500,000.
- The diagonal strips show the ranges within which the Higgs boson should exist based on earlier findings and theoretical calculations. If it were to be found in the range between 115 and 127 GeV/c^2, corresponding to the upper strip, it would mean the stamp of approval on the Standard Model theory. This is because this strip intersects the W boson mass and top

quark mass oval. If it turned out to have a mass beyond 600 GeV/c², it would mean the Standard Model theory would fail, because this lower strip is far outside the largest oval.

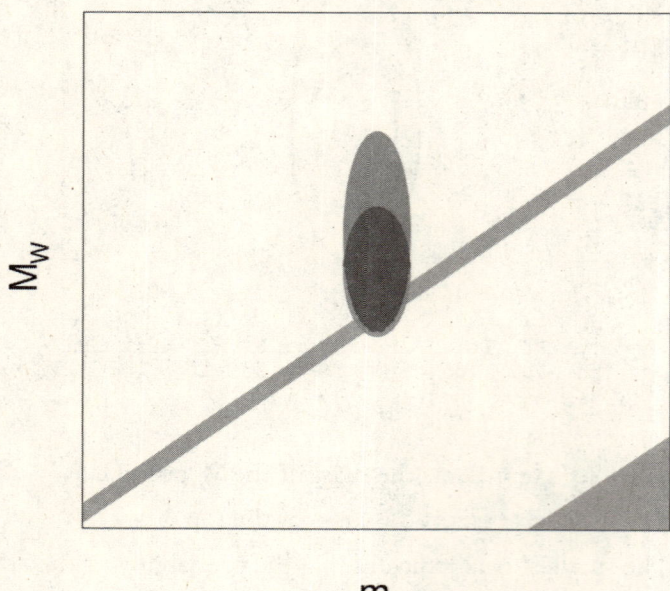

- The larger oval in Diagram 3 represents the previous measurements for the mass of the W boson.
- The smaller one represents the measurement that was announced by CDF and DØ in February 2012.
- The pale diagonal stripe and the shaded bottom-right corner represent the range within which the mass of the Higgs boson could fall, based on all previous experimental data. Depending on what Higgs boson mass the ultimate Higgs discovery would point to, it would either give decisive evidence of the

validity of the Standard Model theory or it would prove it to be wrong.[2]

There was a feeling among American scientists that the Tevatron was losing ground to the newly constructed LHC at CERN, Switzerland. Ashutosh's announcement of the best measurement of the W boson mass in February 2012 proved that there was a great deal of energy in the American scientific establishment. Ashutosh also showed the mass range in which the Higgs boson would be found if the Standard Model was correct. The LHC had achieved ascendency at the high-energy frontier because the Tevatron at Fermilab could not reach the collision energy of the LHC. Although it was more difficult to find the Higgs boson at the Tevatron, scientists at Fermilab were still working on the data to track the footprints of this particle. The Higgs boson search at Fermilab was conducted by tracking a different set of footprints than the ones being pursued at CERN. This complementarity had great scientific value. Ashutosh's contribution to this process was immense. Now Fermilab had also achieved the magnificent record of accurately establishing the mass of the W boson.

At the same time, Ashutosh was also conducting data analysis at CERN's ATLAS (**A** **T**oroidal LHC **A**pparatu**S**) experiment. A new particle was announced by CERN on 4 July 2012, coincidentally the US Independence Day! Its mass was 125 GeV, within the range that Ashutosh had predicted. This was the Higgs boson and the forty-year search had finally come to an end.

---

2   These diagrams are reproduced from the famous academic journal, *Physical Review Letters* (*PRL*) issue dated April 2012. The figure, accompanied by a summary, made the cover; it was the lead story of the issue.

CERN announced the finding of a new particle with the Higgs boson properties at an international conference in Melbourne. Ashutosh was present at this conference to present a paper with a light heart full of enthusiasm. On 1 July, he was writing this secret news to his colleagues from the airport in New York, on the way to Melbourne. He was repeatedly lauded and congratulated for this discovery. His nature was not one to rest on his laurels but immediately turn back to his work with concentration and steadiness. With his student, Benjamin Cerio, he began to study the characteristics of the Higgs boson.

He also began to scan the data from ATLAS from new perspectives. In this quest, he was assisted by another student, Chris Pollard. Are there more than three dimensions to the universe? Ashutosh was sure that a study of this new particle would offer some leads to this question. Is the Higgs boson really elementary, as postulated in the Standard Model theory, or is it made of even smaller constituents in a manner consistent with extra-dimensional theory? If the Higgs boson is composite, then so could be the top quark, because the Higgs boson and top quark have the largest affinity to each other. With Chris Pollard, Ashutosh launched an investigation into this kind of substructure.

'*Manzilein aur bhi hai* / Miles to go before I sleep.' That could have been Ashutosh's motto as he proceeded to work on the W boson. Since the flow of data at the Tevatron had continued, instead of 1 million there were now 4 million W bosons to be studied. As more W bosons are analysed, there is the possibility that their mass accuracy could be improved. With the additional data, he would like to improve the accuracy by another factor of two. Having achieved 0.02 per cent, Ashutosh wants to bring this accuracy down to 0.01 per cent. Reducing this uncertainty is a difficult task. Since the Tevatron has since shut down, he is using the full dataset produced at CDF during the entire Run 2.

At the Snowmass Workshop in 2013, it was suggested that with the larger number of W bosons produced at the higher energy of the LHC, this uncertainty might be brought down to 0.006 per cent or 5 MeV. It will take some time to solve all the difficult problems at this very detailed level; until then, Ashutosh has been working with all the data from CDF to reduce the margin of error. Once he has finished analysing the data, he will use the ATLAS data and aim for an accuracy of 0.006 per cent.

By 2012, Ashutosh had been working on the mass of the W boson for seventeen years and had published several papers. Many other scientists have used his W boson mass papers as reference material in their research papers and so his papers have received 979 citations as of date. Ashutosh's papers on the 2012 result alone have received 338 citations, qualifying as 'famous papers'.

High-energy physicists from the European Union working at CERN have brought out a book series called *Advanced Series on Directions in High Energy Physics (World Scientific, 2016)* in which they published a collection of essays titled 'The Standard Theory of Particle Physics—Essays to Celebrate CERN's 60th Anniversary'. In the context of the W boson, Ashutosh has already been recognized as the world leader. As such, in this referral volume on the latest techniques and results in particle physics worldwide, Ashutosh's essay on the W boson mass measurement finds a prominent place.

Large Hadron Collider

Fundamental to the nature of particle physicists is an unending fascination with the unknown. They are always in pursuit of unknown principles of nature, which manifest as new particles. This has been the grand obsession for the last century.

They have been using quotidian particles such as protons and electrons, accelerating them to high energies and getting them to collide with each other. Out of the debris of such collisions, exotic particles may be discovered. The heavier the particle, the greater the energy required, and larger the machinery needed.

∽

The History

It was at Berkeley in California that the first cyclotron was set up in the Radiation Laboratory or Rad Lab, in 1931. Ernest Lawrence won the Nobel Prize for this invention. The first cyclotron was about 4.5 inches in diameter and achieved energies of up to 80 keV. The next, an 11-inch cyclotron achieved a million electron-Volts (MeV). Other bigger cyclotrons followed; a 27-inch cyclotron in 1932 with an energy of 3.6 MeV, a 37-inch cyclotron in 1937, a 16 MeV 60-inch device in 1939 and in 1945, a 730 MeV 184-inch device. After that many accelerators were built in other parts of the world. There are now 1,200 cyclotrons used for research in nuclear medicine.

An accelerator is an expensive piece of machinery. CERN in Switzerland has the world-famous Hadron Collider which began working in 2008 and cost $5 billion to build. Its circumference is 27 km. A more advanced one, the Superconducting Super Collider (SSC), was to be built in Texas. Two billion dollars were spent on digging one-third of the tunnel. The entire circumference was going to be 87 km. The cost overruns were just too high, international contributions did not arrive, and the construction was behind schedule, so in 1992, the work came to a halt. The project was cancelled in 1993.

Building LHC

Largely, the machinery that had been built to chase down the Higgs boson was at an energy level of trillion electron-Volts. Thanks to the LHC, research was being conducted on the 6.5 x 2 = 13 TeV scale. Close to Geneva in Switzerland, the LHC sits in a tunnel that is nearly 90 metres underground. It is the most expensive, the largest and most prestigious scientific instrument ever built. Thanks to the TeV level of energy used, it is possible to examine phenomena taking place at the 0.1-nano-nanometer level. With the advent of the LHC, there was a general feeling that the golden age of particle physics had dawned.

A truly high-end microscope capable of huge magnification is needed to determine whether the Higgs boson, the quarks, the W and Z bosons have any substructure. The resolution of this microscope has to be smaller than the size of the object that is being studied. This means that the instrument must have the ability to probe truly fine distances. In other words, if the instrument is to measure objects that are one-tenth of a millimetre, it must be calibrated at sizes smaller than that.

LHC is therefore the world's largest and most sensitive microscope. Starting with 7 TeV, the LHC now functions at 13 TeV. Its capacity has been upgraded greatly. Accordingly, its resolution has also improved substantially.

The LHC superconducting magnets generate a magnetic field that is 150,000 times that of the Earth, in order to bend the high-energy protons around the circular path. These are placed at 1232 points along the LHC's 27-km circumference. The vacuum in the beam pipes of the LHC is emptier than the vacuum of outer space, in order to avoid collisions of the beam particles with air molecules.

The ATLAS and CMS experiments at the LHC operate like giant digital cameras, each with a resolution of 92 million and 65 million pixels, respectively. These detectors operate very fast; every second, 40 million pictures are captured.

In July 2012, when the Higgs boson or the god particle was discovered, the LHC became a household word. Ashutosh was significantly involved in the LHC and the search for the Higgs boson at the LHC. During the time that the LHC was being built (1998 to 2008), Ashutosh often travelled to Switzerland and surveyed the construction. In 2006 and 2008, when he returned to India, he addressed gatherings of his friends in chaste Marathi, telling them stories of this exciting enterprise and the possibilities that it held for science.

The LHC had been built with the specific purpose of hunting down unknown subnuclear particles such as the Higgs boson or disproving their existence. And so it came to pass that on Einstein's birthday, 14 March 2013, proof positive of the validity of the Standard Model theory and the existence of the particle that Peter Higgs had predicted, was announced. After the 4 July 2012 discovery, additional data had been used to confirm that the properties of the new particle were indeed the same as the predicted properties of the Higgs boson.

On 10 September 2008, high-energy proton beams were first circulated in the LHC. On 19 September 2008, the LHC stopped working after nine days. There was a problem with the electrical wiring of the magnets. On 30 March 2010, after repairs, it began to function again. Two 3.5 TeV proton beams streamed forth and collided with a combined energy of 7 TeV to create a world record. This was 3.5 times more energy than the previous record held by the Tevatron.

Apart from the Higgs boson and other achievements, the LHC has also been able to recreate the quark–gluon plasma that was first observed at the Relativistic Heavy Ion Collider (RHIC) at the Brookhaven National Laboratory in the US. At the end of 2012, after each beam's energy had been raised to 4 TeV, the LHC was turned off so that its energy could be upgraded again. When it went live again in the spring of 2015, each proton beam's energy was 6.5 TeV, the highest ever. In recent operations, the LHC experiments produce 90 petabytes of data per year. This data is crunched by the CERN data centre and by 140 computer centres in 35 countries. These centres are linked on a grid-based computer network.

At every level, the LHC's position becomes even more special; for the kind of work it can be made to do and the kind of information it generates, has no equal in the world.

26

The Higgs Boson

THE FUNDAMENTAL PARTICLES OCCUPY THE SAME POSITION IN particle physics and cosmology as DNA does in biology. Now that the Higgs boson has been discovered many things that were mysteries are now being resolved. Without the Higgs boson, mass for elementary particles cannot come into being. Without it, the histories of the universe, the Earth and humankind would never even have begun; the electron would be massless and the atom would not form. As Einstein's theory of relativity tells us, the energy of all massless particles would have wandered around in all directions at the speed of light; and the notion of experiencing time—such as the past, the present and the future—would not have come into being. Since it has this central position in the functioning of the universe, the Higgs boson has been referred to by some as the god particle. In his book *The God Particle: If the Universe Is the Answer, What Is the Question?* Nobel Prize-winning physicist Leon M. Lederman refers to it as 'that god-damned particle'—an expletive occasioned by its evasiveness and timorousness—and this led the publisher to coin the title, or so the story goes. But in truth, it is not the god particle. It is not the beginning point of the universe. It does not reveal the story of the primal moment of creation.

The Higgs boson is a very special and unique kind of subatomic particle. As with all fundamental particles, the concept of intrinsic angular momentum, or spin in quantum mechanics is applicable to the Higgs boson also. It has a definite spin value. Though it is a boson, unlike other bosons (W and Z bosons, gluons, photons and the as-yet-undiscovered graviton) it is not a gauge boson. Gauge bosons are the elementary force carriers in the Standard Model. In this sense, the Higgs boson does not mediate a force. The difference between the Higgs boson and the gauge bosons is highlighted by their spin values. The Higgs boson is unique because it is the only elementary particle with a spin value of zero. It means that the Higgs boson has no sense of direction; it looks the same from all directions. In contrast, the gauge bosons have a sense of directionality in space. For example, the W and Z bosons, gluons and photons, when rotated, behave like a vector would behave in 3-dimensional space. This behaviour under rotations is determined by the spin value. The Higgs boson's spin value of zero gives it the unique property of being independent of direction. This is why, when the Higgs field fills all of space, the laws of physics remain the same in all directions.

In particle physics, the Higgs boson plays the role of bringing the mass of elementary particles into existence. In the Standard Model theory, out of the twelve quarks and leptons and the four types of bosons, only photons and gluons do not have mass. But without the Higgs boson, it is rather difficult to construct a theory for how the other particles could have any mass. The Standard Model theory states unequivocally that without the existence of such a boson, no other elementary particle could possibly have mass. However, the model is silent on what the mass of the Higgs boson itself is. Thus, scientists had to look for the Higgs boson at all possible high-energy levels. They had to study millions of trillions of proton collisions to do so.

And thus, the Higgs boson has earned its reputation as an elusive particle. It is an unstable particle with an extremely short lifespan. The Standard Model also maintained that after the decay of the Higgs boson, certain particles would be emitted in certain patterns. These were the patterns that were being studied and their traces were being sought in the data.

When Ashutosh was working at the ATLAS experiment with his students during 2010–2012, the first three types of traces of the Higgs boson were found. Ashutosh wrote the reports on one of these methods. He co-authored three papers on the Higgs boson which were published in international journals. These were the first papers on the findings at ATLAS.

A Tough Job

In the search for the Higgs boson, trillions of protons were swirled around in the Large Hadron Collider. Two streams of protons were created and shot at each other.

Their speed was within 1 millionth of 1 per cent of the speed of light (or 299,792,455 m/s, only 3 m/s less than the speed of light of 299,792,458 m/s, which is about 300,000 km/s). Because of their near-light speed, the protons achieve 11,000 rounds per second of the 27-km circumference. Each proton's energy is about 6,900 times more than its own mass. Because of this immense energy, when these particles collide, tiny flecks of flame are produced, a miniature model of what must have transpired in the first microsecond of the Big Bang when the universe was being created. Among the scatter of particles created by these collisions, the Higgs boson was hiding. Of the trillions of protons shot at each other, only a few collide and produce those flecks of flame and even fewer of these would be the site for the production of a Higgs boson.

The elusiveness of this elusive boson can be described in this way:

- In 1 bunch of protons, there are 100 billion protons.
- In each beam, there were 2,800 bunches going around the ring at any given time.
- Each beam would cross the other beam travelling in the opposite direction at four points, approximately 31 million times per second.
- How many collisions could be expected when two bunches cross? Between ten and sixty collisions, depending on the beam intensity.

And while all these extraordinary events were going on, a Higgs boson would be produced every 2.5 seconds on average. The production rate is proportional to the beam intensity and has increased to about one per second at the highest intensity achieved.

This was the attempt being made at ATLAS and CMS to find the Higgs boson. The huge amount of data generated by the LHC had to be analysed to see if a pattern that the Higgs boson might have left behind could be found. In order to identify a person, one needs to have that person's fingerprints, retina scan, facial features or DNA. In the same way, there were certain unique 'footprints' that the scientists knew the Higgs boson should leave behind. These footprints would be the way in which the Higgs boson would announce itself. Scientists were scanning the data to look for all the characteristics of the Higgs boson that had been assumed to exist.

All of this hard work and ingenuity has led to a momentous discovery in accordance with the theoretical model. For the first time ever, an elementary scalar particle was found; a scalar particle is one with zero spin and therefore no directional property. The mass of this boson and its other properties seem to fit in the range that the Higgs boson was expected to have, given the accurate estimate established by the W boson mass, the top quark mass and other electroweak data.

The production rate of the Higgs boson is also consistent with our current knowledge of Quantum Chromo-Dynamics or QCD and the structure of the proton. QCD is the quantum theory of the strong force, describing the interactions between quarks and gluons. What happens is, two gluons, one from each proton, collide to produce a top quark and a top antiquark, which is the process of creating matter–antimatter out of energy. Why top quarks? Because they have a very large mass, which means the Higgs boson has a high affinity to them. This top quark pair then annihilates to produce a Higgs boson. The observation of this production process fitted in with the prediction of the Standard Model.

At first glance, all of the Higgs boson's production and decay processes seemed to fit in with the predictions of the simple Standard Model theory. The word 'simple' here is to be read as that which minimizes the axioms of the strong and electroweak forces and the Higgs mechanism, consistent with the symmetries of quantum mechanics and the special theory of relativity.

On 4 July 2012, when the Higgs boson discovery was announced, it was said that the discovery had a 5-sigma significance. In other words, the probability of it being a statistical fluke was 1 in 3.5 million. A 2-sigma significance means that one could say with 95 per cent certainty that the evidence from the experiment was not a statistical fluke, which also means there is a 5 per cent chance of it being a statistical fluke. The norm in high energy physics for an observation to be called a discovery is a 5-sigma significance.

Both protons and neutrons are made up of quarks. The mass that the quarks acquire, thanks to the Higgs field, accounts for only one per cent of the mass of the protons and neutrons. The rest 99 per cent of the mass of the visible world is the energy of the gluons in these nucleons. In other words, most of the mass of the protons and neutrons is contributed by the binding energy that holds them together. Or you could say, of the mass of the visible universe, only 1 per cent is contributed by the Higgs boson. But this 1 per cent is crucial because it includes the electron mass that is necessary to form atoms. Furthermore, the up and down quark masses, though small, are necessary for certain mesons to have mass, which in turn mediate the strong force inside the nucleus at low energies. Thus, the Higgs boson has a profound influence on atomic and nuclear properties.

Ashutosh finds the study of the Higgs boson deeply fascinating. There are unanswered questions about the Higgs mechanism. When the answers to these questions are discovered, he believes that it will mean a revolution in particle physics. This revolution could be of the same importance as the one brought about by the theories of relativity and quantum mechanics, a century ago.

Ashutosh has the mind of a true scientist. There is a great thrill in the chase but there is also a shade of gloom in it; when the prey is caught, the chase is over. He says, 'It is true that there is great happiness when a scientific prediction is proved to be true. But it is far more thrilling for a scientist to find lacunae in a model or a theory. It means the start of an even bigger treasure hunt.'

After the Higgs Boson

The Higgs boson discovery was an unprecedented event in the history of science. The Higgs boson has brought forth an extraordinary and mysterious face of the universe for the first time. If the Higgs boson exists, then it was obvious that the Higgs field also must exist. It is startling to think that 'empty' space is not just a vacuum.

The Higgs field presents a host of interesting possibilities and studying them will be possible thanks to the LHC. The new challenge for particle physicists will be to understand and describe all the properties of the Higgs field.

The Standard Model theory does not have answers to some other questions that the universe poses. One of these is the existence of dark matter! Astrophysics and cosmology have already proved its existence. We know that the Higgs boson is concerned with visible matter, but we do not know if the Higgs boson is connected with dark matter or not. There is five times as much dark matter in the universe as there is visible matter.

There is a lot of work to be done in particle physics. It is possible that dark matter consists of completely different particles. All the galaxies are engulfed by clouds of dark matter. Would it be possible to generate these particles at the LHC? The theory of supersymmetry suggests that it might be. But one would need a huge amount of data from the LHC to be able to answer this with any degree of certainty. At present, the LHC is the best tool we have to study dark matter by actually making it.

One of the constant problems of physics is an old one. It cannot be explained in terms of quantum physics. This is gravitation. Gravity does not fit into the Standard Model theory. In order to understand gravity in terms of quantum theory, one would need dimensions of space over and above the three that we experience.

The LHC is the best and most sensitive microscope we have. Our best chance of finding these mind-boggling extra dimensions is the LHC with beams of very high intensity. It might be the instrument with which Einstein's dream of understanding gravity at a quantum level could be realized.

Finding the god particle was of great importance. The assumptions and suppositions that the physicists had made about the way elementary particles acquire mass did get support. But there are still secrets that nature has withheld from us: these include dark energy, dark matter and gravity. To study dark matter and gravity, and of course the Higgs boson properly, it was felt that the scope and power of the LHC had to be improved. Ashutosh began to work on the upgraded ATLAS experiment for much higher intensity. The scope of this project was to be much greater than before in order to be able to study the aforementioned mysteries. The project will be inaugurated in 2027 and will run up to 2040.

When considering the possible future projects in particle physics, the discussions always start with the scientific motivations, before moving on to the considerations of technology, feasibility and funding. Both in the US and in Europe, there was intense activity to assemble the scientific arguments in favour of upgrading the LHC. The US scientists participating in ATLAS wanted to organize their efforts to present the physics case. They selected Ashutosh as the Physics Advisor to advocate for the upgrade and to serve as a scientific consultant to the managers of the US ATLAS project.

Ashutosh and colleagues agreed to supervise the project. The beam intensity of the accelerator would be five to seven times greater than it was earlier. The upgrading of the LHC will be in progress till 2027. In the decade after that, it is expected to generate ten times more data than before; a huge amount of new information.

The Higgs boson will not be the only object of study; many other subjects will be studied in great depth.

The LHC of Tomorrow

After the Higgs boson discovery, many workshops were set up to study the next steps of the LHC research programme and other opportunities in order to set priorities. In the US, the American Physical Society's division of particles and fields established a year-long study for the entire particle-physics community and a series of workshops were also organized for dissemination and discussion. Historically, these meetings were held at the Snowmass Mountain Resort near Aspen, Colorado, and so this community-wide planning exercise has been called the Snowmass study.

Ashutosh was selected as the co-convener of the electroweak physics group in the Snowmass 2013 study. Under his leadership, study groups came up with many suggestions about research projects that could be undertaken. The detailed study of the Higgs boson, the search for dark matter and the search for new subatomic phenomena emerged as the top priorities. To pursue them, a project proposal of $1.5 billion for the upgrade of the LHC's intensity was made to the European Strategy Council and the funds began to be collected. Beyond the twenty-five-year horizon for the upgraded LHC, the idea of a much larger seven-times higher-energy proton collider was also floated and R&D for new superconducting magnet technology was encouraged.

We have mentioned how the investigation of dark matter makes the LHC a valuable tool. The possibility of dark matter came to the fore when astronomer Vera Rubin measured the velocity of the stars spinning around the centre of the galaxy. In order to keep such massive objects in circular orbits around the centre requires the existence of a centripetal force. The greater the velocity, the greater the force. This velocity of the motion of stars is greater than can be accounted for by the gravitational force exerted by all the visible mass of the galaxy. One hypothesis is that there is mass which is not visible with light and so cannot be seen, but it does produce gravity. This is dark matter.

Research in astrophysics and particle physics has thrown up some wonderful possibilities. Dark matter might well be a dark galactic cloud of extremely heavy particles. These particles could be heavier than atoms of gold. Once the LHC has been upgraded, there's a good chance that these particles will show up.

The probability of detection of dark-matter production will depend on the properties of these particles. Various mathematical models of such dark matter are being developed and studied by Ashutosh and others. These studies and detection strategies are in preparation for dark matter detection at the upgraded LHC.

If dark matter is produced, the next challenge is its detection. Since it is invisible, much ingenuity is required for detecting it. Ashutosh is developing a very fast electronic circuit using artificial intelligence techniques, that can detect a particular kind of dark-matter signature extremely fast, in 25 billionth of a second, which is as fast as the proton collisions occurring in the LHC. No other method has been developed that can match this extreme speed.

As the data from the LHC increases, if dark matter production is proven, it will revolutionize our understanding of how the galaxies took their present form, and perhaps the nature of the cosmic void, the vacuum, and of space and time itself.

Another heart-stopping possibility is that, thanks to the LHC, we might be able to understand the gravitational force in quantum terms with greater clarity. The best explanation we have for gravity is Einstein's general theory of relativity. Quantum theory accounts for the other forces. Through the last century, physicists have been trying to fit gravity into quantum theory. Einstein himself was preoccupied with this task. It has proved a tough nut to crack for theoretical physicists. The graviton has been postulated as the quantum mediator of gravity. Einstein's gravity is based on real space and time. If the graviton is actually found, we will be able to understand gravity and the concepts of space and time better.

These discoveries could have far-reaching and unimaginable consequences.

The forty-four American institutions participating in the ATLAS experiment chose Ashutosh as the physics advisor of the team that was directing the ATLAS upgrade.

∽

Black Holes

Although Ashutosh is an experimental scientist, he has always had an interest in theoretical physics as well. His knowledge of black holes is theoretical. He published a paper on black holes with colleagues from the J.W. Goethe University in Frankfurt, titled 'Black hole relics in large extra dimensions', and he co-authored with his post-doctoral research associate Christopher Hays a paper called 'Production and decay of spinning black holes at colliders and tests of black hole dynamics'.

Ashutosh studied the phenomenology of tiny black holes, which could be produced at the LHC if extra-spatial dimensions exist at small distances, beyond the three known dimensions. These extra dimensions were first proposed by string theory. The idea of extra dimensions can be used to explain why the force of gravity is so much weaker than the electromagnetic force. In this scenario, when collisions between particles take place at high energies, microscopic black holes can be produced. When the LHC was being built, it was dubbed by some opponents as 'the machine that would end the world'. These were the kind of statements that might frighten the uninitiated. Some scientists including Ashutosh were certain that no such thing would happen. At such a time, Ashutosh felt that scientists have a duty to reach out and explain things clearly to the lay public. When he was in India in March 2008, he wrote an article for *The Times of India* on black holes. Some sections have been reproduced below.

> In a recent lawsuit in the USA, there has been discussion of these particle accelerators possibly being 'doomsday' machines capable of recreating the Big Bang or creating microscopic black holes or 'strange matter'. A concern has been raised in the reported lawsuit, whether any of these phenomena could cause macroscopic destruction of the environment.
>
> While these concerns were duly addressed by the scientific teams and the US Government, it is interesting to consider the probability of these occurrences on scientific grounds. A number of arguments, based on solidly established data, can be made which strongly suggest that these catastrophic occurrences are practically impossible. Firstly, even though a given collision can produce a very high energy particle such as might be present soon after the Big Bang, the total energy is more than a hundred orders of magnitude smaller than the then-prevailing Big Bang conditions, when every particle on average had this energy. To put the particle energy in perspective, the energy of

a microscopic black hole, if formed, will be about a microJoule, which may at best raise the temperature of one grain of sand through 1 degree Celsius. Secondly, the diameter of such a microscopic black hole would be about 10^{-20} metres, which is so small that there is no additional matter within this radius to fall into the black hole. In comparison, the radius of the proton is about 10^{-15} m, which is one hundred thousand times bigger than the black hole. Thirdly, the black hole is likely to decay in less than 10^{-27} seconds, in a process akin to Hawking Radiation. Thus, the black hole will decay much faster than the time it would take for it to absorb any surrounding matter from even one proton.

In other words, a proton's volume is a thousand trillion times bigger than that of this microscopic black hole. The possibility of this black hole aggregating any macroscopic amount of matter to 'eat-up the earth' is thus ruled out.

Another statement that has been made in the reported lawsuit is that the collider could spit out something called a 'strangelet' that would convert our planet to a shrunken dense dead lump of something called 'strange matter'. In reality, 'strange matter' is nothing more than protons and neutrons containing 'strange' quarks instead of the 'up' and 'down' quarks normally found in them. The name 'strange' quark is purely historical. Since the observation of hadrons containing strange quarks 60 years ago, this quark has been produced copiously in particle collisions and decays rather quickly in an understood way to the common 'up' quark.

In fact, strange matter particles are constantly being produced in the high-energy collisions of cosmic rays bombarding the earth from outer space.

The discovery of microscopic black holes at particle colliders would have truly profound implications for our understanding of the gravitational force and indirectly about the existence of additional spatial dimensions. Furthermore, this discovery could provide the first experimental information ever about the quantum theory of gravity, which many physicists have worked on for decades, including Einstein himself.

This was Ashutosh's attempt to calm the fears produced by these rumours. He also said that if infinitesimally tiny black holes were indeed created, the measurements of these black holes would help fit gravity and quantum mechanics into a single, more universal theory.

Honours and Achievements

Sloan Fellowship

Alfred P. Sloan (1875–1966) was a famous US industrialist and humanist and a remarkable philanthropist. He took the General Motors Company to all corners of the world. Every year, the foundation he set up distributes $3–4 million in research grants to deserving scientists, engineers, mathematicians and economists in the form of Sloan Research Fellowships. These fellowships were set up in 1955. By 2000, it had distributed $87 million in research grants to support young scholars.

Thousands of young scholars in the fields of physics, chemistry, computer science, mathematics, neuroscience, molecular biology and economics send in applications every year, hoping for a grant. Out of these, about a hundred people are chosen as Sloan Fellows. Research scientists who are likely to increase the store of human knowledge are chosen and given healthy funding support for their work. The foundation notes with pride that fifty-one of the scholars it has supported have gone on to win Nobel Prizes and hundreds of others have won other prizes and fellowships.

Every year, the foundation brings together an expert panel to assess all the entries it has received. These are high-ranking professors from prestigious universities such as Harvard, Cornell, Stanford, Princeton and MIT. The winners of the fellowship have the freedom to follow the research projects they have dreamt of. This is to allow them to conduct their research without let or hindrance; and to apply the funds to the spheres they think fit. It is unsurprising then that to a young researcher, this fellowship is a boon.

In the year 2000, Ashutosh won this $40,000 fellowship.

Outstanding Junior Investigator Award

In 1978, the American Federal Government's Department of Energy started the Outstanding Junior Investigator (OJI) Award. The idea behind the award was to identify young physics researchers early in their careers, to get some idea of what their research interests were, and to give them research funding along the way. Every year, five or six high-energy physicists are chosen for this award. This was also to keep the energy and enthusiasm for research in physics high at the university level.

The media helped play up the award. This meant the programme succeeded in getting the nation to sit up and pay attention. This also helped many young people to make up their minds to opt for research as a career. The US National Academy of Sciences congratulated the US Department of Energy for this initiative, comparing the OJI award to other prestigious awards like the Sloan Fellowship and the Presidential Young Investigator Award.

One has to apply for this award. The applications are vetted at the university level. They are then scrutinized by handpicked intellectuals from the field who advise the government on the merits of the applicants. Only five per cent make it to the final cut. Competition is stiff.

The amount awarded is based on a combination of research merit and the needs of individual applicants. Once the award is made, the applicants are free to use it as they judge best for the purpose of research without interference from the department. One can apply for salaries of assistants at the doctoral or post-doctoral level, research material and equipment costs, and travel costs. After the establishment of this award for high-energy physics, many talented young people were attracted to the field which witnessed a flowering.

In 2000, Ashutosh won this award. His proposal's title was 'Precision Electroweak Measurements on CDF II'.

In subsequent years, Ashutosh was twice invited by the Department of Energy as a member of the selection panel for these awards. The panel discussions were conducted over multiple days, with in-depth scrutiny of each applicant's merit and the quality of the proposal. It is a meticulous and confidential process, designed to uphold the high standards of this award.

American Physical Society (APS) Fellowship

In November 2008, the American Physical Society (APS) conferred an honorary fellowship on Ashutosh. APS is known internationally as a research institution that represents all the various branches of physics. It has more than 49,000 members all over the world. Half a per cent of these get an honorary fellowship. The following information has been mentioned in this regard:

Ashutosh Kotwal has worked over the last seventeen years on the design and construction of large particle detectors, and on the computer programs used to analyze the electronic data and produce physical interpretations. He is a world leader in the field of precision mass measurement of the particle which mediates radioactivity via beta decay, which is called the W boson. He recently published the world's best measurement of the W boson mass, which has generated a very important prediction for the masses of the undiscovered Higgs boson and Supersymmetric particles. The APS cited Prof. Kotwal's significant and unique contributions in the field of High Energy Particle Physics, through his precision measurements of the W boson's mass. Prof. Kotwal has co-authored over 300 papers, which have been published in the premier journals of original fundamental research sponsored by the APS.

The American Association for the Advancement of Science (AAAS) Fellowship

Finding the Higgs boson became a lot easier because it was relatively light ... if it had been four or five times heavier, it would have taken a lot longer to discover its existence. The mass of the W boson, measured with an accuracy of ± 0.02 per cent, pointed to a light Higgs boson and gave its search a big boost. The scientific community sat up and took note of this achievement.

Ashutosh was cited by the AAAS Council for performing 'a series of high precision, world-leading measurements of the mass of the W boson, and for stringent tests of the standard model of fundamental particles' when they conferred the honorary fellowship on him in 2012. Each year the council elects members whose 'efforts on behalf of the advancement of science or its applications are scientifically or socially distinguished'.

AAAS is the world's largest organization of scientists; established in 1848, it has 10 million members. It has conducted a campaign to spread science all over the world. It publishes one of the most prestigious scientific journals in the world, *Science*, which has the largest paid circulation of any peer-reviewed general science journal. It was initiated in 1880 with seed funding from Thomas Edison. Its worldwide readership is estimated to be more than a million.

Ashutosh was the youngest Indian to receive this fellowship.

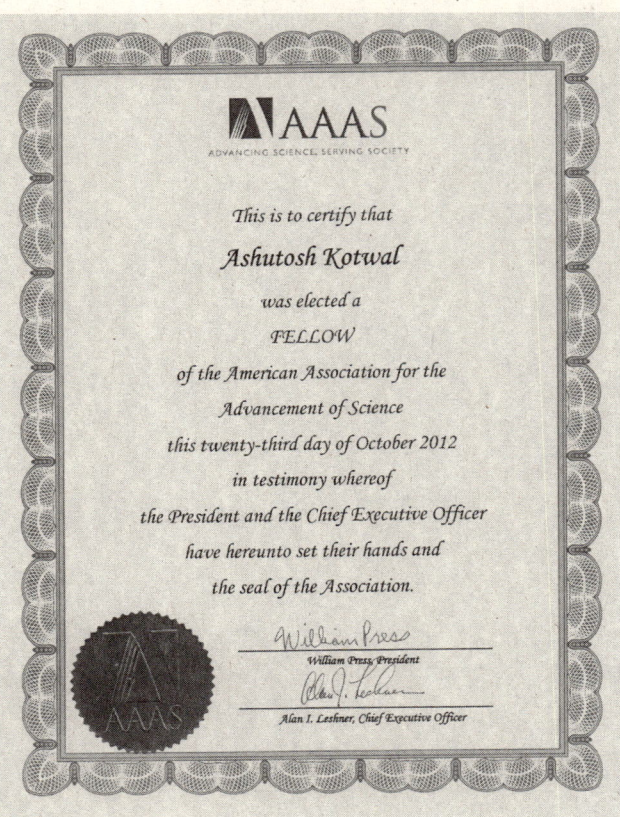

HOME SWEET HOME

First home and car in America.

Birds soaring high in the blue skies have to have their roots in terra firma. They too must have bonds of love and companionship with someone. When there is mutual understanding about their likes and dislikes, their priorities, their views on life, the two individuals become soulmates. While making their nest-like home, they experience zest and joy. Let us peep into the home and hearth of Ashwini and Ashutosh—always a warm and welcoming place.

27

Jab We Met

Choosing a Life Partner

MOST CHILDREN GROW UP IN THE FAMILY CREATED BY THEIR parents, then they begin their independent lives and set up their own families. In our tradition and according to our custom, parents feel a responsibility to help find a suitable partner for their child. Besides, there seemed to be no possibility of Ashutosh finding his own bride. He had always studied in co-educational schools and colleges. While he was friends with a number of girls in the railway communities in which we lived, he never thought of any of them as a 'girlfriend'.

In 1995, his PhD thesis was accepted, and he got his doctorate. His father had also retired from active service. Ashutosh was getting close to thirty and we began to think of his marriage. There were of course many good proposals that came from friends and family and our social network.

We had the usual expectations: she should have an attractive personality, she should be well-educated and aesthetically inclined.

I also felt that she should be a courageous person who had a clear view of her own future, who should know what she wanted to do and which field she wanted to pursue. Since Ashutosh was devoted to his work, she would need to have a life of her own.

Vijayrao wanted a capable and confident girl for his son. But he had some reservations. This has its roots in his family history. Vijayrao's father's sister had been married as a child but lost her husband soon after. As such, she had lived her life in her brother's home. It was said in Vijayrao's family that this mishap took place because of the presence of 'Mangal' (the planet Mars) in her horoscope. Thus, Vijayrao had developed some phobia about Mangal. When we began considering marriage proposals, he became very sensitive. And so, this idea of a bride without Mangal in her stars became an issue. Ashutosh made it clear that his would be the final word. He was not concerned with astrological predictions. He might have differed from his father's views but did not discuss it very much. Later, in a lighter vein, he would say that Mangal or not, the only thing that ultimately mattered was that he and Ashwini met and that she married him.

If someone contacted us, we would say that the girl's parents were welcome to visit us. Then we would have a cup of tea and some conversation. I had some hypotheses of my own that I would check. I would allow conversation to flow freely. Often, the parents of the young lady were younger than us. I would pay careful attention to their way of speaking, their behaviour. I was looking for a family that was comfortably well-off, tasteful and cultured. I was looking for parents who would have left the right kind of imprint on their child.

In Ashutosh's absence, we considered nearly 750 candidates from all our sources. We went through the motions of looking at the photographs of the young women and meeting their parents.

There were many beautiful young ladies from good families who unfortunately had Mangal in their horoscope.

Among them were the daughters of two well-known writers from Maharashtra. One of them was the granddaughter of a Bharat Ratna; she came to see us with her parents. She, too, was studying in America. The two of them met in Denver but found no common ground.

When Ashutosh arrived in September 1996 on a short trip during the Ganpati Festival, there were five or six young ladies on our shortlist. Of those, two or three had visited us with their families. The elders—that's us—would sit upstairs and talk. Ashutosh and the young lady in question would sit on the swing in our garden and chat for an hour or two.

During this visit we had many conversations. Sitting on the swing, Ashutosh would discuss his choices with me. Why did I think he should get married? What expectations did I have of his married life? Which would be better, a working wife or a homemaker? These were the questions we discussed. I could not gauge his thoughts.

And then it was time to meet Ashwini Phene.

Ashwini and Ashutosh met at Garden Court at Chandni Chowk in Pune. The Phene and Kotwal parents sat talking in the neighbouring Banjara Hills Hotel. After a couple of hours, Ashwini and Ashutosh returned and Ashwini left with her parents. (Later, she would tell me that she had told her parents that she had made her choice in two minutes.) In our home, the central protagonist had taken an oath of silence. But a couple of days later he said, 'I would like to meet her again.' And so they did, and us parents got to know each other more closely as well.

On Sunday morning, he was beginning preparations for his return to the US. We were to leave for Mumbai that day. On Monday,

Ashutosh had to deliver a speech at TIFR. Tuesday night, he was to fly back to the US.

We were kept in suspense until Saturday evening. Saturday was a dramatic day. All day, Ashutosh lay on the couch, watching the rain with dreamy eyes, while his father would try, from time to time, to get him to say something.

Finally in the evening, at exactly 6 p.m., as promised, he declared his choice. His father roared with delight. When we called the Phene family, Ashwini's father, Deepak Phene answered the call on the first ring. They had also been waiting for his decision.

On Tuesday, 15 October 1996, the engagement was celebrated in style in Mumbai at Ashwini's aunt's house in Prabhadevi.

28

A Happy Family

On 23 December 1996, Ashutosh and Ashwini got married. There was a nine-and-a-half-year gap between them, but Ashwini's unusual maturity bridged it. She had an undergraduate degree in accounting and a master's in business administration in finance. When she went to the US, she started the rigorous study needed to qualify as a certified public accountant (CPA). She and Ashutosh were then living in Batavia, where Fermilab was located. Ashwini had to attend university in Chicago. She once said, 'When I had a full day of study or when the exams were on, Ashutosh would often handle the kitchen.'

Ashwini did very well in her examinations. It is very difficult to clear these examinations in the first attempt, but she did. She is now the founder and chief executive officer of a healthcare company.

In January 1999, when Ashutosh became a professor at Duke University, the two of them bought a beautiful house in the town of Durham, but only after giving the matter a great deal of attention.

It was a house chosen so that both of them would have an easy commute. They chose elegant, tasteful furniture. It was around this time that Ashutosh was travelling to countries like Japan, Russia and Israel as well as some European nations; he would buy many things to decorate their new home from these places. The house was maintained beautifully and tastefully as both of them like it to be. Whenever we would travel to the US, Ashutosh's father would keep an eye out for things that would suit their home. Each of these objects occupies pride of place in their home.

All Creatures Great and Small

Once, Professor Sadanand Varde (otherwise known as Anu Kaka) and his wife, Ashutosh's Sudha Aatya, went to stay with them as guests.

Ashwini was pregnant with Gautam in 2000. Somewhere in a garden she found the second avatar of Vishnu: a tortoise. Ashutosh was firm: the little reptile would have to be confined to a single room. When he found it wandering around the house, the family was introduced to a startling new aspect: Ashutosh in Rudra Avatar, or angry mode.

He had taken this firm stand about the tortoise being incarcerated because he was worried that if his pregnant wife or his elderly uncle and aunt were to trip over it, the tortoise would no doubt suffer some damage, but the mishap could be much worse for the humans. He felt it was his responsibility to look after all the people in the house, especially his wife.

Ashwini had been told that she would deliver on 20 October. We had planned to arrive on 30 September. But baby Gautam had other plans and arrived six weeks early, on 10 September. It was so sudden that Ashwini and Ashutosh had to finalize the choice of his name while driving to the hospital. At the same time, Vijayrao had a problem with his spine; the pain was so severe that he had to be admitted to a hospital. And then his passport went missing. This meant that we missed our 30 September flight, and finally arrived in the US on 4 November.

It is tradition in the US that the husband should be present at the time of delivery. Since it was all very sudden and the birth was premature, Ashutosh was worried, but he kept his fears to himself and concentrated on giving Ashwini support and confidence. He told her jokes and kept her amused, or so Ashwini told me. Ashwini said, 'He kept me laughing so I did not have time to consider the gravity of the situation. But even as he kept me in good spirits, he was worried. This was a new responsibility and when the child was born, I was frightened at first. The baby boy was delivered safely but he was so small and so weak that he could only be fed milk one drop at a time from the tip of a finger. He could not breathe and was kept in the intensive care unit for three days, suffering from jaundice.' But by this time, Ashutosh's confidence had returned in full force. He told Ashwini that they were going to bring up this child well. He got the traditional Marathi foodstuffs; he called up and got the recipes for them and cooked them for Ashwini.

When we arrived, the little fellow was seven weeks old and was beginning to gain weight. After dinner, Ashutosh had made it his business to clear the table and the kitchen counters and load the dishwasher so that his wife could get some rest. He kept things so clean and sparkling that I was sometimes put to shame!

There would be many barbecues on the patio. It was Ashwini's job to marinate the meat and fish; it was Ashutosh's job to light the barbecue and grill the food. In the kitchen, the electric stove was covered in glass, flat as a page. One could not do deep frying there. One was not allowed to have a naked flame in the house, only outside. It was very windy outside. If the menu had something like bhajiyas or batata wadas, then the frying fell to Ashutosh. He did not want me hovering around.

In 2004, Vijayrao suddenly needed a bypass surgery. Before this development, Ashutosh had talked with his father a great deal on the phone about his busy schedule and important commitments in the following days. Since the operation was imperative, according to the doctor, Ashutosh had to be told about it. He and Ashwini dropped everything and came to Pune with Gautam. He served his father with great devotion and was a great support to me.

The relationship that Gautam and Ashutosh had seemed different from the one Ashutosh had had with Vijayrao. But then Ashutosh knew that Gautam's upbringing could not be modelled on his own. Gautam would grow up in the US and in a much wealthier home. Ashutosh knew that there would be some fundamental differences in the ways of bringing up his son.

Be that as it may, I could see the image of Ashutosh as a boy in the young Gautam. Gautam's way of speaking, his wholehearted laughter, reminded me of his father. Both of them are stubborn. And yet his nature is very different from his father's. Gautam cares about people around him being happy with him; Ashutosh, as a young person, did not care much what everyone thought about him. Ashutosh has a deep appreciation of the arts; Gautam might become an artist himself. He has an interest in performing arts like dance and theatre. Both have an aptitude for mathematics, but I feel Gautam is keener on the arts. He plays the piano beautifully and writes heart-warming poems. Although he does not have a great fascination for science, he still sits with his father and tries to understand what he can. Gautam does have a flair for leadership. He enjoys being a leader of his peer group and being the centre of attention. While Ashutosh has been elected or nominated to various positions, I always thought that Ashutosh harboured a preference for intellectual rather than organizational leadership.

The Economics of It All

Ever since Ashutosh went to the US, he had become completely financially independent. After the tenth standard he won a scholarship in the National Talent Search. Even if he had stayed in India and continued to study at IIT, he would have been able to pay his fees and for all his books, from that sum. Since I was teaching at the Cathedral and John Connon School, he did not have to pay any fees for the eleventh and twelfth standards. And since he did very well in the ICSE board examination, he won many prizes from the school. His name was put down on the Cathedral School honour roll.

There was no tradition of giving undergraduate student scholarships in America. Nor were international students allowed to work outside campus to earn their keep. The law did not allow us to send money abroad. Nor was there any tradition in India of giving economic aid to undergraduate students. But an Ivy League university like UPenn made an exception and waived his tuition and housing charges. They sent him home for two Christmas vacations; and for one year, his scholarship even covered his study at the University of Edinburgh in Scotland. Ashutosh also earned a little money by conducting research in the laboratories over the vacations. He had managed his money and his financial affairs with great skill from a very young age.

In the early years of their marriage, he and Ashwini were sticklers in matters of finance. When they shifted house in 1998 from Chicago to Durham, they packed their belongings themselves. They were their own movers and packers. They did their own repairs and assembled new furniture at home; they enjoyed doing these things.

Recently I heard of an incident that took place in 1994. Ashutosh had bought a second-hand Nissan in 1991 from a friend. When we visited America in 1992, we toured the US in this very car. When it broke down in 1994, Ashutosh repaired it himself. After a while, it totally broke down. This happened during a winter of terrible snowstorms, and Ashutosh was left without transport. His PhD work was at its height. He was cooking at home for himself and spending late nights in the laboratory. That meant he would often miss the shuttle bus. Every day he would trudge through the snow for a couple of miles each way to the lab, facing the terrible cold of the Chicago winter of 1994–1995.

After all these years, when I heard this story, my heart went out to him but I was also proud.

∽

Lifestyle

Our grandson, Gautam, was born in September 2000. We stayed there for about one-and-a-half years. I took charge of Gautam, and Vijayrao took over the garden and backyard and brought it to bloom. In the evenings, father and son would pore over gardening catalogues. Then we would visit the huge garden centres and buy the seedlings and other materials. On either side of the front garden there were two exquisite rose beds. North Carolina has excellent air and water quality, and the land is rich. These roses would be in full bloom all through the summer. On a slight rise, a carpet of green, and then a huge spreading maple tree, a small juniper tree, a patch of lilies, and then the front steps leading to the house. Around the patio at the back, honeysuckle and purple hibiscus ran riot. We would sit there, with the breeze carrying the scent of the flowers and watch jewel-like hummingbirds dip and swing around the flowers. With a spade and shovel in hand, Ashutosh dug eight pits about 2 feet deep each in the ground. He planted various fruit trees like pears, peaches, cherries, plums and raspberries. It became a little orchard. Wild rabbits and cranes would visit the backyard. We would often see the North Carolina state bird, the red cardinal, swooping around. In a pond at the back, there were twenty-five to thirty goldfish. Thus, Ashutosh found himself living with the beauties of nature. I would feel very happy to see him wandering about in the garden with little Gautam in his arms.

A love of horticulture runs in the Kotwal family. During the 1950s, in the evenings, Mothe Baba used to spend his evenings with Vijayrao in the huge compound of his government bungalow in Mumbai, spade, shovel and water sprinkler in hand, tending a beautiful garden. He loved to fill the house with baskets of fresh vegetables. In the kitchen he would hang bunches of plantains for his children and their friends, to eat at will.

For Sudha Atya, the morning was not complete until she had plunged her hands into the mud around a tree or shrub. As long as Ashutosh's father was working, he was too busy to do much else but we would have plants, if not flowering ones then those with interesting variegated leaves, the crotons and ficus for instance, in pots. Every morning, he would conduct an inspection, carefully wiping down the leaves with a moist cloth until they shone, he would caress them gently, and study them with deep concentration.

Wherever we travelled, we would always visit the botanical gardens and buy some new varieties of plants there. They would be carefully packed and the railways would transport them back to Pune. What happened to them when they arrived there? Those plans were also made much earlier; they were taken to Kamshet farmhouse. After Vijayrao retired, there were some offers of consultancy. He was now famous as a railway electrification expert. He had decided well in advance that he was not going to do any of that. To satisfy his horticultural passions, he had built a farmhouse in Kamshet (about 50 km from Pune, near Lonavala), five or six years before retiring.

In 1987, he bought land in Bedse village, eight miles from the Kamshet station. The Bedse Buddhist cave temples are visible from there. It was during our time in Iraq (1988–1990) that the farmhouse was built. After the Christmas vacation of 1987–1988, Ashutosh had not visited India for a while. In July 1994, he visited Pune and Vijayrao took him to see the Kamshet house. That year, there were exceptionally heavy rains. By the time we managed to reach Kamshet, there was water everywhere. The roads were completely submerged, the hills now a series of waterfalls. We had to ford a veritable stream to get to the house. But now water was gushing through this stream with force. Father and son were ready to hop in and get across. Village folk warned us against crossing the stream. We saw the house from this bank and then turned right round and came back.

Vijayrao still makes frequent trips there. He has put a lot of money and effort into the garden. He takes many of his friends to see this second child of his. When his female friends of the Garden Club praise this child of his, his face lights up.

There's only one fly in the ointment. There is neither an electrical connection nor running water there. This is because one would have to bribe the authorities and this simply does not sit well with his straightforward attitude.

And so many people advise him, 'Why not sell the house? What use would Ashutosh have for it? What can you do with it?' but his heart has its reasons that reason does not understand. And Ashutosh seems to feel that if his father loves the house so much, it should remain in the family. And he too seems to feel the same way; for be it ever so flying a visit, he has to visit Kamshet. He examines every tree; he helps Gautam climb some of them. He catches the jackfruit that Gautam has plucked with his left hand and thrown towards him. He observes all the cows and buffaloes; he plays with Ranu the farmhouse dog, looking at the silhouettes of the forts of Lohagad and Tikona and others to his heart's content, watching the sun descend to the horizon …

When Gautam describes this as his village to his American friends, Ashutosh feels very happy. When Gautam romps freely in the Kamshet house, Ashutosh and his father are delighted. There lies the value of Vijayrao's dream house.

His Mother Tongue

Ashutosh pays great attention to his mother tongue. When Gautam was young, he thought his father didn't know any English at all. And so, Gautam learnt eagerly to speak excellent Marathi. At his thread ceremony, both father and son chanted the Sanskrit shlokas with beauty and precision and Gautam's rendition of the *Dasabodha* drew much praise from all the guests. The truth of the matter is that Ashutosh did not grow up in Maharashtra, but he has strong Maharashtrian roots. He is aware of the differences in state origin but has no knowledge of caste. When looking for his bride, he said,

'It's a different matter if she's from Bengal or Punjab, for instance; but if she's Maharashtrian she should be able to speak Marathi.' He would insist that I write to him in Marathi. In 2008, when he came to Pune, we had a party in his honour. Everyone wanted to know about his research work. For nearly one-and-a-half hours, he spoke with enthusiasm and energy. He explained many complex scientific terms in simple language but in chaste Marathi. Many of our friends said, 'Ashutosh, you told us so many interesting things but what we felt truly proud of was how well you spoke Marathi.'

He is not very religious-minded but enjoys celebrating festivals. The ritual bath on the dawn of Diwali and the bursting of firecrackers is a favourite. In the US, beautiful firecrackers are set off on the Fourth of July, America's Independence Day.

Ashutosh feels that science and spirituality should not be mixed. 'The god particle, has it been found yet?' I said to him a month or so before it was announced. He replied, 'Aai, don't call it the god particle. In science it has only one name: the Higgs boson!'

His friendships from his bachelor days are still going strong. He and his friends get together at Christmas at each other's houses; they help each other in difficult times. Tejvir and Jasvir Khurana, Dhiman Chakraborty, Arijit Banerjee, Sathyadev Ramchandran and Pasha Murat are good friends of his. When his cousin Abhijeet and his wife Sangeeta were expecting a child, Abhijeet's mother, Sudha Aatya, was flying in from India. When he heard that Abhijeet was going to pick her up from the airport, Ashutosh told him that he should stay with his wife and volunteered to pick his aunt up from Chicago airport and bring her down to Ohio.

In the US, I met some of his senior colleagues and friends. Professor Alfred (Al) Goshaw, Dr Pavel (Pasha) Murat, Dr Arijeet Bannerjee, all of them said that Ashutosh has a soft heart and a willingness to laugh that's visible in his smile. His friendliness with all kinds of people pleases me. He is never late with an email response. He often sits for hours with his laptop. His father often sends him personal emails. Often, he will receive a reply in five minutes. He treats the family with the same promptness that he would respond to a professional email. Even if he is at an international conference at which he will be talking to many important people in his field, he finds time to reply. He does his professional work with promptness and then is free to attend to the personal. There never seems to be a strain. Even if he has been travelling for a long time and has arrived late in the night, he still manages to seem fresh!

When he is travelling with his family, or even just chatting with them at home; when he is playing with Gautam or taking his lessons; when he is joking with Ashwini, he never shows the strain of work.

Most of his work is done on the computer, often late at night. While he is doing this, a film may be playing on the television nearby or Bear Grylls' adventure shows may be on the Discovery Channel. He is never to be seen with a book in his hands, and yet he manages to keep up with the world's happenings and with deep philosophical thought. I think he reads so fast that I mostly miss when he reads.

These days he spends a lot of time with Gautam, introducing him to the joys of learning; and in the night, he writes his internationally celebrated papers. He makes sure he spends a lot of time with Gautam; they run together, go to the gym, hit the swimming pool or play a couple of games of badminton. He and Gautam have gone skiing in Virginia, Wisconsin and Utah. Gautam thus is a good swimmer and a great skier.

When Gautam is with us at home or in a restaurant, we play an interesting game. You don't need any material for this game. It's called 'Would you rather…?' For example, one day, Gautam and I had watched the film *The Sound of Music* again. The von Trapp children and Maria were now friends; they seemed to look upon her as one of them and called her by her name. After that, their father, Captain von Trapp, and Maria get married. After that, the littlest one calls her Maria, and Maria says: 'Uh-hum, not Maria, Mother!'

This must have bothered Gautam. In our game later, he said: 'Would you rather have the little girl call Maria by name or as mother?' All of us gave our opinions and explained our choices. Many other issues were also tabled, which ranged from international politics to the issues of daily life, from business to cultural affairs. This led to a wide-ranging discussion, spiked with lots of laughter.

Vinayatai Phene, Ashwini's mother, raves about Ashutosh. Vinayatai and Ashwini are soulmates and so Ashwini pours her heart out to her mother. Vinayatai is very fond of Gautam, Ashwini and Ashutosh and often spends time with them in the US. Vinayatai is of a spiritual bent and deeply impressed by the vista of Ashutosh's interests, his clear and honest nature, his gentleness and lack of ego.

She often shares her impressions and memories of him with me. She remembers the trips they took when the Phenes visited the US. He would organize people of their age for them to meet; he took care of their food, especially the vegetarian meals that they needed or the special dietary requirements for religious fasts. He made sure they were always comfortable. As if that were not enough, Vinayatai said, 'When we were in a hotel or somewhere like that, if a porter came to help us with our luggage, he would also lend them a hand, and tip them as well.' But he would make sure to hand the money to one of the elders or to Vinayatai to give it to the porter.

Once, all four of them were standing at an airport. A very beautiful girl walked by them. Ashwini and her mother both said, 'Wah' spontaneously. Ashutosh was nonplussed. He had not even noticed the young woman. Vinayatai was delighted. 'My son-in-law only has eyes for his wife,' she said.

How attentive he can be to his wife and child was also the subject of one of her anecdotes. Once, all of them had gone on a trip to the North Carolina mountains. They had rented a beautiful old log cabin, well-appointed and comfortable, in the woods.

Canoeing was available on the river. Ashutosh had learnt how to paddle a canoe in Wales, but the rest were all novices. A canoe could take only two people at a time.

Ashutosh took Vinayatai in his canoe. Ashwini settled Gautam in another with herself. While Ashutosh was paddling dexterously, he had an eye on the other canoe as well.

Ashwini and Gautam were soon in trouble. They were moving in circles in the water. Ashutosh began to row by 'remote control', offering instructions on how to row, on what side, with what force. Ashwini's friend Poorna and her husband were in a third canoe; this one capsized and deposited the pair in the water. The lifeguards had to go out to rescue them.

Conversations on the Ski Slopes

It is assumed that when scientists talk to each other, it is always about serious matters and that they always use jargon incomprehensible to the layperson. That the world-changing experiments happening at the LHC can be discussed while shooting down ski slopes is a rather exciting thought. Whenever Ashutosh goes to Switzerland in winter, he always takes the opportunity to get a little skiing in with his colleagues while engaging in discussions. In his various leadership roles, his work was at several levels: he was to direct the efforts of scientists and students, collate their results and eliminate obstacles when these were encountered. Ashutosh met with other scientists at the laboratory or used video conferencing to stay in touch. But sometimes it would be best to talk al fresco, under an open sky, an unofficial conference of sorts. There they could share their problems or their doubts; they would get some suggestions and solutions from him or even explore alternative approaches. Not surprisingly, even at this level of scientific thinking, personality clashes and political manoeuvring can get in the way of the work since different points of view may not reconcile. But being with nature, out in the open, can often expand one's consciousness and change one's way of thinking. Plans for the future can be discussed; expectations for directions can be argued.

There are many places where one gets a chance to ski. There is even floodlit night skiing on the slopes. He has skied at many mountain resorts in Europe and the US but Ashutosh still remembers his first skiing experience at Glencoe in Scotland. There were no trees in sight, anywhere; just mountains and snow till the horizon.

God Be Praised, My Belly Is Raised!

Ashutosh is not fussy about his food; the Kotwals are generally not and he has followed in their footsteps. He will eat what is available when it's time to eat, in the manner of a ritual. When he is in a rush, or has to get somewhere quickly, whatever simple food is available will serve him well. He loves fruit and cheese; yoghurt and buttermilk are his favourites.

But if there is something special, he will savour that as well. He loves sweet things and has a special love for his mother's puran poli (the Chandraseniya Kayastha Prabhu variation is the telpoli) and kanavle. He has a jar of these on his worktable and pops one from time to time. Moravala (a sweet jam made with amla) and sukeli (dried banana) are also high on the list. Ever since he was a child, he has enjoyed aamsula (dried kokum).

How to retain the nutrition of food while cooking was always my focus. Perhaps he noticed this at some point in his life. When he was very young, he would be with me in the kitchen, sitting on the counter, rolling out little polis or making letter shapes out of chakli dough. Perhaps that was when he noticed. His friend from Boston, Tejvir Khurana (aka Teji) told me, 'Auntie, when Ashutosh makes chhole (chickpeas) in the cooker, he never throws away the extra water; he drinks it!' Satyadev who was doing his PhD with Ashutosh, is an excellent chef who loves to cook but Ashutosh would be sitting at his laptop, working and eating a radish. Although his eating habits are Sattvic and simple, he has a great deal of knowledge about international cuisine.

॰

Family Entertainment

I discovered Ashutosh's talent for acting by accident. When Gautam was born, we stayed with him and Ashwini for about a year and a half. In the chill winters, we would all sit together with the baby. Ash-2, as his Aunt Truus, Ashok Kaka's wife calls Ashutosh and Ashwini for short, have a stock of jokes, riddles and stories. We would also play parlour games like dumb charades. It was always difficult to tell what name or phrase Ashutosh had chosen, but watching the play of emotions on his mobile face or how he used body language to communicate often left me full of pride.

During one of our trips to the US, we went and played miniature golf at an amusement park. We also took him on at billiards and carom. Even as a boy, he would defeat us at the card game 'three-nought-four' and continues to do so. That makes him very happy. Seeing his mischievous smile on these occasions made me feel that my 'Baalusha' is still a little boy at heart. When he was young, we would have to drag him to the cinema so that we could enjoy a film or two. He did enjoy the circus but when we took him to see the film *Mera Naam Joker*, he grew bored.

As an adult, he began to watch a lot of films. Science, history, political thrillers and action films (such as Arnold Schwarzenegger's Terminator series, Bruce Willis's Die Hard series, Tom Cruise's Mission Impossible, James Bond and Jason Bourne series) are his favourites. He watches a lot of films based on these themes. Initially, he did not have a great affection for introspective and emotional stories, but later he grew to appreciate them. There's no question of making time for films; he works on the computer and watches them at the same time. And it is true that he remembers more about the films he has seen than I do, even though I turn my full attention to a film when I am watching it.

I have no idea when my love of film music entered his system. He has never spoken about it. But one day when he was talking to his father about science, he suddenly stopped and said to me: 'Name a song, any song. I will tell you the singer and the film it is from' and he was quite right. He remembered them better than I did.

Once when I was sorting his cupboard, I found an old chocolate box. I opened it and found the words of some of the best ghazals of Mehdi Hassan and Jagjit Singh inside. Once again, I found that he was a fan of refined music, and this when Gautam was an infant. The strains of classical Indian music and the symphonies of Beethoven and Mozart would emanate from Gautam's room. He has a huge collection of film and music cassettes at home.

A Mistake Made

We know that without making a big show of it, Ashutosh is generally on full alert. One day, when we were sitting in the morning and having tea together, Ashwini told us about an incident, bringing to it her own style of narration. And we were all surprised, we found it funny, and gosh! Everything eventually turned out all right but if it hadn't … the thought sent a shiver down my spine. Even God forgives a single mistake, they say, in that state. In Ashwini's words, 'When the universe is on your side …'

From 2008, Ashutosh had been travelling to Switzerland and back to work at CERN. On this occasion, he had an Air France ticket to Geneva, with a change at Paris. The flight to Paris was landing at the international terminal while the flight to Geneva was to take off from the domestic terminal. The border between the two countries was clearly visible, and in order to get to the domestic terminal, he would have to step into French territory. But he did not have a French visa. This requirement was not known when booking the ticket.

The airline authorities considered the matter and rerouted his flight through Zurich, which would depart from the international terminal. They also advised him to get a French visa at the consulate in Switzerland because his return flight would also have him crossing the same border. In Geneva, Ashutosh got in touch with the French consulate. He was told it would take ten days for him to get an appointment. That wouldn't do. When he told Ashwini, she advised him to buy a new ticket. That was unacceptable to him. It was a question of $3,000.

The next day, he decided to take a chance and went to the consulate. The outer doors would not open without an appointment. When someone came out through the door, he slipped inside. No one spotted him. He explained his problem to the visa official who turned out to be an understanding lady. He got a one-day single-entry visa into France.

He finished his work at Geneva. A friend of his, Srini, insisted on taking him to dinner. They had a great time and then it suddenly occurred to him. The restaurant was in the French territory next to Geneva. That meant Ashutosh's single-entry visa had been used up. The good thing was that when they crossed the border, no one stamped his passport.

Anyway, it seemed like the issue was resolved and in the past. Not quite, it turned out. At the airport, he discovered that the return flight was delayed. If the flight were to be delayed any further, his visa would expire before the flight landed in Paris. In that case, he would not be allowed to board. Finally, the flight did depart and when it landed in Paris, he had an hour left on his visa. He needed to get into the international terminal within that hour. When he took his seat on the flight back to the US, he let out the breath he had been holding and sighed with relief.

For the first seventeen-and-a-half years of his life, Ashutosh lived under our protection. But he is a self-made man. A man who is not free with his words but who is still eloquent … a man who regards the universe with an unending curiosity … sensitive and hard-working … a man who maintains his bonds with his work and his friends. Today, Ashutosh is a man who has not only become a great scientist but also a good father and husband. I am proud of this.

THE LIMITLESS SKY

An artist's rendition of astrophysics and particle physics coming together: stars and galaxies in the sky, Fermilab's main building, and particle traces in the underground CDF experiment, where Ashutosh conducted research for many years. Credit: Fermilab

The brain knows no boundaries; imagination has no limits. When one creates another world in the mind with contemplation, the sky is the limit. This was the state of mind of the ancient rishis and of the modern scientists. Science relies on flights of imagination and scientists' wings find the thermals of mathematical logic and rationality; they rise to develop new theories and to invent new experiments to test them.

Ashutosh was always concerned with the future, which direction to take and what he should study next in the field of particle physics. This section is a survey of that field.

29

Tireless Traveller

Ashutosh's nature keeps him on a constant quest, seeking out the hidden, trying to fathom the mysteries of the universe. There are some things in nature that cannot be explained using the Standard Model theory and those are the things Ashutosh is interested in. They can be understood using extended mathematical models.

Ashutosh often speaks about the Standard Model theory as simple and elegant. The theory explains the behaviour of particles in a mathematical framework. So far, the theory has stood the test of time and scientists have been successful in using it; but it is not accepted as the final word on elementary particles. Some questions remain unanswered.

Do the particles which contribute to the visible matter of the universe—quarks, leptons and the Higgs boson—have any further substructures and new symmetries?

Are the four forces simply facets or different forms of one and the same universal force?

How are the dimensions of space decided? Higher dimensions, according to String Theory, could exist at the level of the infinitesimal. Is this true?

There is a theory about the substructure or compositeness of the Standard Model particles. Ashutosh is trying to verify this theory. In the past, he has conducted searches for the electron's and muon's excited states, which ought to exist if there are smaller constituents bound inside them. Having published the best results on the point-like nature of these particles, he has moved on to searching for the substructure of the Higgs boson and the top quark. Since these particles are so heavy, Ashutosh believes that they are more likely to reveal substructure. He is also trying to address the unanswered questions in the Standard Model theory through the application of the principles of supersymmetry. He wants to verify the symmetries between the particles that are assumed to exist and those that are known to exist.

There are two directions research might take. The Standard Model has predicted certain properties such as masses for the particles that we know of, and their production and decay rates. One can measure these properties with higher precision to see if there is a deviation between the measurement and the prediction.

The hunt for new particles

In fact, Professor Richard Nickerson, who was Ashutosh's PhD guide early on, said that Ashutosh had in-depth knowledge and had done a lot of interesting work in the areas of quantum chromodynamics, proton structure and the photon–hadron interaction.

Ashutosh is still leading the way in increasing the degree of accuracy with which we know the mass of the W boson. This mass has a fine sensitivity to the quantum-mechanical effects of new undiscovered particles. The enigma of the Higgs boson is connected intimately with this mass. Had this mass not been measured with a great deal of accuracy, the quantum fluctuations occasioned in the W boson by the Higgs boson would not be visible. Ashutosh and his colleagues have also measured an accurate value for the mass of the top quark, when it decays into two electrons and/or muons. In the history of particle physics, this was the first time that an algorithm based on the biological evolution of neural networks was used. Ashutosh helped develop modern techniques required to find the Higgs boson at the ATLAS experiment.

New theories which are expanded forms of the Standard Model theory are being examined in particle physics. The theory of Supersymmetry and the Grand Unified Theory (GUT), which seek to unite electromagnetic, weak and strong forces, have predicted the existence of new force-mediating particles. Ashutosh has published two papers on these particles from the CDF data. At ATLAS, he made a detailed study of the silicon and transition-radiation detectors in order to maximize the accuracy with which they measure all the particle trajectories produced in collision events. He also wrote the first three papers on the heavy resonances occasioned by their decays into leptons at ATLAS.

Z-Prime Research

After the LHC was set up at CERN, the world's scientists began a desperate hunt for the Higgs boson, but the elusive god particle kept evading them for two years. At this time Ashutosh was deeply involved with Z-prime boson research. He worked for nearly five years on the search for the Z-prime boson. Fewer scientists were paying much attention to the possibility of this particle at the beginning of the LHC since the Higgs boson was the focus of all attention, but Ashutosh felt that research into this particle would throw new light on the Higgs boson as well as other mysteries, because the Z-prime boson was predicted by GUT.

How elementary particles get their mass was still a mystery that was confronting scientists. When the Higgs boson was discovered, this riddle was solved. It was hoped that other riddles would also be unravelled by the Z-prime boson, including the extreme light mass of the neutrinos, the origin of dark matter, the puzzle of dark energy, or why there is more matter in the universe than antimatter.

In April 2011, Ashutosh's colleagues at Fermilab found tantalizing signs hinting at a Z-prime boson in the CDF data. However, these signs were not strong enough to be convincing. These hints had been found in the data containing a high-energy electron–positron (the anti-electron) pair. Ashutosh urged caution before making any announcement. Ashutosh and his team immediately launched a detailed analysis of complementary data containing a high-energy muon–antimuon pair. His argument was, if the Z-prime signature in the electron–positron data were not a statistical fluke, then it should be present in the muon–antimuon data too. Alas, in the muon–antimuon data Ashutosh found no confirmation of the Z-prime boson's signature. But he and other scientists were not disheartened. It is in the nature of scientific enquiry that clues must be diligently and carefully pursued. The search was going to continue at the much higher energy and rate of the LHC.

The Z-prime boson would be the transporter of a new force. There are suggestions in many theories of the existence of a new force. The possibility of the unification of the strong and electroweak forces has only been posited at extremely high energies. In such GUTs, the manifestation of a new force at lower energies is quite natural, because of the mathematical and geometrical nature of the logic of the GUT.

Another possibility is that the Z-prime boson may not mediate a force between known particles but might be the transporter of a force between new particles that are going to be discovered. If these particles exist in nature around us, then their interaction with the known particles must be very weak. In the same way, these new particles may be the harbingers of a 'brave new world' that has been hidden from us, and the Z-prime boson may be the transporter of a force in this 'brave new world'. This is called a 'hidden valley' theory. The particles and forces in the hidden valley would mimic our Standard Model in many ways. The Z-prime boson would mediate a force similar to electromagnetism, but amongst the hidden-valley particles. Such a Z-prime boson is sometimes called a 'dark photon'.

If a Z-prime boson is found, then we might be able to get a glimpse into that concealed world. For instance, dark matter may be made of the particles in the hidden universe and may even interact with the matter of which we are made, albeit very weakly. That is why searching for dark matter is a difficult task. The Z-prime boson might be one of the few ways to make contact with it. In addition to the GUT idea, this shows how many exciting possibilities the Z-prime boson might present in the future. Each force that we have discovered has been the source of a huge amount of knowledge. The Z-prime boson might be the next big one.

Ashutosh has been studying the Z-prime boson for many years, first at CDF and then at ATLAS. At CDF, he wrote two papers and at ATLAS, he wrote five papers on the Z-prime boson search alone. He has worked as the leader of the Z-prime research group. He has devised many advanced techniques to help in this quest. Some of them were used at CDF and others are in use at ATLAS. There have been 1,442 citations of his papers on the Z-prime boson. One of these is a 'famous paper' with 441 citations.

One of the first principles researchers are taught in science is that the absence of evidence is not evidence of absence. In other words: if you haven't found it, that doesn't mean it isn't there. Keep on looking. Use new devices, use new methods, look in new areas but keep looking. This is the principle on which Ashutosh conducts his Z-prime research. He has invented a new method for searching for Z-prime bosons that interact solely with top quarks, rendering the boson invisible in previous searches. His team of fifteen scientists and students is applying his method to analyse all the ATLAS data collected so far for this novel type of Z-prime boson.

30

In Search of Supersymmetry

The year 2015 was the annus mirabilis for particle physicists. The US Snowmass and the European Strategy deliberations recommended the upgrades and improvements to be made in the LHC. Their recommendations were accepted and over the next five years, work at the LHC to develop new technologies began afresh with renewed energy.

The end of the forty-year search for the Higgs boson was a landmark in the LHC book. Now the hunt is on for supersymmetry (SUSY), a search that could have an even bigger payoff. This SUSY theory could be at the root of all the models on which the ambitious particle physics of the future will stand. If the LHC does indeed find evidence of supersymmetry, this will give the work of experimental physicists a new fillip; they will have new fields to plough, new particles to chase down. If such evidence is not found, it will be back to square one and the eternal question 'How did the universe begin?' will have to be reconsidered from other perspectives.

The mathematics of supersymmetry was investigated starting in the early 1970s. It was initially motivated by all the hadrons being discovered in the 1960s. Supersymmetry extends the logic of quantum mechanics maximally while remaining consistent with the rules of special relativity. Further studies of this mathematics revealed that some of its properties would help to resolve certain weaknesses of the Standard Model. SUSY started becoming very popular as an extension of the SM. And since then, it has been playing hide-and-seek with particle physicists.

Both the Tevatron at Fermilab and the LHC at CERN have been in hot pursuit.

SUSY has the answer to a vexing conundrum. The Standard Model theory has a quantum-mechanical explanation for all the known particles and the forces with which they interact, except gravity. Only gravity, which was explained by Einstein's General theory of relativity, has proved recalcitrant: it is not compatible with the rules of quantum mechanics in the Standard Model. However, if SUSY is incorporated into the SM, a path forward towards a quantum theory of gravity is found! This is another big attraction for SUSY.

Earlier, we saw that matter particles are fermions and force-mediating particles are bosons. SUSY makes a bold move by postulating that fermions and bosons are different facets of a single, more complete description which incorporates properties of both fermions and bosons. Automatically, each fermion must have an accompanying boson and vice-versa. This is the idea of a 'partner particle' for each known particle; every SM particle will have a super-partner with a different angular momentum, i.e., spin.

By the original logic of supersymmetry, the super-partner must have the same mass as the SM partner. As we haven't seen these super-partners, this part of the logic has to be modified so that the super-partners are heavier and beyond the reach of past experiments. Now that the LHC is running at its highest energy, scientists are hoping that they will see traces of these supersymmetric particles here; it is their last stand for the next twenty years. SUSY might also explain dark matter because these super-partners might well be dark-matter particles. This is another attraction for SUSY.

But even if these heavy super-partners are beyond the scope of the LHC, that does not mean the end of the road for particle physicists. Not finding something can be as exciting and as meaningful as finding something, so the history of science tells us. In the nineteenth century, scientists believed that light was a wave and a wave had to have a material medium through which to pass. But then how did light from the Sun cross the vacuum of space and get to us? So they decided that the universe must be filled with aether, the material medium through which light passed to cross the vacuum of space.

Then Albert Michelson and Edward Morley, two scientists, disproved the existence of aether in a brilliant experiment. Aether was found to be a dead end. However, that opened a magnificent new road: Albert Einstein's theory of special relativity.

So even if the LHC fails to detect supersymmetric particles, all that will happen is that scientists will believe that there is something beyond the SM about which we do not know. Science looks for that which can be measured, calculated and understood.

The mathematics of SUSY means that space and time themselves have quantum aspects. Ashutosh believes the discovery of super-partners means the dawn of a new age of quantum mechanics! SUSY could be the bridge that links astrophysics, cosmology and particle physics; this mathematical theory can help understand dark matter and gravity from the quantum perspective. 'I believe that SUSY has the potential to unlock many mysteries of nature that are unfolding before our eyes,' he says.

In a lighter vein, one might say that were Ashutosh a gambler, he would consider SUSY a good bet, though not the only bet. But even if he isn't going to write a cheque for it, he will try his best to persuade others to underwrite the effort. In the next round of particle physics experiments, he says that he will have to wear several hats: a sombrero and a baseball cap, certainly.

The sombrero's broad rim helps protect us from the sun. The baseball cap fits the head of the player tightly and the visor protects his eyes and face from the light and heat. The 90-degree angle of the visor creates a sort of tunnel vision that also focuses the attention of the player on the ball. The sombrero-wearer expects to be protected in all four directions.

The sombrero, in Ashutosh's analogy, is to allow him a 360-degree view of the field of particle physics, so as to have some view of the directions it might take. The baseball cap, on the other hand, is to help him focus on the decisions that he must make regarding the ATLAS experiment. He must also make a calculated guess about the needs of particle physicists ten years down the line, if ATLAS is to be further improved.

This means that particle physicists have had to go back to the drawing board and think afresh about the goals of their research. They must decide which experiments need to be tinkered with or designed from scratch, in what ways they can assist each other's work, and what they want to achieve.

Between 2011 and 2013, Ashutosh's group explained in accessible language why $1 billion would be needed to upgrade the LHC. To do that, he had to present the arguments of all the scientists involved. The consensus was that the LHC had to be upgraded to make new measurements and explore uncharted territory of fundamental science.

31

Back to the Future

Ashutosh and some like-minded scientists could see the future of the LHC clearly. There was a focus on their attempts to upgrade the LHC. However, it was not as clear a picture as they would have liked. No supersymmetric particle had been spotted. No one had any idea at what energy level the super-partners of the electron, the top quark, the bosons and other particles would manifest themselves. And so, it was difficult to estimate what means and materials would be needed.

At the national conference called Snowmass, Ashutosh and his team presented the idea of setting up a collider of the future. Snowmass takes place every ten years; this is when a group of international scientists come together at a ski resort and make plans for the future. They set up the research programmes for the next ten years, and estimate the costs and work out the plans. At Snowmass 2013, the idea of setting up a huge collider, bigger than the LHC, was a topic of discussion. This huge collider could be at Fermilab or at CERN. It would not be easy to dig a tunnel 100–200 km in circumference; from Fermilab, it would reach the city of Chicago, and from CERN it would reach the mountains surrounding Geneva. Would such a long tunnel really be needed? Yes, for two reasons. When a charged particle changes direction, it radiates energy. The greater the change in direction, the greater the loss of energy. If the curve is kept gentle, the direction change is small, and the loss of energy is reduced. To do this, you need a large circumference. The second reason is that, to bend a charged particle in a circle, a magnetic field is needed—the higher the beam energy, the stronger the field needed.

Breakthroughs achieved in superconducting magnet technology by particle physicists have made the Tevatron and LHC possible. Further breakthroughs are needed to build even stronger magnets. The highest beam energy is achieved by maximizing the magnet strength and the tunnel radius.

The collider envisaged at Fermilab, which is to be larger and of higher energy than the one at CERN, is called the Very High Energy Proton–Proton Collider. The one envisaged at CERN is called the Future Circular Collider. In our discussion here, for ease of reference, I have referred to both as the Very Large Hadron Collider (VLHC).

The diagram below may help us understand the difference in size between the Tevatron, the LHC and the VLHC.

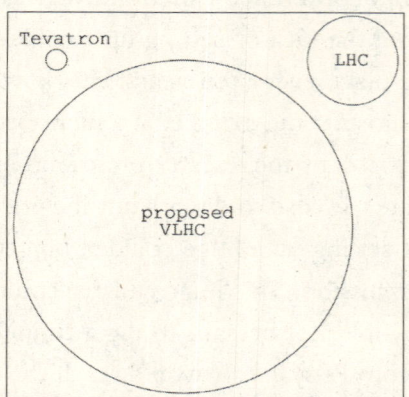

Circumferences: Tevatron at Fermilab, 6.3 km. LHC at CERN, 26.7 km. VLHC about 100 km.

The director of Fermilab, Dr Nigel Lockyer, set up the Department of Strategic Initiatives in High-Energy Physics. The design of this new collider requires a great deal of foresight and planning. Dr Lockyer established a connection with the US federal government's Department of Energy and got Ashutosh appointed as the head of the Future Collider Group in this department. Ashutosh took leave from Duke University to go on deputation to Fermilab.

In June 2014, Ashutosh accepted this new responsibility and moved from Durham, North Carolina, to Naperville, a suburb of Chicago. After the successes at CERN, China and Japan began to feel that they too should have new large colliders. Since the cost of such a project would be in the vicinity of $20 billion, it will need financial, technical and theoretical support. To undertake such a project requires much detailed attention to its varied aspects.

Ashutosh coordinates with the various study groups and designs future policies and programmes. The job involves making an educated guess at the future. What progress will the particle physicists of the next forty years have made? What progress would they like to be making? What equipment and what facilities would they need? At what level of energy would they like the collider to be working? What theory will take centrestage, SUSY or an alternate extension of the SM? Will the dream of unification of the four forces have materialized or how far will it have been realized? What kind of detectors will they need? How much more powerful must the superconducting magnets be? How much more powerful can they be made? All this was now part of Ashutosh's portfolio. In addition, he must offer an estimate of the VLHC's lifespan. He must have some sense of the design and the construction logistics.

The most important concern is that such a project is going to be the last of its kind. This is because even tunnels larger than 100–200 km seem unfeasible. Thus, a crucial aspect of the project is to win the support of the scientific community.

Different nations have different levels of resources, theoretical and technical skills. It will be necessary to study all these and work out a collaborative policy, which will also be an exercise in international diplomacy. It will also be necessary to receive goodwill and support from the public, always an uphill task. When the Higgs boson was discovered, the Nobel Prize went to Europe and this stung the US. In 1993, the project of setting up a very large collider in Texas had to be abandoned after $2 billion were spent on it. This failure is still alive in the consciousness of the US. No one could touch the US in the sphere of particle physics till the 1970s, but Europe has been catching up fast. The onus of keeping the US in numero uno position vests in Ashutosh. Ashutosh's brief includes building up public opinion, making sure of government grants, meeting with and convincing Congressmen and Senators.

And Ashutosh, too, has his expectations. He wonders whether and what new discoveries will be garnered from the Very Large Hadron Collider. In every time period, scientists concern themselves with a primary and fundamental question. In the last fifty years, physicists have been asking: How do elementary particles acquire mass? Although the Higgs boson, which would supply the answer was discovered, that did not mean that scientists could now rest on their laurels. The next question has already surfaced, and it concerns dark matter. No one has any doubt that dark matter exists. But what is its nature? What is the nature of the particles it is made of? What are these particles?

Matter and antimatter were both born together at the time of the Big Bang. But how did an inequality develop in the amounts generated? In order to answer this, the Standard Model theory will have to be modified. Nature has shown a preference for matter.

Protons and neutrons are visible everywhere, but their antiparticles are very rare. Antimatter does not show up on Earth, and it is very rare in cosmic rays. If there were significant amounts of antimatter in other galaxies there should be sources of radiation from matter–antimatter annihilation.

In other words, in the infinitesimal picosecond after the Big Bang, matter and antimatter were locked in battle but somehow matter won. However, according to the SM, this should not happen. Therefore, the Standard Model theory needs to be expanded. Many theories can be floated with the help of mathematical models but they all need to be tested experimentally. For example, it is possible to estimate the neutrons and protons, hydrogen and helium produced from the Big Bang using the Standard Model theory and the measured amounts match up. This proves that, with the correct theory, mind-boggling success can be achieved in understanding nature and the very genesis of the universe.

One of these alternate theories suggests that, apart from the Higgs boson, there must be a second Higgs boson with different properties. The theory also posits its signatures. VLHC may be the site of its discovery. Ashutosh finds this theory appealing and has initiated a search for a second Higgs boson at ATLAS with one of his PhD students and colleagues.

These different theories come from different scientists who form different groups.

Ashutosh keeps in touch with these groups. Ashutosh has to decide which of the theories could be proven at the VLHC and what experimental designs will make for the best results. This is an extremely important job. Deciding how to discover the signatures of the predicted particles takes a high degree of skill. The person who is deciding how to identify particles released from a proton collision must have great technical expertise.

Designing the experiment, working out the prototype, and then testing it are all dependent on this technical knowledge.

It is also necessary to establish what the signatures of particles like the muon, the electron, the tau lepton and the photon would be. It was expected that when the Higgs boson showed up at the LHC it would sometimes decay to a pair of tau leptons. Thus, Ashutosh feels it is necessary to devise a new detector to find the signature of tau leptons with high efficiency.

Plans for this huge construction project have already begun and the accelerator is anticipated to be ready by 2040. Money will have to be found in tandem with the work being planned. The scientific community must therefore be solidly behind the project; this is as important as public opinion. This is a project which can only be achieved with the help of international cooperation.

Snowmass Workshop

By consensus, there are three frontiers of particle physics: the cosmos, high-energy beams and high-intensity beams. There is always an attempt in research to expand these frontiers. In order to do this, one has to think far into the future and have a different perspective. The US has made great contributions in the arenas of leadership, expertise, resource mobilization and technical knowledge.

In the sphere of the cosmic frontier, the goal is to make observations of the cosmos using particle detectors placed on the ground or on satellites in orbit. These detectors observe particles and radiation coming from the upper atmosphere, the Sun, or from astrophysical and cosmological sources. These data provide information on neutrinos, dark matter, dark energy and antimatter in the universe.

In the sphere of high-intensity beams, the goal is to increase the amount of data collected which leads to more accurate measurements and enables the observation of rarer processes. Accurate measurements address fundamental questions by comparing measured values with predictions and a deviation indicates a new physics principle at work. The observation of a rare process can reveal a surprise, a completely unexpected reaction or it can reveal an anomaly in the rate of occurrence of the process. In these cases as well, a new physics principle is indicated. The word intensity here represents the number of beam particles per unit area per second, to which the rate of collisions is proportional. Intensity tells us how many particles can be produced from the specific origin or reaction.

In the sphere of extremely high-energy beams, the goal is to increase the energy of the beam particles so that new rules of physics come into play in the higher-energy collisions. In experiments linked to the energy frontier, high-energy accelerators are used to create specific fundamental particles and to hunt out new, predicted or unexpected particles. The Higgs boson discovery has thrown up many new fundamental questions. In the future, these questions will be front and centre to any experimental designs at the energy frontier.

The Snowmass Workshop considers all the options for the high-energy accelerators:

- Linear electron–positron collider
- Circular electron–positron collider
- Proton–proton collider
- Muon collider
- Photon collider

A collider is an accelerator in which two particle beams are circulated in opposite directions and brought into collision. In this conference, a suggestion for a 100 TeV proton collider (eight times the LHC energy) was floated. It was felt necessary to have a collider of such high energy in order to study the Higgs boson, dark matter and the matter–antimatter asymmetry of the universe.

Instrumentation

It is necessary to have the right instruments to conduct experiments to get solutions for the problems posed. In order to devise these instruments, one has to find the right people who can visualize them, design them and then build them. The results can only be as good as these instruments.

Inventing new detectors takes cooperation from industry, academia and scientific institutions. It is also necessary to get all these people on the same page. A deep knowledge of computer science is also necessary. Both the bandwidth and storage capacity of computer networks must be maximized. It is necessary to have a strong network across the nation and across the world to make all this happen, since enormous amounts of data must be processed at distributed centres. Obstacles must be worked through and sorted out.

Particle physicists will have to find answers to many questions. These include:

- Is the Higgs boson an elementary particle or is it composed of other, smaller particles? In other words, does it have components?

- Why is the neutrino so light when compared to other particles?
- Why is there more matter than antimatter in the universe?
- By far the largest component of matter in the universe is dark matter. What is the nature of dark matter?
- What is it about dark energy that it exerts a force of repulsion on the universe, pushing it apart?
- What was the nature of the universe in the first picosecond of its birth? What did it look like?
- Are there forces at work in the universe that have not been noticed so far?
- Will new heavy particles be found at energy levels of tera electron-Volts (TeV)?
- Whether any new light particles will turn up which interact with very weak forces, such as the 'hidden-valley' particles?
- Will the four forces that we know of come together at very high energies and at infinitesimally small distances?

All the particles that were predicted by the Standard Model have been found. Their characteristics have also been measured. But there are natural phenomena which we are discovering which do not fit into the Standard Model theory. Dark matter is one of these. There are many explanations offered; one is that dark matter is made up of weakly interacting massive particles (WIMPs) which are electrically neutral. These would have been born at the moment of the universe's birth at those unimaginably high temperatures of the Big Bang. The hunt is on now for exotic particles whose mass is around 1 TeV.

EDUCATION: A NOBLE GIFT

The campus statue of James Buchanan Duke, the founder of Duke University. Credits: Duke University

In the section called 'Spreading Wings' I described Ashutosh's career as a scientist. From 1999, teaching at Duke University has been another equally important part of his career. He has managed to unite the vocations of teacher and scientist beautifully. He has inspired many of his students to take up careers in research and has involved them in many exciting experiments.

To describe his career as an educator, I must rewind the clock to 1999.

32

Quick March in New Avenue

After finishing his post-doctoral research at Columbia University under the guidance of Professor Michael Tuts, Ashutosh decided that he would like to teach his favourite subject at some reputed university. He sent applications to many important universities. There were opportunities at Brown and Duke. The hopeful candidates were required to present a seminar on campus. The best candidates are interviewed, and their seminars are audited by the faculty.

Ashutosh prepared intensely for the seminar. The interview and seminar at Brown University went well but he did not get the post. There was a senior professor, Richard Partridge, who wanted Ashutosh to join Brown. Later, he met Ashutosh and congratulated him. 'I have the feeling that your seminar was far too advanced for your audience. You are ahead of your time and this may be beyond them. Don't let this setback discourage you,' he said.

Now Ashutosh threw himself into preparing for the seminar at Duke. The senior professor Al Goshaw enjoyed his colloquium very much. The subject was well-organized. The question-and-answer session went well and his presentation was confident and insightful.

Out of fifty applications, three or four candidates were invited to present a colloquium and then to personal interviews. Ashutosh made a brilliant presentation on his research on the Z-prime particle, the mathematics of it and the data analysis that he had made.

James Buchanan Duke was a wealthy tobacco and electric power industrialist of North Carolina. In 1924, he set up Duke University in Durham with very beautiful Gothic architecture. The beginnings of the university lie in the setting up of Trinity College in 1838, to which James Duke's father Washington Duke contributed generously. James Duke bought up all the land around this college and set up the university, which was renamed in honour of his father. The church at the heart of the new campus and the grounds is aesthetically pleasing; more than 600,000 visitors come to see the 55-acre Sarah P. Duke Gardens. It has its own exquisite lake on which regal swans glide and is well worth a visit.

Duke University appointed Ashutosh as an assistant professor in the physics department. In January 1999, he started working there and bought a grand house in Durham. Newly appointed professors are supposed to be on the tenure track. They must prove their suitability for tenure by producing original research and by writing papers of note and significance. It generally takes about seven years to get tenure. Ashutosh was appointed to the tenured position of associate professor in five years. The heads of other universities keep an eagle eye out for such talent. Professor Goshaw's mentorship helped Ashutosh make good strategic decisions about his research, which in turn raised his profile faster. Goshaw encouraged Ashutosh to go for early tenure.

Generally, 5 per cent of those who get their doctorates in physics become professors. To become a professor, it is vital to continue doing research. The more reputed the university, the more difficult it is to get tenure there.

When Ashutosh became professor, Dr Robert Gates, the ex-director of the CIA, became the president of Texas A&M University. He was a close friend of President George H.W. Bush. Later, Dr Gates served as the US secretary of defense. He did not stay long as the president of Texas A&M, but during his time there, he recruited many talented professors. One of those he wanted to hire was Ashutosh. 'The salary you want, the best schools for your children and a job for your wife that will pay her what she's getting now,' he offered. But Ashutosh turned him down gently.

Having been educated in America, Ashutosh knew the system of education well and as professor he was able to bring into his teaching methods that would enrich the lives of his students. In the American system, there is a great deal of flexibility. Everyone gets a chance to express their individual personalities. One does not have to stay within certain predetermined parameters. For instance, students can take a combination of sciences and humanities as subjects. This helps them expand their horizons. It does not mean that their attention is distracted from their main subject. There, the culture of self-studies is well-developed. There is an emphasis on independent study. The students are encouraged to work on their own from childhood. Students stay in touch with each other, discuss their ideas and projects; tell each other about the latest developments; they read extensively for context. They have developed the ability to listen carefully and understand the underlying concepts; they know how to express their thoughts and doubts clearly and to get the latter cleared up. These are all skills that are inculcated in them from a young age.

There is also a tradition of dialogue between teachers and students. Debate is an important tool of learning. Original thinking is given primacy. Secondary issues and problems are brought up and the students themselves must contribute to the process of resolution. This system of education promotes a deeper knowledge of the subject not only of students but also of the teachers.

Over the course of his career Ashutosh has taught at the undergraduate and postgraduate levels; he has guided several students working on their doctorates. Every three years, the subjects a professor teaches are changed. He has found that while figuring out how to explain a new subject to students, it is often the case that insights are illuminated, and new solutions are discovered. One's thought process gets clearer. One's way of thinking is refreshed. New students bring new ways of thinking and new perspectives to the class. Communicating with them in their language is another challenge. Thus, the teacher enters, with the students, into an unending educational process; this is the speciality of the US educational system.

Much emphasis is placed on analysis. Teaching is not one-directional; concepts are illuminated by discussion and thereby internalized. In this system, the student cannot afford to be a passive spectator. Ashutosh has always looked out for students who show energy and motivation; he tries to channel their energies in the proper direction. The American education system works on the concept of mentorship. Talented and motivated students find this system to be tailor-made for them. The mentor is always on standby to urge them on and to offer a helping hand.

The professor also benefits from encouraging the talent of a student. This is not so much about personal benefit but more about benefiting that branch of knowledge. By drawing the attention of the layperson towards that branch of knowledge, its future is assured. This is a far-sighted way of thinking about it. This is the attitude Ashutosh has always demonstrated. He has always made it his business to seek out funding towards the buying and building of the materials needed for particle physics experiments. He wants to be able to hand over his store of knowledge to the next generation of talented students and this question is one that he mulls over frequently.

It is his desire to further the cause of particle physics. His university has also been proactive in this area. He is proud of the talent and the hard work displayed by the students. He has been keen to mentor Indian students. He has seen that these students are valued by US universities; this has also been his own experience.

Research in the US depends on international collaboration. Thus, students there get to work at a global level. In this way, they get the best exposure and their talents are brought out so that others can observe their abilities.

Ashutosh has always taken good students, whether from US, India, or elsewhere, under his wing. He has involved them in the experiments he has conducted. He has made them co-authors of the papers he has published. Whether he was conducting research on the CDF experiment at Fermilab or the ATLAS experiment at CERN, he got his undergraduate, masters and doctoral students involved, thus promoting the name of Duke University.

And in appreciation, Duke University has offered him appropriate respect. In 2013 he, and the ATLAS team, became the first recipients of the Dean's Leadership Award. It was his research and collaborations that earned him this recognition.

INSPIRING EXCELLENCE

Trinity College of Arts and Sciences
at

DUKE UNIVERSITY

acknowledges

ASHUTOSH KOTWAL

and the ATLAS Team as the recipients of the

2012-2013

DEAN'S LEADERSHIP AWARD

_____
Richard Brodhead
President, Duke University

_____
Laurie Patton
Dean of Arts & Sciences

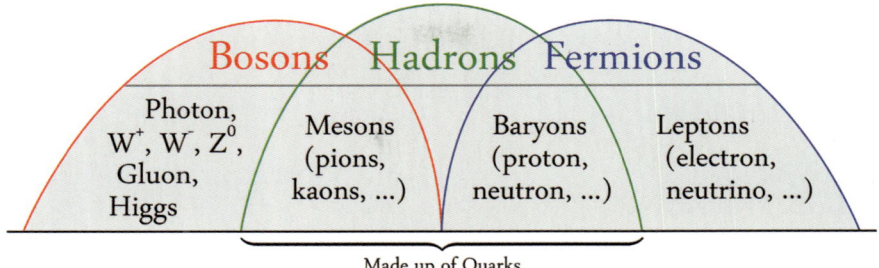

Elementary and composite particles along with their classification based on intrinsic spin.
Credits: Wikimedia

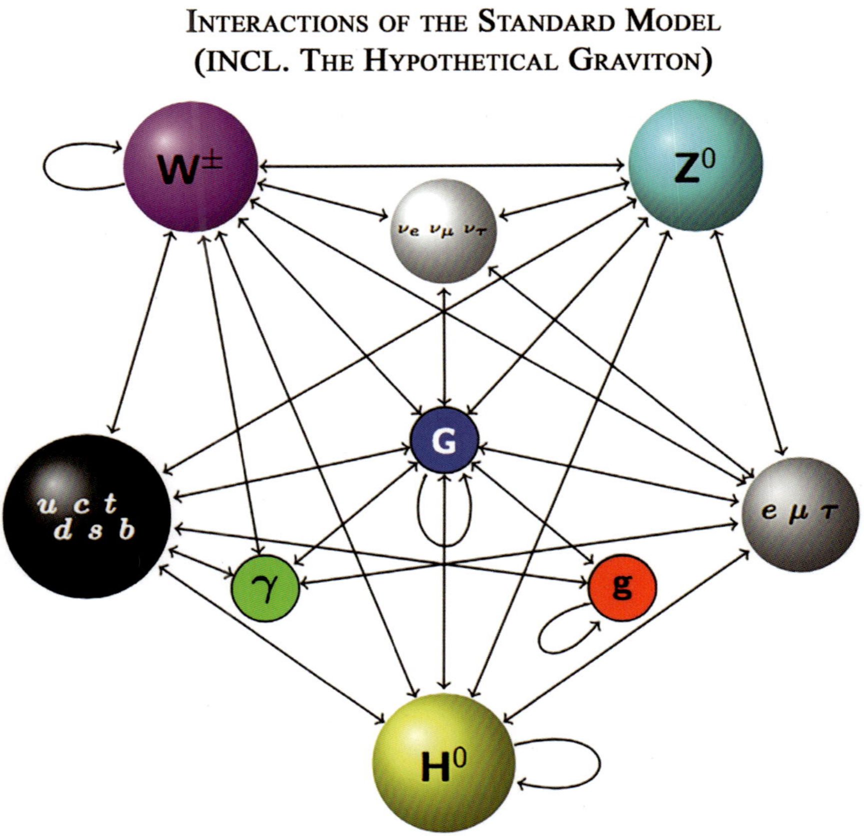

INTERACTIONS OF THE STANDARD MODEL
(INCL. THE HYPOTHETICAL GRAVITON)

Fundamental mediators of forces. Force-carrying bosons and their interactions with matter particles and with themselves.
Credit: Wikimedia; https://creativecommons.org/licenses/by-sa/4.0/deed.en

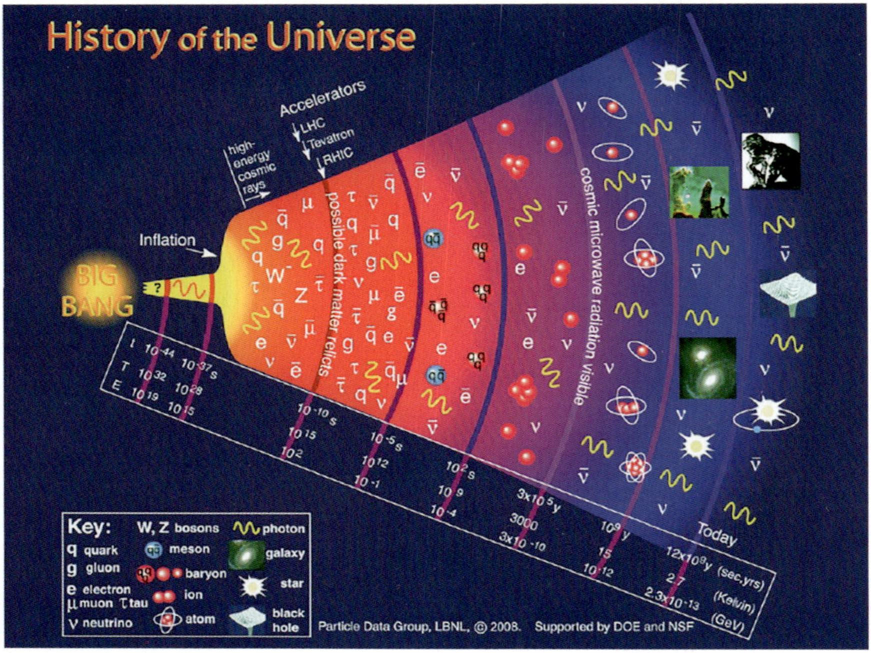

Origin and evolution of the Universe. Credits: Denis Perret-Gallix 2013 J. Phys.: Conf. Ser. **454** 012051
https://creativecommons.org/licenses/by/3.0/

Installation of the CDF experiment at Fermilab. *Credit: Fermilab.*

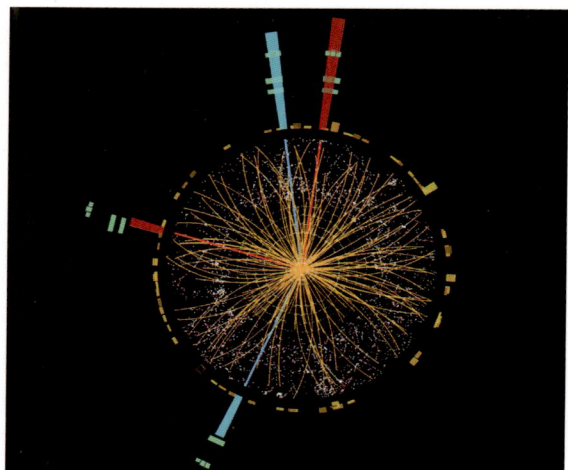

Detection of a Higgs boson event by the ATLAS experiment operating at the LHC in 2012. *Credit: CERN*

The international D0 Collaboration at Fermilab, with significant participation of Indian scientists. The Indian flag is displayed on the back wall. *Credit: Fermilab*

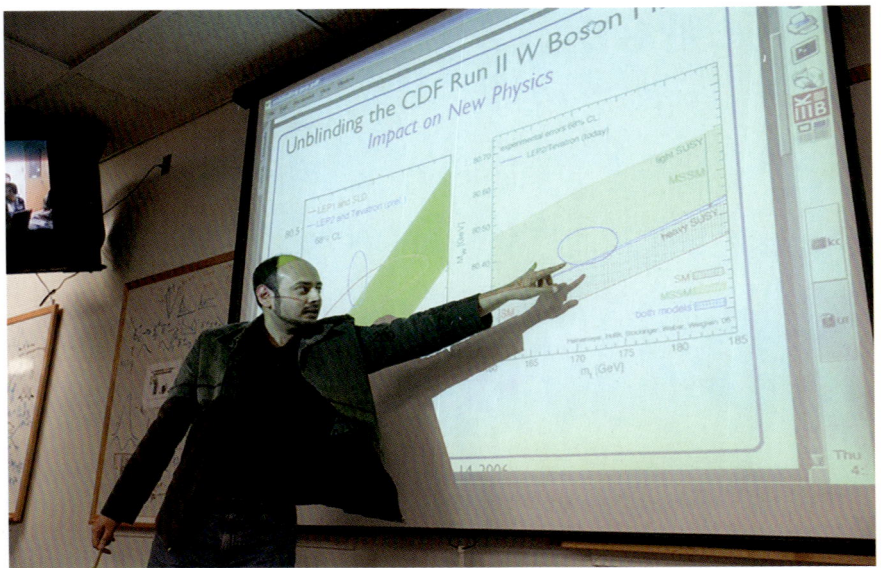

Ashutosh unveiling the W boson mass measurement to colleagues on December 14, 2006.
Credit: Fermilab.

Ashutosh with his PhD student Heather Gerberich.

Ashutosh relaxing at Fermilab.

Ashutosh next to Duke Chapel on the university campus.

Building 40 at CERN where Ashutosh conducts research. *Credit: CERN.*

Ashutosh, Ashwini and Gautam at the Hanuman Mandir at our Maval Shrushti Farmhouse in Kamshet, near Pune, 13 June 2022.

Ashutosh with Padma Shri Dr Govind Swarup FRS and Padma Bhushan Dr Vijay Bhatkar, before delivering a public lecture at Abasaheb Garware College, Pune, July 2011.

With Dr William Press, president of the American Association for Advancement of Science (AAAS), at the AAAS Fellow's Ceremony, February 2013.

With Padma Vibhushan Dr Raghunath Mashelkar FRS (centre), July 2011.

With US Congressman Dr William Foster, February 2015.

With US Senator Kay Hagan of North Carolina, May 2009.

Fritz London Professor Ashutosh at the Distinguished Professor Felicitation Ceremony with Ashwini, Jene Goshaw and senior distinguished professors Haiyan Gao and Robert Bryant, May 2014.

At the Distinguished Professor Felicitation Ceremony, Ashutosh with senior distinguished professors Alfred Goshaw, Daniel Gauthier, Berndt Mueller, Haiyan Gao and Horst Meyer, May 2014.

33

Ashutosh as Educator

As an assistant professor at Duke University, Ashutosh taught electronics for six years. Some of the students were physics majors and others were electrical engineering students. There are generally about fifteen students in a specialized class like this one.

Ashutosh's policy for teaching electronics was:

- To increase the insight of the students into the physics behind electronic circuits.
- To improve the mathematical and analytical abilities of the students while teaching them circuit analysis.

Electronics is generally seen as a handmaiden to technology; for the principles to imprint themselves deeply in the minds of the students, the principles explained in the class would be tried out in a weekly laboratory class.

He also taught classical mechanics and advanced mathematics at the postgraduate level. He had to study the subjects himself first. Simple harmonic motion in multiple dimensions, coupling and decoupling, were in themselves not difficult ideas, but the mathematics involved was formidable. Non-simple harmonic motion and non-linear motion were fascinating subjects. Classical mechanics does not bear much relation to particle physics directly but having to teach it meant that Ashutosh got the chance to study it deeply. Advanced mathematics is the language of physics.

Classical mechanics and advanced mathematics are central subjects for postgraduate studies. Two objectives have to be achieved:

- For a good grounding in classical mechanics, it is important to fully understand the principles behind the equations of the Lagrangian and the Hamiltonian formulations, which are even more powerful and insightful than Newton's laws of motion. Once these ideas have been internalized, quantum mechanics also becomes easier to understand.
- Once the mathematical base is solid, it helps the students achieve PhD-level theoretical thinking and analytical skills. Mastering mathematics makes it easier to understand how nature is thinking.

After this, for nine years, Ashutosh taught physics to undergraduate students who had taken the premedical curriculum. They intended to join medical school for postgraduate studies. To do so, physics was a required subject at the undergraduate level. These students were bright and hard-working but did not have a mathematics or physics background.

Teaching them physics was an important job. Ashutosh developed a different approach to engage these students. It was a difficult course, but many students did very well with his guidance.

In modern times, the electronics industry is in a constant state of churn. New technologies and ideas are implemented swiftly and older ones become outdated very soon. One has to work very hard to find one's feet and then keep one's place. To do that it is necessary to stay up to date with what has been invented, to have an innovative bent of mind and the ability to think out of the box. These were the qualities that Ashutosh sought to develop in his students.

It was for the first time at Duke University that the content of the electronics course in the physics department was highlighted. With the help of computers, circuit-design and simulation tools have become something of a habit with the students who follow this curriculum. This has increased the students' ability to innovate.

When Ashutosh was working on the DØ experiment at Fermilab, he had made much use of an electronics designing software called ORCAD. He had also used it to design the electronics calibration system for CDF. Having worked at the Thomas J. Watson Research Centre of IBM, he had a deep understanding of the way industry works. Ashutosh wanted to make sure his students were industry ready.

Thus, Ashutosh drew up a policy about how the electronics component would be incorporated into the physics syllabus at Duke. Each academic semester, the students have a project. As far as possible, they must show their independent contribution to the project. They are given homework and demonstrations that are designed to get them used to the technology so that they can design their own circuits. Ashutosh guides the students on the literature search, the choice of the circuit to be designed, and its analysis on the computer. They also write an abstract on how the circuit can be used. Their grade is based on the practicability of the circuit and the student's innovative thinking.

Increasing cooperation and coordination is an important goal, according to Ashutosh. Thus, his students work in pairs; they can either work on separate components of the circuit and then bring them together, or one can take responsibility for the design and the other can work on simulation. This is modelled on the work ethic of industrial enterprises. Students, therefore, experience a microcosm of real-world projects. In order to demonstrate this simulation, he uses software like CADENCE and ORCAD. To get permission to do this, he had to contact the makers of ORCAD.

Ashutosh's students have responded with enthusiasm. Some students have offered valuable suggestions about circuits that were given to them for practice. This bolsters Ashutosh's confidence in designing this course. With this new educational experience behind them, the students will find it easy to get employment in industry. And of course, there is the joy of learning something new.

Duke University is located in the Research Triangle Park which comprises the cities of Raleigh, Durham and Chapel Hill. This is a hot shop for America's electronics industry. There are 140 units here that employ 45,000 people. Ashutosh's students look to the Research Triangle Park as a place for summer jobs and for permanent employment afterwards. Ashutosh stays in touch with these companies, understanding their needs and tinkering with the curriculum to make sure his students can hit the ground running.

It is the practice in American universities that the students assess their teachers at the end of the year. These comments are kept anonymous. Talking about Ashutosh's electronics class, one of the students wrote: 'Professor Kotwal's knowledge of electronics is immense. He seems to know everything.'

Ashutosh has been working hard to bring high-energy physics into focus at Duke.

To do this it is necessary to convince the president of the university and other functionaries of the importance of the subject. He is also working on increasing the opportunities that undergraduate students have to do research on campus. Such research opportunities make the undergraduate college experience very special. For more than a decade, Ashutosh and the high-energy physics group have been mentoring six to ten undergraduates in ATLAS-based research every year. This activity is greatly appreciated by Duke, a university that provides generous funding for these undergraduates to travel to CERN during the summer, to experience the ATLAS experiment up close.

Ashutosh has invented a technique of combining artificial intelligence and electronic circuits for the purpose of performing an extremely challenging task—detecting the ephemeral traces of dark-matter production at the LHC within 25 nanoseconds (billionths of a second), which is the interval between beam collisions. Many groups have attempted to solve this tough problem, but to no avail. Ashutosh has published two papers describing this innovation, one of them in *Nature*, one of the two most prestigious scientific journals in the world.

Building this circuit is a project of great attraction to some very talented Duke undergraduates working under Ashutosh's guidance. His team of students started at seven and has grown to thirteen students, who will all be co-authors with Ashutosh on the next paper. These students are extremely excited to build these highly specialized circuits, which Ashutosh has designed to operate 10,000 times faster than modern computers. Ashutosh believes that the future belongs to today's students, and they should be part of projects that define the future from the very beginning.

There was no department of astronomy or astrophysics at Duke. When Ashutosh was director of High Energy Physics at Duke, he thought that the faculty should be enlarged and a high-profile astrophysics/cosmology experiment should be added to the Duke portfolio. He submitted this proposal to the US Department of Energy and it was accepted. One of his colleagues joined this experiment and Duke endorsed this initiative strongly by hiring two new faculty to pursue observational cosmology. The experiment is building a huge digital camera, with dimensions of 1.7 metres by 3 metres and 3 billion pixels, the largest ever constructed. It will scan the sky and gather an enormous number of precise images. Google has made a huge contribution towards this project.

This camera will provide opportunities for research projects of all kinds for students and will also increase the number of students taking physics at Duke. While physics will remain the priority, it will give rise to opportunities for students from other departments to use the information as well. These include computer science, statistics, optics, signal processing, atmospheric science and mathematics. The Department of Energy has chipped in with huge funding. This project will increase Duke's stature and add a dimension to the department's involvement in the field closest to Ashutosh's heart: particle physics.

Cosmology looks into the formation of the Milky Way and other galaxies, going back to the Big Bang. Particle physics also has much to say about the beginning of the universe and its subsequent evolution. Dark matter and supersymmetry, all of which will be studied by the LHC, are important subjects, and are closely connected with cosmology. This means that this dream project that Ashutosh envisages is an extraordinary one.

34

A Benevolent Teacher

In ancient India, under the Gurukul system, students would leave behind the warmth and love of their home, and go to live in their gurus' homes. The guru would then become the parent, teacher, guide and mentor to the child.

In the American system of education, the idea of the mentor is very important. The first duty of the guru is of course to impart knowledge to the student. But beyond this there is the individual dialogue into which the teacher and student must enter. The teacher seeks to understand the personality of the individual student. He who understands the strengths and weaknesses of the individual student's personality and using this knowledge leads the student to the path of success is a true mentor.

At Duke University, Ashutosh's work as a mentor has been strenuous and rewarding. He teaches students who are pursuing their doctorates. Heather Gerberich was his first doctoral student. She would help him in his research. She was intelligent and meticulous in her work. She wrote a fine PhD thesis under his guidance. Ashutosh encouraged and supported her in solving research-related problems.

Students must defend their theses. This is a process in which the student must prepare a presentation on their research and be ready for tricky questions from the faculty committee. Heather was nervous about this presentation and had built it into a bogeyman in her head.

Ashutosh prepped her for this encounter. He did a number of practice sessions with her. At each one, he raised the bar on the difficulty of the questions. Slowly, she began to get better at overcoming her nervousness. She knew her material well; it was just a matter of confidence in presenting that knowledge without fear.

Finally, after many sessions, Ashutosh's questions threw her from the frying pan into the fire. She was flummoxed. Ashutosh had been waiting for this moment of crisis. After she calmed down a little, he said in a sympathetic tone, 'Even if you answer half as well as you have done now, you will still achieve good success. Now mark my words, the real viva will be a breeze in comparison.'

Heather's PhD thesis defence truly went well. The committee congratulated her on a confident presentation. After that she left to do her post-doctoral work at the University of Illinois, Urbana-Champaign. Ashutosh learnt that she became an 'ustadon ki ustad' there. During her post-doctoral research, she conducted her own reviews and became a formidable presence on the review panels. Since then, she has developed a career as a data scientist in an information technology company.

Ravi Shekhar was a US student of Indian origin. He was very bright, diligent and excellent at software. He had joined Duke as a doctoral student but had to switch to the master's degree programme. But he was also possessed of a strong sense of perseverance and commitment. He was determined to acquire research and analysis skills. Ashutosh took him under his wing. Ashutosh would sit in the backyard of his home, watching over Gautam while discussing research for hours on end with Ravi on the phone. Ashutosh understood that it was a question of his future, and he wanted his student to experience the satisfaction of success.

Ravi was ready to participate in the research into the Higgs boson and write his master's thesis. Under Ashutosh's direction, he even published it. Ashutosh secured a grant for him. He sent him to Fermilab to work on the CDF experiment; Ravi excelled there. At this point, he had mastered the analytical skills that he was seeking.

Ravi had always been interested in the environment and earth sciences. The analytical skills he acquired at Fermilab stood him in good stead with the analysis of the data coming out of these fields. His skills at software and analytical thinking became his strong points. Ashutosh wrote a long and strong recommendation letter and Ravi got into the Yale PhD programme. When professors are entrusted with the duty of writing confidential recommendation letters, they must take into account the suitability and talent of the candidate they are recommending. They must be honest and objective. This is important to keep standards in the academic community at the highest levels in the US.

Ravi moved on to studying climate change, weather and geophysics. Ashutosh is sure that he will make a great contribution to the understanding of these world problems.

Christopher (Chris) Hays first came into contact with Ashutosh on the DØ experiment when Chris was Prof. Michael Tuts's doctoral student. Chris and Ashutosh worked together in the summer of 1997 on large-scale testing of the new electronics that Ashutosh had designed. Ashutosh then moved to Duke and the CDF experiment and was recruiting a post-doctoral researcher. By then Chris had completed his doctorate at Columbia and interviewed for this position with Ashutosh. Ashutosh is a good judge of talent. He spotted Chris's abilities before anyone else did and offered him the position.

Ashutosh's work on the mass of the W boson was in full swing at the time. Chris was not interested and so Ashutosh gave him freedom to choose his research topic. From his own experience, Ashutosh knew that one had to be really interested and dedicated in order to study the W boson. Chris began to search for a special kind of Higgs boson that has two units of electric charge. When Chris and Ashutosh wrote this paper, it was the first search paper published from CDF in the newly started Run 2 of the Tevatron. All eyes were on CDF and DØ at the time and the first results were much anticipated by the particle physics community worldwide. After that, their next paper was also greatly esteemed and praised.

Ashutosh had two Canadian doctoral students, Oliver Stelzer-Chilton and Ian Vollrath, for the W boson mass research. Observing their intense intellectual activity, Chris also developed a keen interest in the W boson mass. He began to work on it with all his might, plunging into the depths of its details. This brought him some good results.

Chris's work on the W boson took off and he got a job at Oxford University and now holds a permanent position there. He continued to work with Ashutosh on the CDF experiment. Later, he became the co-convener of the Electroweak physics group and also the Particle Searches group of the CDF experiment.

Starting with their work on CDF, Oliver has also been a successful mentee of Ashutosh's. He is now a senior scientist in particle physics at the Canadian national laboratory, TRIUMF. Their collaboration has continued on ATLAS, where they have written multiple papers together. Oliver has served as co-convener of the Particle Searches group on ATLAS.

Ashutosh sees this as part of his job: to encourage students and postdocs and bring out the best in them. He has had a 100 per cent successful track record in mentoring his post-doctoral associates, who are all well-placed in permanent positions in particle physics. Dr Bodhitha Jayatilaka, whose family is from Sri Lanka, worked with Ashutosh on the Higgs boson search at CDF and on the W boson and top-quark mass measurements. He received the Alvin Tollestrup Outstanding Postdoctoral Research Award from Fermilab in 2012. He is now a tenured scientist at Fermilab. Dr Shu Li was Ashutosh's first postdoc on the ATLAS experiment and worked with him on Higgs boson physics. He became co-convener of the Electroweak physics group and is now a tenure-track professor at the Shanghai Jiao Tong University and a Fellow of the

Tsung-Dao Lee Institute at the university. His most recent post-doctoral researcher, Dr Katherine Pachal, was co-convener of the supersymmetric long-lived particles group on ATLAS and is now a scientist at the Canadian TRIUMF laboratory for particle physics. His collaborations with them on CDF and ATLAS have continued since their advancement and they are still publishing research papers together.

༄

Dean's Leadership Award

In 2013, Duke University instituted the Dean's Leadership Award and Ashutosh was honoured by being its first recipient. As director of particle physics at Duke University, Ashutosh showed exceptional leadership skills with his colleagues and students. Many different departments and universities had to be kept in dialogue and this being done, it was a success. Seven faculty members, six post-doctoral scientists, seven doctoral students and ten undergraduate students were all involved. Thus, Ashutosh managed to get the undergraduate students at Duke University involved in research at the international ATLAS project at CERN, which is no mean feat. Dr Richard Brodhead, President of Duke University, said, 'I am honoured to present the first Dean's Leadership Award at Duke University to Professor Kotwal.'

Speaking on the occasion, Dean Laurie Patton said, 'I am in constant touch with Ashutosh. This [ATLAS] project which has involved graduate and undergraduate students and connected them up with ATLAS is one of great prestige. The students will never forget this experience and will tell their children and grandchildren stories about it. This is a golden moment in the history of Duke University.'

The Fritz London Chair

Fritz London (1900–1954) was a German–American theoretical physicist who was a professor at Duke University. His work on the quantum theory of chemical bonding and of intermolecular forces is still studied today. London co-authored the first paper providing the quantum mechanical explanation of the molecular bond in hydrogen molecules. He also published the first quantum mechanical explanation for how noble-gas atoms could be attracted to each other. This mechanism is now called the London dispersion force and is present between all molecules, and explains why every substance eventually becomes a liquid and solid at sufficiently low temperatures.

London's theories were useful in understanding the electromagnetic properties of superconductors. Fritz London was a recipient of the Lorentz Medal. John Bardeen, the only scientist to be awarded the Nobel Prize for Physics twice, gave his award money to Duke to set up the Fritz London Memorial Prize in low-temperature physics and to establish the Fritz London Memorial Lectures at Duke. Every year, a prominent lecturer is invited. Up to now, twenty Nobel laureates have delivered this lecture. Many of London's friends and well-wishers got together to contribute to establishing a chaired professorship in his name. This chair had been left vacant as there were no suitable candidates for a while. In 2014, the university announced that Ashutosh had been appointed to the Fritz London Chair as a Distinguished Professor of Physics. Goshaw was a strong supporter for Ashutosh to be named to this Chair.

We watched a video recording of this award ceremony when we visited Ashwini and Ashutosh in Chicago. Gautam gave us commentary on what Duke President Richard Brodhead said about Ashutosh. We were filled with pride.

WORDS OF ADULATION

Happy moments: Ashwini, Ashutosh, Aai, Gautam and Vijayrao

When a seventeen-year-old youth leaves home to travel to a strange land, what is he equipped with? His emotional state is likely to be very delicate and vulnerable. Even if one is intellectually gifted and endowed with self-confidence, one is not yet exposed to real-life experiences which make one mentally strong and mature. In the Author's Note and in the section, 'The Nest', I wrote about certain aspects of Ashutosh's mindset that I knew as a mother. Later, even while he was away, we were always keen to know about the development of his personality. He turned fifty as this book was being written. By this age, one generally becomes a complete person. I am now trying to take stock of certain aspects of his personality at this juncture.

35

In the Eyes of Others

Even as I took up the task of writing this book, I knew that some readers would assume that they would hear nothing but paeans of praise from a mother writing about her son. Throughout his educational career, since his childhood, we would always hear words of appreciation about Ashutosh and feel gratified. At various times, Ashutosh had to get recommendations from his teachers and others. They were unstinting in their praise. At the time of admission to US universities, a questionnaire is often sent with the admission form. Answers to these questions must be written as essays. It is an attempt to get to understand the student and assess their intellectual and mental abilities in a scientific manner. This was the first encounter that the US universities had with Ashutosh; he was at the time around sixteen years old. Many universities recognized his talent and invited him to study there and offered financial assistance.

The Green Card

In order to do his work, Ashutosh has to travel to many other countries. After the terrorist attacks on 11 September 2001 in the US, it became even more difficult to obtain citizenship. In June 2005, he had to go to Spain for a conference. The embassy of Spain was in Washington; Ashutosh then lived in North Carolina. Twice or thrice, he applied and did not get the visa. It was difficult to give up his work each time and travel to Washington DC. Each time, there would be a new reason for refusal, or they would ask for more information.

It was an unwritten rule that non-US scientists get their international visas in their countries of origin. This seems to have been the established practice. That was when Ashutosh decided that it was time he became a US citizen. In 2004, he and Ashwini applied for US citizenship. Gautam had been born there and so he was a natural-born US citizen. Ashwini had to go for an interview to Charlotte, North Carolina and she was soon granted citizenship. It took much more time in Ashutosh's case. As he had worked at national laboratories and travelled widely, perhaps the background checks had to be more stringent in his case. On 24 November 2008, he received a letter confirming his citizenship.

Before that, in 1999, he had decided to get a green card (permanent residency), for which he had to get recommendations from famous scientists. 'If the US is to keep its leading position in the world of particle physics, we need to keep scientists like Ashutosh in our country,' or so everyone said. The US Immigration Service expedited Ashutosh's green card as an 'outstanding professor or researcher'.

Ashutosh had worked with Professor Michael Tuts of Columbia University at the post-doctorate level. Prof. Tuts has led the DØ construction project for the Tevatron Run 2 and he has led the US contribution to the ATLAS construction project at CERN. He wrote about Ashutosh:

> Prof. Kotwal is one of the leading young researchers in experimental particle physics in this country. ... The research carried out by Prof. Kotwal on the DØ experiment focused on the most important precision measurement carried out by experimental groups at Fermilab, the measurement of the mass of the W boson. ... These precision measurements could reveal an inconsistency with the Standard Model, which would be one of the great scientific breakthroughs in the field of particle physics in the last decade.

Paul Grannis is a renowned professor of physics. In 1997, the Department of Energy recognized his work with an exceptional service award. He is a recipient of the W.K.H. Panofsky Prize, the highest prize for particle physics from the American Physical Society. For many years he led the DØ experiment at the Fermilab. In 1995, he found the top quark. Professor Grannis said about Ashutosh:

> Professor Kotwal is an internationally recognized researcher in the field of experimental elementary particle physics. ... Professor Kotwal has been responsible for developing new experimental detectors for improved measurements of particles produced in very high-energy collisions. He is a recognized expert in analogue and digital electronics. He has developed new electronics that will enable the energy-measuring calorimeter detectors to operate at 25 times the rate previously used. This project is a $4 million effort, and Kotwal's contributions were essential in making it a success.

> These developments are at the cutting edge of modern electronics capabilities and will enable much superior measurements in the next phase of the experiment. ... He is an excellent colleague, clear in his thinking and presentations of his work. He is a responsible and careful scientist whose ideas command respect. He has shown the capability to lead the work of others. He is recognized internationally as a leader in his field.

Dr Thomas Ferbel, professor of physics at the University of Rochester, served as the head of the LHC funds disbursement programme at the Department of Energy. Praising Ashutosh's path-breaking research, he said:

> He has made several important advances in this field, among which were his measurements of the mass of the W boson and of the proton and deuteron substructure. ... Dr Kotwal's works have been published in the most prestigious scientific journals, and the results have attracted world-wide attention and interest. ... He has had great impact on several important analyses and made remarkable progress. This can be attributed to Dr Kotwal's clear focus on the objectives, his enormous energy and his deep insight. Dr Kotwal's scientific strengths and his exceptional enthusiasm account for his success and point to a future leadership role in research programs that will expand our understanding of the fundamental properties of matter.

Ashutosh's leadership skills have impressed many people. Here is Prof. Dr Norbert Schmitz, Director of the Max Planck Institute for Physics in Germany, on the subject:

Dr Kotwal is an extremely talented young scientist with a bright intelligence and quick understanding of complicated contexts. He is inventive and finds solutions also to tricky problems. ... In his talks, he has demonstrated his special talent to explain complicated things in a clear and understandable way. ... He is a hard and devoted worker and feels responsible for the quality and correctness of his work. Due to his exceptional abilities, Dr Kotwal is very well qualified to take over leadership positions in science. Finally, he is a very pleasant and helpful person, so it has always been a pleasure to work with him.

Dr Hugh Montgomery led the DØ experiment and served as the associate director of research at Fermilab and the director of the Thomas Jefferson National Accelerator Laboratory. He had this to say about Ashutosh:

Dr Kotwal made seminal contributions to the fundamental measurement of the mass of the W intermediate vector boson. ... This quantity is one of about five which define the primary basis for physicists' attempts to describe the whole universe. ... As a result of his preeminence, Dr Kotwal was chosen to lead one of the five major analysis groups within the experiment. As such he was one of the few physicists among the many, who was setting the directions for the research and physics results from the experiment. ... As a colleague Dr Kotwal has a reputation as one of the hardest working, willing and helpful of people. He is particularly adept at conducting discussions of contentious technical issues with no posturing, whether those participating in the conversation are university professors or starting graduate students. His work is conducted with the highest standards of professional ethics. He is a credit to our field.

Ashutosh first met Dr Montgomery when he came to Fermilab during the summer of 1989, between his first and second year at Harvard, to build electronics for the E665 experiment. One evening, Ashutosh was walking back from the Fermilab main building to E665. Mont (this is how everyone, including his wife, referred to him) drove up and asked Ashutosh if he needed a ride to E665, since it was more than a mile away and Ashutosh did not drive back then. Mont asked him about Harvard and the E665 project. When Ashutosh relayed this conversation to a colleague at E665, he found out he had just gotten a ride from the leader of E665! Later, when Ashutosh joined E665 for full-time PhD research, he and Mont had many conversations. Mont was a great mentor, tough and demanding but also very supportive of hard work and creative ideas.

Once, Ashutosh had a debate with Mont on a theoretical point in quantum mechanics. Ashutosh had just studied quantum mechanics at Harvard and thought he knew his theory. Mont offered a different logic. A few days later, Ashutosh ran into Mont at the Fermilab cafeteria having breakfast. Professor Mark Strovink of the University of California, Berkeley, walked past and Mont told him about their debate, since it pertained to a proposed Fermilab experiment. Strovink had been the chair of the Fermilab Physics Advisory Committee (PAC) and was a well-known scientist. Referring to Ashutosh's argument, Strovink said, 'Nobody on the PAC thought about that argument.' After Strovink left, Mont said to Ashutosh, 'So you got some support there from Strovink.'

Ashutosh felt really good about the whole thing and got a big confidence boost. Many years later, Ashutosh realized that his logic was wrong and Mont's logic had been correct all along. But he let Ashutosh learn the correct logic for himself, and never insisted.

Ashutosh remembers many evenings spent discussing his PhD research with Mont. Later, when Ashutosh was nearing the completion of his PhD and interviewing for post-doctoral positions, he applied for the position with Professor Michael Tuts of Columbia University. He had heard great things about Prof. Tuts and the upgrade project he was leading on the DØ experiment. By this time, Mont was the co-leader of the DØ experiment, along with the founder Professor Paul Grannis of Stony Brook University.

Ashutosh had other postdoc offers and was trying to decide which offer to accept. Heidi Schellman told Ashutosh, '...plus, Tuts is good friends with Mont.' And so that settled it, Ashutosh accepted Michael Tuts' offer and joined DØ as a Columbia University postdoc.

It turned out that Michael Tuts had also obtained his PhD from Stony Brook University. Ashutosh's association with Grannis, Mont, Schellman and Tuts has continued to this day, even though he moved from DØ to the CDF experiment more than twenty years ago.

Leadership Qualities

In the sphere of research, Ashutosh has taken on many leadership roles. Right from being the chairman of the conveners of the DØ experiment to being CDF offline project co-leader, the chair of the Fermilab users executive committee, the US ATLAS physics advisor and the head of the future facilities group, he has done it all. All those working in high-energy physics tend to be highly talented individuals. Their working styles and personalities are likely to be different and very individualistic. Power struggles and ego clashes are common and discord is a very strong possibility. It is difficult to handle all these people and their egos to get work done specially when one has been given a leadership role.

But it is necessary when one is working at this level with scientists from all over the world to get everyone on the same page and to keep them there. The scientists participating in these experiments can be of different social, cultural and socio-economic backgrounds. To keep all these people motivated and headed in the same direction indubitably requires a certain amount of skill.

One aspect of this skill is to be able to communicate one's thoughts clearly and lucidly to others, which requires an understanding of the background and where the other person is coming from. From the time Ashutosh was a child, he has been a person of few words, which were very well received.

My principle as a parent was that one should not interfere with the basic nature of the child. Ashutosh by nature was a reserved person. On one side he prefers brevity of speech and still by dint of effort, he has become a good communicator. He has made sure that his own personality and personal choices have not become problematic in his career. He has had to make presentations at many international seminars. At his public lectures, we have experienced his ability to use language with dexterity and inventiveness. As a child and as a teenager, his reticence was thought of by many as a shortcoming and was pointed out in the context of his departure for America. I admire the finesse and self-confidence and grace with which he handled these judgements. Without submitting to social pressure, he fruitfully employs his linguistic abilities whenever he feels the need.

Most of Ashutosh's experiences with the Americans have been positive. Although he is not into self-promotion, he has been fortunate to meet people who have appreciated his work and his talent and who have been instrumental in helping him achieve his next goal.

One of these persons has had an exceptional role to play during Ashutosh's years as a professor, but it took him some time to recognize Ashutosh's talent.

Dr Nigel Lockyer has been the director of the Fermi National Accelerator Laboratory (Fermilab) for many years. After spending many years as professor of physics at UPenn, he left for Canada to become the director of TRIUMF, the Canadian national laboratory for nuclear and particle physics. He has made a deep study of accelerator technology.

He was a co-spokesperson and co-leader of the CDF experiment. In 1999, after completing his post-doctoral research at Columbia, Ashutosh joined Duke University as an assistant professor. Before this, his work on the DØ experiment had been remarkable. And yet at the beginning he was treated on CDF as an unwanted newbie. Various technical projects had already been apportioned when he joined the CDF experiment.

Thus, he did not initially get to work on a project that he liked. He spent some time being bounced around between groups.

Dr Lockyer's counterpart as co-spokesperson and co-leader of CDF was Prof. Al Goshaw who was professor of physics at Duke. It was he who recruited Ashutosh to Duke. Goshaw had a post-doctoral researcher as an assistant. He was working on a very important software project, but he was getting nowhere fast. Goshaw asked Ashutosh to take over the job of getting the postdoc to deliver the goods. Ashutosh did not have much experience with software and he wasn't even very interested in this new job. He had a solid background in hardware and had won many plaudits for his work there. But this software was of vital importance for the measurement of the mass of the W boson. And this was the sphere of activity to which Ashutosh wanted to devote his attention. In that spirit, he accepted this rather challenging role.

Ashutosh believes in the motto, 'Every problem is an opportunity in disguise.' To identify this opportunity and to turn the situation to one's own advantage is an important human skill which gives fulfilment to life. Ashutosh took over all the work that the other scientists had left behind. He studied the software and its problems with great intensity and depth. He offered the postdocs working under him a series of innovative suggestions and got the software going.

The new software was demonstrated to Nigel Lockyer and other scientists. There was a specific software application for identifying cosmic ray muons in the CDF experiment. There had been many software developed at CDF earlier for this purpose. The one developed by Ashutosh proved superior to all of them. It was therefore decided to use his software thereafter. Not only this, Ashutosh's postdoc Chris Hays was chosen as the leader of the team that developed all the software for measuring energies and directions of all charged particles produced in the collisions. Ashutosh was now looked at in a new light. Lockyer congratulated Ashutosh.

Then came 2002. The convener of the Electroweak physics group had to be appointed. Al Goshaw thought that Ashutosh should be appointed to this post.

Ashutosh had significant experience with electroweak physics analyses and understood the issues and priorities. He was also pleased with Ashutosh's performance with the software project.

In any experiment of this kind, the detector is the heart and the soul of the experiment. All the technical work was divided between the online project and the offline project. The online project handled all aspects of the detector hardware—maintenance and operations and getting the data recorded. The processing of the recorded data—calibrations, software and computing, were the domain of the offline project. Getting all this work done involves large numbers of scientists, working night and day, at full capacity.

Nigel Lockyer was the online leader. He disagreed with Al Goshaw's suggestion that Ashutosh be the convener of the Electroweak Group. Lockyer felt that Ashutosh should get his turn after two years. A tough discussion followed. It was decided that Ashutosh would become the convener of the Electroweak Group.

This is a post that lasts for two years. For three days each week, Ashutosh would come from Duke to Fermilab in Chicago to handle the work. In addition to the Electroweak group coordination, he continued working on the critical software. He was developing improvements in this software and making it work. Some of his innovations were novel and he published them with his postdoc Chris and PhD student Heather as co-authors. These innovations became the experiment's standard from then on.

His colleague Dr Pavel (Pasha) Murat was the Electroweak group co-convener and was a Fermilab-based scientist. One night in 2004, at 11, Ashutosh arrived at Fermilab from the Chicago airport. He had just flown in from Durham. He went to Pasha's office to discuss a few things that evening since the next three days were going to be busy. In the middle of their discussion, someone came into Pasha's office and said, 'Wow, my two favourite people are here!' And then this person took Ashutosh off to his office.

He had a proposal to make. Ashutosh's term as the convener of the Electroweak group was coming to an end and the post of the offline project leader was also vacant.

His understanding of the offline project work was indeed extraordinary. This the person knew full well. Ashutosh indicated that he was not averse to the idea and said, 'Talk to the others and let me know.' The answer came immediately. 'I've already done the talking and everyone has agreed happily. Now say yes, sign on the dotted line and you will be the offline project leader from this day on.'

That person was none other than Prof. Nigel Lockyer.

Between 2002 and 2004, Ashutosh's work on the mass of the W boson had picked up speed. The analysis was being led by Ashutosh. More and more data was being accumulated. Nigel Lockyer was eager to get some of the results published.

But Ashutosh was opposed to the idea of preliminary results since he wanted to be sure of his measurement. He held off Lockyer until December 2006. He wanted to be utterly certain that there were no errors, that everything had been double-checked, and only then an official announcement could be made.

Ashutosh's research profile was on the ascendance as the years passed. Nigel Lockyer became the director of the Fermilab. The American scientific community was intent on seizing centre stage in particle physics. Lockyer set up a specific post that would handle the physics proposal of the next big collider and the experiments that would be required. He got permission for this from the US Department of Energy.

Goshaw was very fond of Ashutosh. He wanted Ashutosh to take on more projects in the ATLAS experiment at CERN, Switzerland and earn the US more international plaudits. Again, there was a tug-of-war between them over Ashutosh. This time Nigel Lockyer wanted Ashutosh for this job and Ashutosh was appointed the first convener of the Very Large Hadron Collider project at Fermilab. Ashutosh was handed a challenging job by Lockyer, a job that almost looked like fighting and winning a huge war.

36

His Hidden Talent

Although Ashutosh is not in the habit of talking too much about his hobbies and pastimes, it might be interesting to discuss them briefly here because one can see, even in that, his single-mindedness and his enthusiasm.

Ashutosh enjoys and appreciates every form of art, be it natural or man-made, and wishes to understand them thoroughly. When he understands its magnificence and significance, he is overwhelmed and impressed.

But for many years, I felt that he was cold to one particular form of art. When he was in the mood to talk, he would begin a discussion with me with a well-chosen question; I would of course fall for it and pour my heart out. I have always had an attraction for art but his remarks would make me feel that he found my choices filled with unreal sentiment and showy language.

When I talk about the aspects of Ashutosh's personality, perhaps it would be natural for me to discuss the questions: 'What does he read? Who are his favourite authors?' I thought this would not yield much. I wondered if I would have to embroider the truth to demonstrate the versatility of his personality; so I asked him about his reading habits with some trepidation. I got a pleasant surprise.

I never saw him actually studying hard except for the time when he was at our dining table in Mumbai, studying for the IIT entrance examination. He would do the homework he was assigned from school, and that was all the studying he did. Nor did I ever see him buried in a book. There were Shakespeare's plays assigned for study in the tenth and twelfth grades. The day before the examination, he would wave the book at me and say mischievously, 'This is the first time I'm opening this book.' This was the Ashutosh I remember.

His letters from the US would mention books like Alex Haley's *Roots* and Mario Puzo's *The Godfather*, and it would occur to me that he was starting to relate more to human-interest stories. But when he went to Harvard, I was reading Erich Segal's *Love Story* and told him about it over the phone only to be greeted by a cold response. And so I was slightly suspicious of his opinions on books and literature. It did not seem to me that he had read much, and if he had, I had no reason to believe that it had made any impression on him at all.

But once he started talking (on the phone), he would leave both his father and me wonderstruck. In his childhood, his father had brought him many general knowledge books; he had a great liking for them. It was only at this time that I found out that he had also read the books I gave him, like the Panchatantra, Aesop's Fables, the Ramayana and the Mahabharata, stories of Chhatrapati Shivaji Maharaj and other great leaders, stories from the Upanishads and the Puranas. We read Tintin together, and on his own, he read Enid Blyton, Hardy Boys and The Three Investigators, followed by the mysteries of Agatha Christie (especially the Hercule Poirot series) and all of Arthur Conan Doyle's Sherlock Holmes mysteries.

At school, he had the opportunity to read Munshi Premchand's stories and novels, Bhagwaticharan Varma's *Chitralekha*, and he told us now of the effect these books had had on him. I still have his school workbooks. The answers to questions are concise and to the point; no excess.

He also told us that he would sit in the balcony of our Badhwar Park apartment in Colaba, Mumbai, which looked out over the Arabian Sea, and read *Gone with the Wind*. We had a large collection of P. G. Wodehouse and W. Somerset Maugham books, and he had read them all. He said that I had inspired him to read Wodehouse and my mother had inspired him to read Maugham. He and his grandmother read *Roots*, taking turns with it. At this time, I was busy with the multiple demands of teaching, the social life of the railway community, the elders and their health issues and such so I must not have noticed all his reading, or so I think.

Favourite Authors

Michael Crichton is someone I heard of around the year 2000, when Gautam was born. Ashutosh read him in 1979 or 1980 and liked his writing even then. He writes about important issues. His stories are set in the worlds of technology, medicine and engineering, but there are historical and societal issues buried in them. In one of his books, *The Great Train Robbery*, he describes the methods by which the heist was pulled off. Crichton conjures up the world of these daring robbers with accuracy as he does a great deal of research. The book also offers insights into the state of society at various economic strata in Victorian-era England. Ashutosh had read this book when it came out and enjoyed it tremendously. Ashutosh can still read a Crichton novel even today. He has reread *Congo* and *The Andromeda*

Strain. *Congo* tells the story of modern explorers going to Africa in search of a special type of diamond that has industrial applications. It is the story of the obstacles they faced, the hard work they put in, the intense rivalry, and the deaths of some. In the backdrop there is information about the culture of high-tech industry and the historical exploration of Africa by Europeans. *The Andromeda Strain* tells the story of the return of a space capsule sent into orbit. It brings back a crystal that kills through instantaneous blood clotting. When people begin to die, a laboratory that was already set up to investigate new life forms is used to quarantine the survivors and conduct research.

Since this is a science thriller, it would appeal to Ashutosh. But now his understanding is deeper and more holistic. Now he pays greater attention to the psychological make-up of the characters. He says, 'The people who will work in the laboratory are chosen on the basis of their psychological profiles as well as skills. Some are researchers from medicine, some from biology. One of them is a young male surgeon. So who chose him? And why? Because this man carries a great burden of responsibility. If anything goes wrong, he must detonate a nuclear bomb at the base of the laboratory, to eliminate any possibility of infection. This man must have the ability to make such decisions and to carry them out.'

Arthur Hailey is another author Ashutosh enjoyed reading. His novels, *Airport*, *Hotel*, *Final Diagnosis*, *Wheels* and *Moneychangers* are full of minute details on the way these institutions run, all based on meticulous research. However, Hailey never loses sight of the fact that these huge modern operations are handled by people. And so, he writes vividly about human interactions.

Frederick Forsyth and Jeffrey Archer were also favourite authors of Ashutosh in high school. As long as Ashutosh lived with us, I had the feeling that he was not interested in reading fiction because he believed that it dealt with some make-believe world. I believed that the study of English, psychology, economics and other humanities that Ashutosh encountered while at UPenn helped him develop a humanistic perspective and a deeper holistic understanding of society. He began to understand human reality better. And his reading has also developed in a more rounded manner.

It is also true, though, that I had not realized how much he had been reading before going to college. Perhaps this is what prepared him for the non-scientific part of his curriculum at UPenn.

Ashwini is also a voracious reader. She has introduced him to a number of other authors. He also enjoys legal thrillers by John Grisham. I reminded him of the authors of his childhood, the ones recommended by Indutai. He said, 'Indutai led me to "The Happy Prince", a story I liked very much. I didn't understand all of her other stories, but my interest was piqued. So I read Thomas Hardy and Somerset Maugham's *Of Human Bondage*, *The Razor's Edge*, *The Painted Veil* and all his short stories. I read A.J. Cronin's *Hatter's Castle* and *The Judas Tree* and realized that Gulzar's film *Mausam* was based on the latter. Of course, the ending has been changed and made a happy one to fit with the expectation of Hindi cinema's audience.' *The Judas Tree* has a legend attached to its name. Judas was a disciple and friend of Jesus. For thirty pieces of silver, he betrayed Jesus. He repented and tried to return the silver but it was refused. In despair, he supposedly hanged himself from a tree that bears his name. It is a leafy tree, which grows all across Asia in large numbers. In the spring, it is rich with purple-pink flowers. Maugham and Hardy were English, whereas Cronin was Scottish and Oscar Wilde Irish.

Ashutosh also read the short stories of Anton Chekhov and William Sydney Porter (aka O. Henry). These authors deal with the universal subjects of human strength and weakness. Their stories are based on human fallibility. Their characters feel themselves to be defeated by circumstance; they have no support in the world or so they feel. An exception, Ashutosh found, was in Maugham's *Of Human Bondage*. The protagonist is born with a club foot and every night, he prays for release from his disability. It is an article of his faith that the Divine can do this. But not relying on the Divine alone, he completes his education and becomes a successful doctor. His club foot is never taken from him, but his faith gives his life direction and meaning. This novel was an illumination for Ashutosh.

When Ashutosh came of age to read literature, Hindi cinema was dominated by the figure of Amitabh Bachchan, the angry young man. Simultaneously, it seemed that society was seized with the notion that one must fight one's way out of the 'fell clutch of circumstance'. At around the same time, the figure of the rebel who fought society was taking shape in American literature. This literature had a deep impact on Ashutosh, these are still the books he turns to today. He gets a great deal of pleasure from reading books that have a huge canvas on which universal themes are played out and the human spirit is always valued. When he takes Gautam to the library for his schoolwork or otherwise, as he believes that the library habit is a good one for a child to inculcate, he is always drawn to the literature section.

The Hemingway Effect

Ashutosh has always been deeply influenced by Ernest Hemingway, an author who can pull off the alchemical magic of creating mysterious lives run by their own principles with the fewest words.

Ashutosh once told me that the following quote has been attributed to Hemingway, 'There is nothing to writing. All you do is sit down at a typewriter and bleed.' He may have never said it, but it's in his style.

Ashutosh added, '*The Old Man and the Sea* is a book that offers timeless encouragement. The book takes you beyond defeat, despair and discouragement. It is a hymn to the human spirit. It is only one hundred and twenty-five pages, not an excess word but something to treasure for a lifetime, the story of a pitched four-day battle between a seventy-five-year-old fisherman and a fifteen hundred-pound fish. Over those days, they put their lives on the line, and they begin a dialogue with each other. It is a mental battle, but each is respectful of the opponent. Eventually, the old man wins the battle. He draws the fish in, but he is full of respect for his fallen enemy. He wants to take him home with full honours. But on the way, the sharks are waiting. The old man manages to kill one of the sharks with his harpoon but in the process, he loses his harpoon. And then the sharks begin to feed, taking forty to fifty pounds of the fish's flesh with them. He fights the sharks with his knife. The knife breaks. Now he does battle with the sharks using whatever he has, his hooks for instance. When his weapons are lost, the sharks take over and dispose of most of the fish. Just one big skeleton is left when the old man reaches the shore! He pulls the boat ashore and sleeps the sleep of the just. The neighbours are in a ferment. The parents of a little boy say, "He isn't a good fisherman." The little boy shouts, "I want to go fishing with him the next time he goes out."'

Ashutosh loves the fisherman's famous thought: 'But man is not made for defeat. A man can be destroyed but not defeated.'

Ashutosh also enjoyed reading about Hemingway's personal life, which was colourful and exciting: fishing expeditions in Cuba, living in the African wilds in a tent and going out big game hunting, travelling through Italy as an ambulance driver during the First World War and as a war correspondent in Europe during the Second World War … all this seemed thrilling to him.

In Paris, Hemingway would meet with his artist and writer friends at his favourite bar. These meetings came to an end when Paris fell and the Vichy Government took over. When the two armies of the Allies liberated the city, Hemingway sauntered back to the bar. The bar was called something like Coronation, Independence or Revolution, but I can't remember. I said this to Ashutosh and he said, 'When Hemingway was writing *A Farewell to Arms*, the end was not going the way he wanted. Hemingway estimated that he wrote and tried out thirty-nine different endings. Later, research revealed that the actual count was more like forty-seven endings. His friend F. Scott Fitzgerald suggested an ending too. None of the endings were cheerful.'

In 2014, Vijayrao and I went to Chicago. I do a lot of reading when I am there. Gautam asked me to read *Holes* by Louis Sachar and discuss it with him. However, when he asked me to read *The Lord of the Rings*, I did not have the courage. I revisited *To Kill a Mockingbird* by Harper Lee. I was re-reading Bhalchandra Nemade's *Kosala,* and in that wake, told Ashutosh to get me J.D. Salinger's *The Catcher in the Rye*. Ashutosh also read it and felt that this was a very different book.

It has the status of a cult book in the history of US literature for its depiction of a teenager, whose alienation and angst cause him to reject the superficiality of the society he sees around him. Writing a book like this is always a gamble. Ashutosh explained the title to me. The rye is growing all around, deep and rich and high. The children are unaware of the dangers that surround them. The catcher stands in the middle of the rye; he is there to warn the children, to catch them before they fall off a cliff. The young man feels he is the catcher in the rye. He detests the hypocritical way that adults behave, the way they talk. Children need to be children, they need to be allowed to grow up at their own pace.

This young narrator finds it difficult to stay in any one school. His parents are tired of him. He is sixteen and tells his ten-year-old sister that he wants to live away from society, in the hills. He loves his sister and expects her to understand him.

His sister gives him the money she has saved up for Christmas. The young man is in a state of upheaval; through the medium of his sister, he begins to develop a relationship with the adult world. His desire to run away to the jungle or leave home dissipates when his sister insists on accompanying him. She is well-adjusted in society, very bright and on the path to success. But she is willing to give it all up to accompany him. He is not the catcher; he is one of the children playing in the rye. It is his sister who is the catcher.

Ashutosh enjoyed this realistic description of the tumult of a teenage mind.

Through the narrator's experiences, Salinger makes a number of insightful observations. This is about as much as Ashutosh said about his reading; however, when he manages it and how he retains the details is still a mystery to me.

I am often up late into the night, and from his study, I hear the sound of the television playing. When I put my head around the door, he will be hard at work on something serious and on the television will be a film like Schwarzenegger's *Terminator* or a Bear Grylls documentary on Discovery channel, or even an Amitabh Bachchan film where the dishoom-dishoom is interspersed with dialogue-baazi.

Ashutosh does not read Marathi literature but all three of them—Ashwini, Ashutosh and Gautam—can read and speak

Marathi well. It is true that after the eleventh and twelfth standard, Ashutosh began to read less Marathi and Hindi, and the influence of English increased. But until that time, he enjoyed reading Marathi and Hindi as well as English.

Having read, enjoyed, and imbibed hundreds of books, wisdom lies behind Ashutosh's composure.

37

Ashutosh and Indian Scientific Organizations

Here I would like to mention that each time Ashutosh has come back to India since 1994, he has made presentations on the new developments in research on particle physics at TIFR, Inter-University Centre for Astronomy and Astrophysics (IUCAA) and the University of Pune.

Dr Naba Kumar Mondal and Dr Shashi Dugad and some other scientists of TIFR, Mumbai, would travel to Fermilab and CERN to conduct experiments. Dr Mondal and Ashutosh were in constant contact. Whenever Ashutosh came to India, Dr Mondal would expressly invite him to deliver a lecture on the latest developments in the field.

This was also true of IUCAA, Pune. In 2006, he was introduced to Dr Jayant Narlikar. Doctorsaheb and his wife, Mangalatai, and Ashutosh had a long and free-flowing conversation. Ashutosh gave two lectures at IUCAA and the University of Pune.

In December 2008, a particle physics conference at Varanasi was convened by the Government of India's Department of Atomic Energy. Ashutosh was invited to deliver the keynote address at this high-level conference, which was attended by 300 scientists, many from abroad. Ashutosh described the search for the Higgs boson. He shared the new measurements of the masses of the top quark and the W boson. He chaired the conference sessions that were discussing the research done at the LHC.

Dr Narendra Dadhich, the then director of IUCAA, arranged for him to give a lecture there when he returned to Pune and, afterwards, took him out to dinner. Two other senior Indian scientists, Vijayrao, and I were also present. I will always remember how these senior scientists asked Ashutosh many questions and listened to his answers attentively.

Ashutosh's public lecture at the Abasaheb Garware Sabhagriha in Pune in 2011 was a huge success. Respected intellectuals like Dr Govind Swaroop and Dr Vijay Bhatkar were among those present. Dr Raghunath Mashelkar and Ashutosh had a special appointment at which they talked extensively. He also met with the directors of IISER and the National Chemical Laboratory (NCL) in Pune; he presented a seminar at IISER. NCL scientists also attended the seminar. At this meeting, the idea of a collaboration between IISER, NCL and Duke University came up. The possibility that the scientists of IISER and NCL might work on a new sensor for particle physics experiments was proposed.

Ashutosh expects India will be able to produce such materials that will not change their inherent structure when exposed to intense radiation. In the coming decades, the intensity of particle beams is going to increase thirty-fold and hence there is a need for new particle sensors that remain immune to the increased radiation.

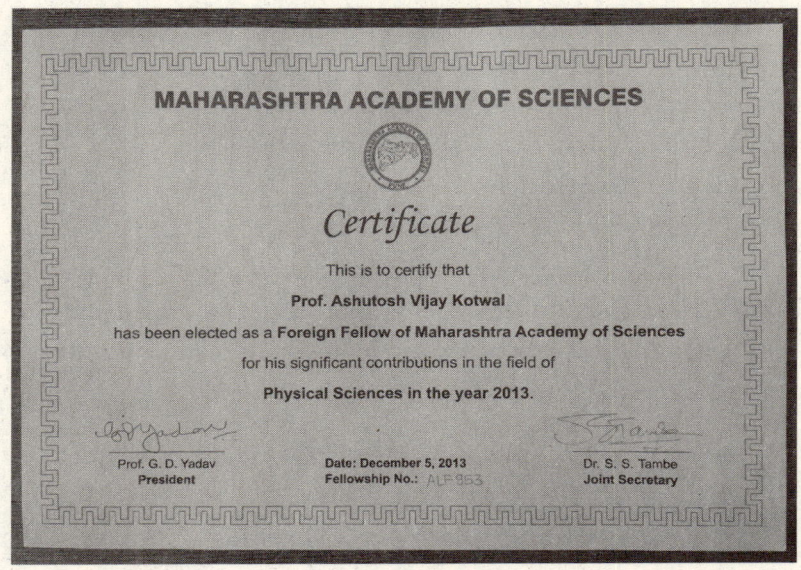

The sensors that we have up to this point may prove incapable of keeping up.

It will not only be in particle physics but wherever there is intense radiation that these sensors will find use. Silicon sensor technology is very highly developed. But the silicon crystal's structure and conduction characteristics may slowly prove inadequate, though they are still working well. What Ashutosh is looking for is a similar material with a greater ability to work with higher levels of radiation. It is important to do a lot of research on this topic. Ashutosh feels that the scientists of IISER would be able to develop such materials that would stand up to this requirement.

What we call sapphire is actually a crystalline form of aluminium oxide. It is, of course, found in nature but can also be made artificially. When Ashutosh presented a seminar at IISER, with scientists from NCL also present, he discussed his idea of using sapphire as the substrate for sensors and integrated circuits.

Between 2024 and 2027, the LHC will be upgraded for much higher intensity. It will take more time to investigate the properties of the sapphire crystal to see if it will work for particle sensor applications. But there is enough time before the VLHC starts operating for this research to be conducted. Indian institutions like BARC have the research and development infrastructure. RRCAT in Indore, BARC in Mumbai, VECC in Kolkata and the Inter-University Accelerator Centre in New Delhi have tied up with Fermilab to collaborate on superconducting acceleration science and technology and in the research and development of superconducting materials.

Atomic Energy and Thorium

The question of India's energy production is a vital issue. The use of fossil fuels must be reduced to reverse climate change and to protect the environment. In the next hundred years, atomic energy, wind and solar energy are going to be the next big options. India has the largest reserves of thorium though we have little to no uranium. For thorium to be used to generate atomic energy, special reactors have to be built. The other option is to use a proton beam to induce fission in thorium. The second option has the advantage of being able to control the nuclear chain reaction by manipulating the proton beam, whose source remains outside the reactor.

There is economic support available to set up such a proton accelerator, with the benefit that it has applications in particle physics research. An added benefit is that such research invariably contributes to industrial progress. Another significant point is that in the generation of atomic energy, production of highly radioactive waste is inevitable. Disposing of this waste safely is a big issue. The proton beam can make the disposal easier by nuclear transmutation of the waste.

There is much research being conducted in China on atomic energy generated by proton beams, which are called accelerator-driven systems. We need to start similar programmes in India for this might be the answer to the nation's power needs; and once those are met, there will be long-term benefits in both the industrial sector and in the social space. The government must step forward to offer support and encouragement to such research so that our international role may be enhanced. Such initiatives also accelerate the development of ancillary technologies such as large-scale computing and silicon integrated-circuit technology. We need to create the kind of opportunities and work culture that will attract talented young people, who are now looking for jobs in the US, to study and work in India.

The Importance of Analytical Ability

Here, Ashutosh offers an out-of-the-box idea.

Students who went to the US had to spend some time understanding the American way of life, as indeed Ashutosh had to. These students had to face some challenges and had a certain amount of struggle, but when they found their feet, the doors to economic success began to open for them. These students have got the best of both educational worlds. And their children, in turn, born and brought up there, have had the benefit of an educational system that emphasizes the need for analytical ability. If those young people could come to India and work here, the results would be interesting.

This 'analytical ability' is of great importance in this day and age. In large companies, crunching data is of prime importance. In the US, this is a sunrise industry. Duke University has begun to teach courses in big data analysis. There is a great demand for this kind of skill. When students or scientists actually start working, right now, they learn by experience. Particle physics is one field where students get exposure to big data analysis. Astrophysics, cosmology and climatology also have great masses of data that are challenging to analyse. There is a great demand for those who can do data analysis in the industrial sector, the atomic sector, national security, the medical field, etc. When data analysis is carried out in the appropriate manner and with the correct tools, problems can be clearly identified and pursued. This is a field that is not taught in India, no examinations are conducted in it, but when you study particle physics, this is integral to the learning process.

In this age of globalization, young Indians are coming out of their cocoons and taking their place on the international stage. This is a matter of great pride for us. A great national asset is this young generation's talent and hard work, its assiduous nature and its ability to handle huge challenges. Ashutosh feels that this must be allowed to continue without hindrance.

Love for Motherland

It gives me great pride to know that Ashutosh has become a scientist of some standing. But it gives me even greater pride to know that he has become a good person.

Ashutosh left his homeland when he was quite young. He arrived in a world that he knew very little about; he was a stranger in a strange land but by degrees, he settled down and made a place for himself. He has internalized their style of education and their work ethic. But he has not lost touch with his roots. He has always been concerned with the development of his motherland and draws from its philosophies; to me these are also marks of a good person.

'Will Ashutosh return to India? And if so, when?' we are often asked. Neither his father nor I have ever asked him to come home. This decision will always be his and Ashwini's to make. We never discuss this. But we know quite well that his career and its successes are all linked to his being there. Without making a big thing of it, I can say quite honestly that while I know how much he admires the lifestyle and the educational and research atmosphere of the US, it is not as if he would find it difficult to work in India. However, the kind of work he does and the level he has reached make it inevitable that he should live in the US.

On the other hand, I can often see that the two of them consider the possibility of coming back to India, to live in Pune or Mumbai. To this end, Ashutosh did make some inquiries in Pune. He has made arrangements for a nice plot of land and an elegant apartment in good locations. Through these investments, one could say that one gets a glimpse of their long-term thinking for their personal connection with India. They were guided in these decisions by Deepak Phene, Ashwini's father.

These are topics of personal interest. But when he speaks about the topics he feels strongly about, such as science and its impact on society, specifically on Indian society and the emergent younger generation, all considerations of personal interest fall away and one can see the depth of his intensity.

The US's Science Campaign

Ashutosh has been witness to the way in which the US has launched an outreach campaign, almost a movement, to popularize science and the scientific temperament. This is an attempt to reach all sections of society to increase their awareness of and information about science. It aims at dispelling some of the misconceptions about science and increasing people's liking for the subject.

One cannot expect everyone to be able to solve scientific problems. Nor can one expect them to know all the laws of science. But the outreach programme wants people to know that in every sphere of life, in every activity we undertake, there is some science involved. It seeks to remind us all that science arises in the human brain and that there is a deep and unbreakable relationship between science and culture, whether it is in artistic, social, political, philosophical or spiritual endeavours. It seeks to give science a human face. Ashutosh has seen that an intellectual encounter with science tends to give rise to a more thoughtful and intelligent citizen.

India and Science

Ashutosh has some observations to make in this matter. Science is always phrased in the language of mathematics. It is a language of concepts that are abstract. This idea of the abstract is an important part of the Indian culture and mindscape. Many important concepts in mathematics had their origin in India. Mathematical analysis, which is a vital part of much scientific investigation, is also a field that appeals to the Indian imagination. But he feels that in present times the difference between fundamental science and technology is not well understood in India.

He wonders whether we understand the difference between flights of the imagination and scientific truth. The history of science is based on reliable evidence that must be understandable and accessible to everyone. There is a particular discipline to working in science, which must be maintained rigorously. It is only then that the results generated take the form of scientific knowledge. Curiosity, experiments, observations, analysis and rationality are all the stages in the acquisition of such knowledge. Scientific analysis must be universal and objective. The personal experiences of a single person and any observations or conclusions made thereon cannot be considered scientific truth.

Science has no room for personal allegiances and subjectivity. An experiment conducted by one person should be replicable, i.e., other scientists should be able to do them and arrive at the same results. Then the conclusions drawn must seem logical and must be acceptable to the scientific community. These conclusions must also yield to statistical analysis and must be workable into a formula. There is no evidence of this kind of scientific tradition in Indian history.

Modern India has made great strides in technology. The success of the Mars Orbiter Mission, Mangalyaan, is an entirely Indian one. Our atomic bomb tests and missiles are all examples of technology, not of science. However, these are offered as examples of Indian successes in science. Indians are drawn to technology and have achieved many successes in this field; but today's technology is only the result of yesterday's science, science that has been around for the last fifty years. Ashutosh is not sure whether this difference is clear in the Indian mind. When there are advances in fundamental science, these may be transmuted into technology over time.

Fundamental science is complex, so many do not find it accessible. Since it does not have form, it is abstract, it is conceptual, and thus seen as unfathomable. But it is science that gives rise to the technology that we all know, which we can see, which we can use, which has form and shape. A society with no respect for science cannot progress. The need for freedom of thought and the space to question must be protected, and this must be something that everyone in society should be aware of. You cannot afford to ignore fundamental science to gain leadership in technology.

Indians are very proud of our achievements in the fields of atomic and space technology. These are often made much of on national platforms. They are sustained by huge government grants. But the smaller laboratories that might become the centres for excellence in fundamental science are ignored. These spaces should be encouraged because they are the centres where the upcoming generation can be challenged and drawn to science.

There is a huge inequality at work in the way the cities progress based on technology while rural India lags behind. Thus, the city exerts an irresistible magnetic pull on the rural young. In order to build a bright future, they feel they must go to the city.

This is where they will get a good education, good medical facilities, good entertainment and all the other necessities of life. This is why the cities end up overcrowded and slums proliferate.

The Growth and Improvement of Scientific Education

Ashutosh believes that the future lies in improving the quality of science education in our country. When the rural youth have equal access to scientific knowledge as the urban do, there will be a sea change in the countryside. The opportunities for employment will automatically increase; it will be possible to redirect some of the produce of the countryside to improve the condition of rural India instead of sending it all to the cities. There must be a multipronged approach to the improvement of scientific education in India:

- It is essential to uproot the blind faith and lack of scientific understanding that has been passed on from generation to generation.
- We will have to teach the young generation to look at their environment, both natural and man-made, with an objective eye.
- We will have to teach them how the world actually works. We will have to learn which of our actions will lead to the betterment of the world and which will not. Now is the right time to increase the number of opportunities in the field of science education and scientific employment. It is, therefore, of prime importance to choose the facilities that will be needed to make this happen. If done with rigour, it will be possible to generate employment opportunities in the villages. Those with merit in the younger generation can take the lead in this.

∽

India's Contribution to International Scientific Research

India has contributed 2 per cent to the construction of the LHC in terms of superconducting magnet technology. As an Indian, Ashutosh is proud of this. Even the most advanced nations have not contributed more than 10 per cent. And at TIFR and BARC, some components required in the accelerator construction were manufactured and supplied. Indian scientists from the Indian

Institute of Science (IISc), Bangalore; Delhi University; Punjab University; Variable Energy Cyclotron Centre (VECC), the Bose Institute, the Saha Institute of Nuclear Physics, all based out of Kolkata; Raja Ramanna Centre for Advanced Technology (RRCAT), Indore; the Indian Institutes of Technology; and the Indian Institute of Science Education and Research (IISER), Pune have all contributed to research at the LHC.

Globalization has helped collaboration between India and America in the field of information technology. Ashutosh believes that Americans are masters of economics, management and organization and have the ability to communicate effectively. But he thinks that the economy of the future also demands conceptual thinking and the perseverance required in design work. These qualities are well developed in the Indian mind. These are also important in the pursuit of scientific knowledge.

Ashutosh feels that successive Indian governments have shown an interest in encouraging fundamental science. Thus, there are more opportunities now than there were in the past. India seeks to be self-reliant, knowing that this will be beneficial in the future and that it will also help build the reputation of the country. A great change can be wrought if the younger generation begins to believe that they can do fundamental science while remaining in India and that they would earn enough money as well as some measure of respect and fame. Ashutosh says that if he had been a student in India today, he might not have thought it necessary to go to the US for further education.

He says that he is happy that some welcome changes have been made to the IIT curriculum. Students now receive some exposure to literature, sociology and the arts, subjects from the humanities that encourage them to think about the society and the country they live in and offer them a way to do so.

Ashutosh's experience leads him to believe that primary and middle school education in India is quite good but it is in higher education that we have a lot to learn from the US. America is a nation of immigrants. Coming from advanced European countries, these immigrants appreciated the importance of higher education. Many universities were immediately set up. The Founding Fathers understood that there should be a class of people who did not have to do daily operational work, who could instead think and write and read and discuss. They knew these people would provide the nation with direction and guidance. Many industrialists contribute significantly to the development and building of universities.

―∽―

Education, Agriculture and India

The Tatas are an example of a company that seems to have taken its cue from the American system. We need more affluent people to think in the same way. At Duke University, where Ashutosh is a professor, the Dukes were industrialists who established tobacco and electric power companies. They retired at fifty and gave a huge amount of their earnings to Duke and other educational institutions, as well as local communities.

Duke University has many departments including art, economics, literature, sociology, history, music, classical and other cultural studies as well as science, engineering, law and medical departments. Far-flung topics are studied at Duke and other US universities; for example, half of Sanskrit studies occur in India, but the other half takes place in the US.

There are many more universities in the US than there are in India. Some say that this is because Indian industrialists did not benefit from government policies. There may be a germ of truth in this, but it is not the only reason. The immigrants who founded America had fled repressive regimes; in the 'New Country' they were determined to set up a nation that was free. They wanted low taxes and small government. India, on the other hand, took its model from the British. It was only in 1990 that liberalization began. That, says Ashutosh, was the right moment for it.

He also says: 'For liberalization to succeed, the justice system must be strong. Otherwise we will not be able to reap all the benefits of liberalization. The Americans love to talk, and the number of lawyers there is huge. But this comes with the benefit that judicial decisions are made quickly; people receive extensive damages when they have suffered losses. This generates confidence for setting up new ventures. They have realized that it is best to do things right; they have faith in the judicial system. They know that it is better to earn money and use it well than to be underhanded in one's dealings. From this arises a discipline and doing business becomes easier. India can match the US but only if and when our justice system is strengthened. In parallel, education in high school must emphasize the development of creativity and the ability to analyse and think independently.'

Ashutosh has done a lot of thinking about the topic of analytical ability, and he offers some ideas. We will talk about them a little later. He has also offered some ideas about the Indian agriculture scenario. In the US, there is a lot of rain, so it is possible to have standing crops throughout the year. Due to our irregular and monsoon-dependent rainfall, much of our tillable ground lies fallow. Providing guidance and support to farmers is an old tradition in the US. Saving one's money, investing it and paying taxes are all part of the psyche there. It is not only a question of scientific temperament but the idea of the collective good; and so, laws, discipline, and collective thought, are all embedded in their psyche. Thus, Americans, even those who leave their place of origin, continue to think even two or three generations later: 'I have come here alone, there is no one to help me. I must do what I need to for me and my family to succeed.' This deeply ingrained idea focuses them on social discipline, which entails collective good.

Talking about the US economic depression, Ashutosh says that those who founded the US were clear thinkers. Saying that they were self-sacrificing would be going too far, but they did give their best. The generation that came after 1990 saw a great deal of prosperity. This was not a generation that had witnessed the World Wars, nor had they been through the fires of Cuba, Vietnam and Korea. And so they had little foresight. 'It is going well. Let's live on credit. Let's buy a big house. If you give up a job, there's always another. The economy is booming. What can go wrong?' These attitudes were shaken a little by the Iraq and Afghanistan wars. By that time, the loan brokers for easy money had already made their pie. People were in deep waters due to their greed, irrational exuberance and complacency, and the loan sharks were at their door for recovery of the dues. This economic depression gave everyone a reality check.

༄

Indian Constitution—Democracy

Ashutosh also has some views on the Indian Constitution and the Indian democratic system. Our Constitution is a fine document. In many ways, it resembles the Constitution of the US. But he maintains that the representative form of government has been beneficial to US citizens. At the time of elections, the citizenry investigates their choices with care, they ask them tough questions and only when they are satisfied do they elect them. So their representatives can make decisions aggressively. Our system causes the Prime Minister to be constrained while making decisions when there is a coalition government. Our democracy is far too complicated, and it needs a mature electorate to handle it.

The relationship between Russia and India has been a robust one in the past. In comparison, our closeness to the US is a new development. This may have an effect on our relationship with Russia. Ashutosh feels that any nation that becomes another's puppet eventually pays the price. 'India is a great nation and its Constitution is a magnificent document. We have a rich cultural heritage. Our people have great intellectual ability. India's position as one of the world's primary nations is independent of its friendship with Russia in the past and its friendship with America in the future.'

America has realized that it cannot remain for long as the world's only superpower. The US can see how China is catching up. China is aggressively buying up American debt. Thus, it would be beneficial for the US to have a robust relationship with India.

∽

India's Strengths

Our knowledge of English is an asset. It is possible for Indians to express many imaginative and creative ideas in it. In the next hundred years, the value of creative thinking in the fields of biotechnology, electronics, and pharmacy is going to increase. Thanks to our Constitution, democracy, language and culture, it is natural that there should be an affinity between the US and India. Compared to other places, it is easier for an Indian living in the US to preserve their 'Indianness'.

The US often praises the intellectual progress India is making. Now that India has managed a Mars mission and the nuclear tests without outside assistance, it has become clear that India has an impressive pool of intellectual talent. The Americans of Indian origin have been making waves in every sphere, and there is growing appreciation of their merit.

India's independent stance has helped the nation keep its head high in international relations. India also has to fight terrorism. Although it is very clear now that the roots of the problem are in Pakistan, India has dealt with its neighbour with rationality and intelligence. It would only be to India's advantage if there were a stable government in Pakistan and if democracy were to take deep roots there.

India has made a significant contribution to the LHC at CERN. Our scientists have also made remarkable contributions to the experiments being conducted in the US and Japan. In India, too, there have been great advances in research in the field of cosmic ray physics and neutrino physics and more projects are in the pipeline. There is much scope for the students of these organizations. These students write strong undergraduate, master's and doctoral theses and contribute significantly to the writing of papers. Indian students have a reputation for being talented and diligent; thus, many reputed universities welcome them to help them enhance their research. Many scientific projects in the US, especially those dealing with fundamental science, must bring in talent from across the globe. This gives Indian students a chance to show their skills on a world platform. It gives them great exposure and an opportunity to become part of an international campaign.

If the work on the LHC goes well, then there will be even greater opportunities in the Very Large Hadron Collider. Research and design of its construction will be at an extremely high level. There is an independent branch of knowledge called materials science that deals with the study of material properties. IISER Pune has a very good department of materials science. There is great scope for the professors and students of this department to help with the construction of the collider. Many fields will come into play including computer science, materials science, accelerator physics, sensor technology and electronics.

Ashutosh believes that if reputed universities like Delhi and Panjab University, IITs and IISERs and scientific institutions such as National Physical Laboratory (NPL), National Chemical Laboratory (NCL), Bhabha Atomic Research Centre (BARC), TIFR, IISc, RRCAT, SINP and others were to come together to enter into dialogue, good synergies will come from it.

38

Ashutosh's Reflections

Science is Ashutosh's passion. Science means the study of nature; science means the study of the principles that underlie nature; science means an analysis of how the systems of nature have evolved and how they are likely to evolve. Mathematics is inseparable from the study of science for the world of nature can be beautifully expressed in mathematical terms.

Science has another meaning. It has made a special role for itself in the development of mankind. Science develops best where there is freedom of thought and expression and where views may be freely exchanged. Thus, these two truly important human values get a fillip from science. It is only when flaws are found in earlier scientific hypotheses or models that new investigations begin. A great deal of mental energy must be expended on this. Scientists must be objective, keeping their personal opinions away from what they are studying. It is only through the rigorous exercise of this discipline that one gets clarity of thought. Over a period of time, without one even being aware of it, this begins to influence one's entire lifestyle. The study of science can give humankind the ability to see our lives in a wider perspective.

The production of scientific knowledge and the establishment of scientific laws require a great deal of accurate measurement. The first steps of this process involve the devising of instruments of measurement, the acquisition of knowledge of how to use such instruments, and then actually making those measurements. The next steps involve making sure these devices are error free; this is an even more difficult step. Only when these steps have been taken can real scientific knowledge be produced. This verified scientific knowledge raises one's confidence level, and one can begin to share this knowledge with others.

Modern thinking is based on science. Science concerns itself with bringing the unknown into the realm of the known. That we have so many miles to go, so many horizons to explore, keeps us humble.

Particle physics is the study of nature at its most elementary level. Ashutosh is often confronted with questions such as: Isn't the study of these conceptual and imperceptible particles just a chase after a will-o'-the-wisp? His reply: 'Certainly not. The entire world you see and feel around you is built of these particles. Everything from the atom to the human mind is made of these particles. These atoms and their molecules and their chemical characteristics are all dependent upon these particles.'

The applications to human life are also immense. Two concrete examples of the benefits of this technology include the nuclear power reactor and the positron emission tomography (PET) scanner. With the help of this scanner one can investigate the interior of the human anatomy with an unprecedented level of precision. This scanner can detect problems without invasive surgery. Radiation therapy and microchips, superconducting magnets, magnetic levitation ... behind all of them is the scientific pursuit of particle physics. In fact, the world wide web is a result of solving the need for massive data transfer in this field and was invented at CERN. Our daily life has changed dramatically thanks to the web. The digital age and our new tools of medical diagnosis stem from technologies developed in particle-physics experiments.

In the modern age, the citizens, especially the citizens of a democracy, must remain well informed. Science and the technology that it produces can give a society immense economic power, which empowers the political economy as well. The thread that runs between fields as diverse as atomic and electronic weaponry, communication technology, media, medical technology, computers and information technology and winds its way through business and industry and leads to political power is a convoluted one, but citizens who have a scientific temperament and are well informed will be able to figure out these connections.

Going further, humankind has always had an unending and fundamental curiosity about its own existence and its surroundings, and science has gradually found many answers to these questions. The first fundamental revolution in the human worldview was brought about by Galileo. He brought about a radical change in our collective thinking that we were at the centre of the universe. Three centuries later, in the twentieth century, thanks to the theory of relativity and quantum theory, our knowledge has penetrated from the subatomic to the cosmic levels. New perspectives are being generated on the meaning of human life.

This is a collective intellectual journey. In order to allow the layperson to participate in this intellectual journey, outreach programmes ought to be organized. It is necessary that more people take science as a career, and it is equally necessary that more people should try to understand what science is about, its basic principles and develop a scientific temperament.

This should be a collective movement. Ashutosh feels that everyone should know what influence science has on their lives. I have studied Hindustani classical music. I can see the link between music and science, specifically physics. Qualities such as measurement, simplicity, balance, beauty and grace apply in both physics and music.

Music appeals to the aesthetic sense of the listener when its elements of sonority and rhythm are in full play. These two are based on the physical principles of sound and time.

Ashutosh respects and enjoys music as much as he loves science. He pointed out that in the modern age, computers not only play music but also create new music. Computer programs can produce beautiful music and will no doubt generate their own cultural forms. It would not be wrong to say that the twenty-first century has generated a new music industry. Physicists have had a lot to do with the technology behind this industry.

I am saying all this to point out a simple fact: whether you choose your field for love or money, it will veer towards science, says Ashutosh. He feels that if the young generation gets the opportunity to understand the intellectual delight, the adventure and the excitement of science, and turn towards it, they will find that many unexpected doors will be thrown open and their lives will find a new direction. He tells many stories to illustrate this.

When globalization begins in industry, business or other economic activities, it soon becomes a talking point. But the fields of science including particle physics have always been globalized. Science surmounts barriers such as nationality, religion and lineage. For everyone, the focus is on the acquisition of knowledge.

Scientific research takes a huge investment in machinery, which many countries may not be able to afford. Similarly, different countries have different levels of knowledge and capability. Each country, therefore, brings to the table what it can. In this sense, science has been an international collaboration and cooperative across the world from the very beginning. Scientific knowledge has always been freely shared.

It was in school that Ashutosh began to develop an interest in physics. He found a huge intellectual excitement in the subject. Thus, he was drawn to the technology developed by microelectronics. He began to see the relationship between physics and electronics. He took a degree in electrical engineering with an emphasis on electronics. He was interested in economics and finance. Therefore, he took advantage of the double-degree option offered by UPenn and acquired a degree from the Wharton School as well. But at the postgraduate level, he turned to physics and now his entire focus is on particle physics.

It was his deep, abiding love that made him want to conduct research in the subject. He acknowledges that it might seem sentimental, but he still wants to say that in particle physics, you see a reflection of the thought of God. It is therefore a search for the ultimate truth. He believes that to study particle physics is to try and read the mind of the maker.

He saw his future as being part of the great ocean of research and knowledge. As far as his choice of workplace, the most important criterion was intellectual freedom. For him the most important thing was to be able to obsess over a question that was interesting to him even if it did not seem to yield an immediate use!

There are many branches of fundamental science. Both the study of nature and the study of society are incorporated in their scope. When you are studying different sciences, it is necessary to separate them. These divisions are based on the methodologies of the study. While explaining this to me, Ashutosh offered this summary which I liked very much and so have outlined below:

- Reductionist approach. Break things down to the smallest possible components and study those components.
- Complex-system approach or collective behaviour: The study of the interactions between large numbers of particles and the results of these interactions in big systems.

Particle physics is an example of the reductionist approach. It would not be possible to, say, study the forms and appearances of life or the systems of the brain using this approach. This is because when the billions of cells that constitute life come together, or the cells of the brain interact with each other, the system characteristics emerge. If one knows the characteristics of a single cell, one does not automatically know how the system will behave as a collective.

The particle physicist studies the characteristics of the particles that make up the atom. But when the atoms combine to form molecules, predicting the characteristics or behaviour of the molecules is not part of their remit.

In the complex systems approach, the emergent behaviour of collections of particles in the combined form is not necessarily just a reflection of the behaviour of the particles in the independent state.

Fundamental science thus has two clear frontiers. Or one might say that there are two roads to new, interesting and revolutionary science. Both the approaches mentioned above are important.

In the social sciences such as psychology, sociology and economics, it is the complex systems approach that takes precedence. In biology, the brain is a perfect example of a complex system where billions of neuron cells send messages to each other. In each cell, the nucleus contains the genetic information needed for the production of proteins. The neurons of the humblest worm, and the neurons of Einstein show no huge difference. The difference is in number and connectivity; the human brain has a hundred billion neurons, and each neuron makes 10,000 connections on average. Thus, the human brain can accomplish things that worms are incapable of. Imagination and creativity are the gifts of these billions of cells and their hundreds of trillions of interactions.

The human body is made up of a number of machines all working together. It is a machine that relies on its various organs carrying out their respective roles. How complex it would be to try and understand the entire body's functioning starting from individual cells. It would require countless equations to figure out the interactions of about 30 trillion cells in the human body. When neuroscientists or biologists make a deep study of this, they must use the complex systems approach. Although it is very different from the reductionist approach of particle physics, cutting-edge science happens here too.

Economics, too, uses the complex systems approach. Noted economist Adam Smith offered a theory. When people have to make choices, they make them in the simplest way possible. Each person's focus is on getting the best possible deal for themselves and for their family from their earnings. They allocate their earnings on the basis of their needs. Their labour is directed in order to maximize their earnings. Even though each individual is motivated by self-interest, the collective effect is to create an 'invisible hand', as Smith called this mechanism, by which the overall interest of the community is served best. This is the basic hypothesis on which the free market is based.

John Nash saw the shortcomings in Smith's theory and posited game theory application in economics. Nash thought it to be too idealistic. Every person does not exist in a cocoon in which their decisions are made in isolation; when people come together, they begin to interact and their decisions will depend on their knowledge of how others will make their decisions. This interdependence of everyone's decisions, according to Nash, was what Smith had left out of his theory.

One person cannot affect the economic behaviour of a society, but many people interacting with each other determines the economic behaviour of society. The Nash equilibrium is defined as the stable state of any interacting game between participants in which no participant has an incentive to change their position if no other participant changes their position.

In Smith's theory, the notion of the economy behaving like an interacting game of many participants did not play a central role. It is only in societies where such collective behaviour is negligible that Smith's theory works. Where game-style collective behaviour does operate, the opposite can happen; the Nash equilibrium may end up being detrimental to everyone's interests. For the economic system to remain strong and vibrant one must prevent such situations. This is the role of good government and a working system of justice. This means that to keep societies running smoothly, an external force is often necessary, so that the society does not get stuck in a poor Nash equilibrium.

It may so happen that the participants do not have the ability to do this themselves. From time to time, some extraordinarily talented person who has an independent way of thinking may happen along and increase the potential of the society. This person may set right an unpropitious turn that society has taken and set it on the high road to prosperity.

We have seen so far that the complex systems approach is used in neuroscience, biology, economics, etc. It is used in physics as well.

One example is the currently voguish nanotechnology. About thirty-five years ago, 60 atoms of carbon were bound up into a ball. When these are placed in a layer, a new hexagonal layered form of carbon called graphene is created which has entirely different properties.

Another experiment of a similar kind. When certain elements or compounds are cooled to very low temperatures, they begin to demonstrate superconductivity, meaning that they can conduct electric current without resistance. This collective phenomenon is so interesting that it has occupied physicists for more than a hundred years. It also has enormous practical applications. However, it takes significant effort and resources to keep temperatures this low in order to create superconductivity. Now experiments are underway to see if superconductivity can be induced at ordinary temperatures.

The two examples above were offered to explain the nature of collective behaviour or complex systems. Thus, we see how the two ways to study fundamental science, the reductionist approach and the complex systems approach, lead to an understanding of so many phenomena. One might reiterate that particle physics is one of the best examples of the reductionist approach.

From Ashutosh's analysis, I discovered the depth of his respect for and love of the knowledge system called science. He enjoys its maturity, its profundity, its comprehensiveness and, most of all, its honesty. To him, it is the field that brings scientists, technocrats and governance together. It is the space where those who are searching for the secrets of nature work together in harmony, accept the technological challenges therefrom, look for solutions and devise experimental methods to test them, all for just a glimpse of the Creator's mind. This is a project for all of humanity. The knowledge produced here will belong to all of humanity.

And as he grows more and more absorbed in this quest, it occurs to him that the human intellect is the greatest of all of the Creator's works for we are the only ones who can think about all this. Einstein's famous saying echoes often in his head: 'The eternal mystery of the world is its comprehensibility … the fact that it is comprehensible is a miracle.'

Epilogue

nature. Humans cannot reproduce every condition of nature; today it is not possible to invent a million trillion (10^{18}) GeV accelerator. At this energy level though, we may get proof of the unified theory and quantum gravity.

And yet humans will never cease the restless striving, the forward march on the path of discovery because we will be driven by insatiable curiosity and a sense of wonder. As the late eminent physicist Stephen Hawking said, humans live 'on a moderate-sized planet, orbiting around a very average star in the outer suburb of one among a hundred billion galaxies'. A group of such inspired physicists take it upon themselves to understand the vast expanse of the universe, its origin and its machinery. This pursuit of science is a magnificent story of our achievement and courage. The grit, the confidence and the zealous spirit of ours, we who are a minuscule part of the complete design, are awe-inspiring.

The journey of this field of endeavour is amazing; it looks into the heart of the extraordinary. Setting foot on this path can only be because of certain innate motivations. The first is irrepressible curiosity and the other is a rebellious spirit. One begins by accepting what one's elders and betters have hypothesized and discovered. But then the true scientist begins to look for the flaws in the argument, the limitations of the theory, the puzzles of the observed world. She seeks then to correct these errors, to expand the theory, or even overthrow it. This struggle, this fight, this constant endeavour to better what has been done before is the history of science.

When this dialectic began, it meant the end of Aristotle's view of the universe and the beginning of Galileo's 'modern science'. Newton said he stood on the shoulders of giants; his work followed Copernicus, Galileo and Kepler in order to understand the nature of the universe. The theories of motion and gravity provided the basic pillars on which the edifice of modern science was built. The unified theory of electricity and magnetism followed in the nineteenth century. In the twentieth century, the third scientific revolution expanded the horizons of science in all directions. Physicists like Galileo, Newton, Maxwell, Einstein, Bohr, Dirac and Feynman determined the path and the direction of the future of physics. This is the road that the physicists of the future must also tread. Each teacher hands over a flame of knowledge to the student who must take care to keep it alight and aloft. After a difficult apprenticeship, he works as a nishkaam karmayogi, he who does what he does from pure motivation with no thought of reward. But he has to have the support of society; he must have a government that understands the value of his work and nations that understand that the single-hearted pursuit of science must transcend narrow identity politics for scientists to work together under the banner of humanity. Only then can this journey be completed, and at some point in the future, we will be able to celebrate the goodness of human life.

This will happen, it is inevitable. That is because, after everything is said and done, humankind has one thing on its side. In the words of the poet Kusumagraj, who puts them as Columbus addressing the ocean:

Ananta aamuchi dhyeyasakti,
ananta ana aashaa,
Kinaara tula paamaraalaa!

(Boundless is our devotion to our goal,
limitless our aspirations
O poor little ocean, it is only you
Confined by your shores.)
So be it!
Amen
Tathasthu

Appendix I : Ashutosh V. Kotwal's Career

Professional Preparation

University of Pennsylvania, Moore School:

Bachelor of Science in Electrical Engineering, majoring in Microelectronics, Summa Cum Laude, 1988.

University of Pennsylvania, Wharton School:

Bachelor of Science in Economics, majoring in Finance, Summa Cum Laude, 1988.

Harvard University:

PhD in Experimental Particle Physics, 1995.

Appointments

2014–present: Fritz London Distinguished Professor of Physics, Duke University.

2012–2015: Associate Chair, Department of Physics, Duke University.

2010–2014: Professor of Physics, Duke University.

2005–2010: Associate Professor of Physics, Duke University.

1999–2005: Assistant Professor of Physics, Duke University.

1995–1998: Post-doctoral Research Associate in Physics, Columbia University.

Fellowships, Awards and Grants

ABP Maza Sanman Award from Chief Minister, Maharashtra, India, 2022.

Fellow of the Maharashtra Academy of Sciences, India, 2013.

Dean's Leadership Award, Duke University, 2013.

Co-recipient of the High Energy and Particle Physics Prize, European Physical Society, 2013.

Fellow of the American Association for the Advancement of Science, 2012.

Programme Director and Principal Investigator of Duke High Energy Physics, 2009-2015.

Fellow of the American Physical Society, 2008.

Alfred P. Sloan Foundation Fellow, 2000.

Department of Energy's Outstanding Junior Investigator Award, 2000.

Leadership Activities

US Physics Coordinator of Global Very High Energy Collider Project, 2014–2016.

Head of Future Collider Facilities Group, Fermi National Accelerator Laboratory (Fermilab), 2014–2016.

US ATLAS (LHC Experiment) Physics Advisor, 2013–2014.

Electroweak physics co-convenor, APS Division of Particles and Fields (DPF) community study for long-range planning, 2013.

Chair, Information Technology Advisory Committee, Duke University, 2012–2013.

Chair and Vice-Chair, DPF Nominations Committee, 2010–2011.

Chair, Fermilab Users Executive Committee, 2008–2009.

Co-leader, Collider Detector at Fermilab (CDF) Offline Analysis & Computing Project, 2004–2006.

Co-convenor of the CDF Electroweak Physics Group, 2002–2004.

Co-founder of the Tevatron Electroweak Working Group.

Co-leader of CDF Simulation Group, 2003–2004.

Co-convenor of DØ Experiment at Fermilab, Electroweak Physics group, 1997–1999.

Advisory and Review Committees

Standing Committee on Misconduct in Research, Duke University, 2019–2025.

Standing Committee on Conflict of Interest and Commitment, Duke University, 2019–2025.

DPF Nominations Committee, 2021.

External Evaluator for Natural Sciences & Engineering Research Council, Canada.

ATLAS Upgrade Physics Committee, 2013–2015.

US Department of Energy (DoE) Selection Committee Early Career Award, 2013.

ATLAS Forward Physics Upgrade Review Committee, 2012.

US–ATLAS Upgrade Review Committee, 2011–2012.

Information Technology Advisory Committee, Duke University, 2010–2013.

DoE Selection Committee, Outstanding Junior Investigator Award, 2008.

Fermilab Users Executive Committee, 2007–2009.

Joint DoE and National Science Foundation (NSF) Review Committee of US LHC Software and Computing Project, 2007.

Open Science Grid Council, 2004–2007.

Fermilab Collider Physics Task Force, 2005.

Reviewer, Physics Letters B and Physical Review Letters.

Reviewer, Research Proposals for US Department of Energy and Research Corporation, 2017.

External Evaluator for European Research Council, 2017, Academy of Finland and Portuguese Foundation of Science and Technology, 2013.

Conference and Workshop Organizations

Co-convenor, Workshop on *Probing Dark Matter at Very High Energy pp Colliders*, Fermilab, December 2015.

Co-convenor, Workshop on *Electroweak Phase Transition and Baryogenesis at Very High Energy pp Colliders*, University of Massachusetts, Amherst, September 2015.

Co-convenor, Workshop on *'Future of High Energy Physics'*, Hong Kong University of Science and Technology, January 2015.

Programme Committee, US–ATLAS Workshop, University of Washington, August 2014.

Organizer, Workshop on Electroweak Physics, DPF Study for Long Range Planning, Duke University, February 2013.

'Higgs and New Physics' Session Convenor, European Physical Society, July 2011.

Organizer, W Boson Mass Workshop at Fermilab, October 2010.

Chair, Programme & Organizing Committees, Fermilab Annual Users Conference, June 2009.

Co-convenor, Electroweak Physics Session, DPF Conference, July 2009.

Member, International Advisory Committee, Hadron Collider Physics Conference 2004–2008.

Chair, Hadron Collider Physics Symposium, Duke University, 2006.

Organizing Committee, Precision Electroweak Physics Workshop, Fermilab, 2004.

Co-convenor, Very Large Hadron Collider Group, Snowmass Workshop 2001.

Organizing Committee, Workshop on Monte Carlo Generator Physics for Run 2 at the Tevatron, 2001

Particle Physics Research Collaborations

The ATLAS collaboration, since 2010 (co-author of 1,257 publications)

The CDF collaboration, since 1999 (co-author of 436 publications)

The DØ collaboration, since 1995 (co-author of 137 publications)
The E665 collaboration, since 1990 (co-author of 8 publications)

Mentorship

PhD advisees: B. Cerio, H. Gerberich, E. LeBoulicaut, C. Pollard, S. Sen, Y. Zeng

Master's thesis advisees: C-H. Yeh, J. P. Tuttle, R. Shekhar

Post-doctoral advisees: C. P. Hays, B. Jayatilaka, S. Li, K. Pachal, N. Ribaric

Appendix 2: Research Interests of Dr Ashutosh Kotwal

Executive Summary

- Search for dark matter: The large amount of dark matter present in our and other galaxies is still unrecognizable except for the gravitational force it produces. How can we meld two fascinating ideas from technology and physics—use artificial intelligence incorporated in silicon-integrated circuits to see the footprints of dark matter production at the LHC.
- The deep significance of the mass of the W boson, the mediator of the weak force: Even after 125 years of its discovery in nuclear beta decay, the weak interaction continues to puzzle us. How the accurate measurement of the W boson mass influences the future direction of particle physics.
- The Higgs boson and the top quark that fit into the currently accepted Standard Model theory may not be the last word.

How to pursue the kaleidoscopic behaviour of the Higgs boson and the extremely massive top quark, which may unlock the secret of the excess of matter over antimatter in the universe?
- The importance of the theory of supersymmetry in getting a handle on the quantum theory of gravity.
- The quest for evidence of the grand unification of forces.

Description

Prof. Ashutosh Kotwal's research focuses on the physics of fundamental particles and forces at high energies. He was a key member of the team that discovered the Higgs boson at the Large Hadron Collider. The Higgs boson arises from a completely new mechanism, never before seen in nature, to impart mass to all elementary particles. While this discovery has solved a major fifty-year-old puzzle in fundamental physics, it has brought a new set of questions to the fore. How does this Higgs boson happen to have just the required properties? What is dark matter, how is it related to normal matter and how is it produced? Is there a connection between dark matter and the Higgs boson? Finally, why is there more matter than antimatter in the universe, when the experimentally tested theory of particle physics called the Standard Model predicts that there should be no such imbalance? Prof. Kotwal is pursuing these questions experimentally using two approaches—precision measurements of fundamental parameters, and direct searches for new particles and forces.

Prof. Kotwal was the US physics coordinator of a global effort to build a very large hadron collider of 100–200 TeV in collision energy, in a circular tunnel of 100–200 km in circumference. This project is about five times bigger and ten times higher in energy than the LHC. In connection with this responsibility, he has served as the head of the Future Collider Facilities Group at the Fermi National Accelerator Laboratory (Fermilab) in the US. He headed an international study group of 300 physicists producing quantitative physics publications on the discovery potential of this future collider, and developing detector concepts using futuristic technology. Europe, China, Japan and the United States have shown interest in hosting this huge collider. Prof. Kotwal coordinated this project with the leaders of US National Laboratories, the European CERN Laboratory and the Institute of High Energy Physics in China.

In his own research, Prof. Kotwal leads the world in measuring very precisely the mass of the W boson, which is sensitive to the quantum mechanical effects of new particles or forces. In particular it is directly connected to the mysterious properties of the Higgs boson. If the latter are derived from a new, super-strong force hiding at very small distances, the quantum fluctuations associated with this new force will be revealed in a measurable change in the W boson mass.

Using data from the CDF and DØ experiments at Fermilab, Prof. Kotwal has repeatedly published the world's best measurements of the W boson mass, each time with more data and improved techniques. Most recently he led his team to achieve a precision of 0.01 per cent, which is unprecedented. The arc of this research project and its significant implications are presented in Appendix 3.

Prof. Kotwal and his collaborators have also published the most precise measurements of the top quark mass in the dilepton channel. His latest measurement used, for the first time in particle physics, neural network algorithms based on biological evolution. This method showed how to solve certain optimization problems based on ensemble properties.

Prof. Kotwal developed improved techniques to search for the Standard Model Higgs boson. On the CDF experiment at Fermilab, he published three papers describing the search for the Higgs boson, each time using more advanced techniques. He used one of these techniques for the first time in the ATLAS experiment at the LHC to search for the Higgs boson in the vector boson fusion process.

Prof. Kotwal's research on the ATLAS experiment at the LHC is also motivated by the possibility of Higgs and top quark compositeness. He initiated a new idea to search for top quark constituents by looking for top-antitop resonances in events with four top quarks. In this project, he has been joined by colleagues from Harvard, France and Germany. He is also pursuing the vector boson fusion process as a method to measure important Higgs properties and to detect new particles in the Higgs sector, both providing incisive tests of an alternate theory of a composite Higgs boson which has constituents.

The second part of Prof. Kotwal's ATLAS research is motivated by dark matter, which was discovered on the galactic and cosmic scales via its gravitational interaction. If dark matter consists of particles, these may be produced from the decay of heavier, short-lived charged particles which in turn can be produced at the LHC. With his colleagues from Duke, Harvard and Genoa, Prof. Kotwal is searching for heavy short-lived charged particles using the silicon pixel detector. This work is closely aligned with Prof. Kotwal's expertise in particle tracking and efforts to improve tracking algorithms for ATLAS. His group is working to improve both the efficiency and speed of these algorithms so that such rare signatures can be recognized and separated at very high rates. This project is a key component of the LHC upgrades to collect vastly more data over the next two decades.

Prof. Kotwal has also worked with his students, post-docs and collaborators on searches for rare, exotic signatures of new interactions. He has published searches for charged and neutral gauge bosons mediating new weak forces, the Higgs boson in theories that extend the Standard Model, and excited states of Standard Model fermions. These particles are predicted in theories where the weak interaction has both left-handed and right-handed couplings (as indicated by neutrino oscillations), in supersymmetric theories which impose a fermion–boson duality, and in grand unification theories.

In the ATLAS experiment at the LHC, Prof. Kotwal has performed detailed studies of the silicon and transition radiation detectors. His students have published searches for new particles decaying to top quarks as well as Higgs boson measurements. He wrote the first three ATLAS papers on searches for heavy mediators of new forces that are predicted by grand-unification theories.

Prof. Kotwal has developed cutting-edge electronics for particle physics experiments. He built high-speed digital electronics for the E665 muon-scattering experiment, fast and very sensitive analogue amplifiers for the DØ experiment, and an ultrastable timing calibration system for the CDF experiment, all at Fermilab. Most recently, he has invented a technique of combining artificial intelligence and electronic circuits for identifying charged particles in the silicon sensors of the LHC experiments. These circuits can identify all high-momentum charged particles in real time, keeping pace with the 25 nanosecond interval between beam collisions, which is a hundred times faster than alternate approaches. Prof. Kotwal plans to use his invention to search for short-lived charged particles decaying to invisible particles such as dark matter.

In addition to his experimental research, Prof. Kotwal has done theoretical work in the phenomenology of black holes in extra-spatial dimensions. Extra-spatial dimensions have been motivated by string theory and to explain why the gravitational force is so much weaker than the electromagnetic force at large distances. In this scenario it is possible for the gravitational force to be strong in the high-energy regime of particle colliders, leading to the production of black holes. Prof. Kotwal has published a theoretical analysis of the production and decay of rotating black holes and their experimental signatures. Prof. Kotwal has also co-authored a paper on black hole relics, which are postulated to resolve the 'information paradox'—after the black hole evaporates by Hawking radiation, where is all the information swallowed by the black hole during its lifetime? The information may remain locked up in these black hole remnants.

Prof. Kotwal is heavily invested in mentoring young physicists. All his post-doctoral mentees have flourished in the field; Christopher Hays is on the faculty at Oxford University, Bodhitha Jayatilaka is a senior scientist at Fermilab, Shu Li is on the faculty at Shanghai Jiao-Tong University and Katherine Pachal is a scientist at TRIUMF, the Canadian national laboratory for particle physics. His students are well-placed in high-tech industries and in academics; Chris Pollard is on the faculty at the University of Warwick. In addition to this group of young physicists at Duke, he has mentored scores of students and postdocs in his various leadership roles in international collaborations.

Appendix 3: Upsetting the Standard Model of Physics

Ashutosh's paper titled 'High-precision measurement of the W boson mass with the CDF II detector' was published as the cover story in the world's most prestigious journal *Science* on 7 April 2022, brought out by the American Association for the Advancement of Science (AAAS). This measurement reveals the biggest crack ever observed in the Standard Model of physics.

The paper has generated worldwide attention. The Communications Office of the Fermi National Accelerator Laboratory (Fermilab) has estimated that this paper received 850 media mentions, reaching a potential readership of 1.6 billion people. It has been accessed 190,000 times and has a very high Altmetric score of 2940. According to the public archive of scientific papers, this paper received the maximum number of citations amongst all physics and astronomy research papers published in 2022.

Ashutosh and his team of 400 scientists at Fermilab had been working on the analysis of fundamental particles called W bosons produced at the Tevatron particle accelerator in the CDF II experiment for the last 10 years. In November 2020 at a meeting on zoom they decrypted the result on the mass of the W boson.

The result was a pleasant shock for everyone. Ashutosh and his team had worked till then on encrypted data so that the numbers should not influence their analysis. The central value and the uncertainty of the latest mass measurement is $80,433 \pm 9$ MeV/c^2, where c is the speed of light in vacuum and MeV represents million electron volts, a unit of energy. Compared to the predicted mass of $80,357 \pm 6$ MeV/c^2 from the Standard Model theory, it is nearly 77 MeV/c^2 higher. In the language of statistics, this disagreement has the significance of 7σ, meaning that the chance that this difference is a random statistical fluke is less than one in a billion. The scientific community conventionally accepts a significance of 5σ, or the chance of a fluke lower than one in 3.5 million, that the physicists must clear to claim a definitive discovery.

The new measurement of the W boson mass is the most precise measurement ever made of this fundamental quantity. It provides a rigorous test of the Standard Model (SM); a set of equations, developed between the 1940s and the '70s, that describe the basic building blocks and forces of nature. The SM has been one of the most important theories in all science. Over the last seventy years, of the 161 Nobel prizes awarded in all branches of physics, forty-nine of them, or 30 per cent of the prizes were awarded for contributions to the Standard Model of physics.

Ashutosh's measurement is significantly different from the theory. This could indicate a new principle at work in nature. The new measurement of the W boson mass is our biggest clue yet that we do not completely understand the weak nuclear force or all the particles that experience this force. This is reminiscent of a similar disagreement observed with classical physics a century ago—the observation of the atomic nucleus by Rutherford, which paved the way for the emergence of quantum mechanics and defined modern physics. Therefore, this upset to the Standard Model may well point towards exciting new discoveries in particle physics for years to come.

For the latest measurement, Ashutosh and his team used a large sample of 4 million W bosons collected during the entire CDF II run from 2002 till 2011. He used established techniques from previous analyses but more importantly, he developed many new analysis techniques that eventually paved the way for this discovery. He implemented new ideas to use the data in novel ways to calibrate his experimental apparatus much more precisely than in the past. He also incorporated new information about the colliding protons' structure that the particle physics community has collected over the decade. Importantly, the analysis procedure demonstrates several precise checks of internal consistency, which no other experiment has demonstrated at this level. The combination of a dataset four times larger, more insightful methods and new ideas of using the data, and new information about the proton structure improved the precision of this measurement substantially.

In this paper Ashutosh and his team have described fifteen new ideas or improved techniques which were developed over the last ten years, since their 2012 publication of the W boson mass. That measurement, which had an accuracy of 0.02 per cent, predicted the range of the mass of the Higgs boson before its discovery at the Large Hadron Collider (LHC) at CERN in Switzerland. In the latest publication of 2022, he has improved the accuracy by another factor of two, to an unprecedented 0.01 per cent.

There is another factor which led to a more precise measurement than all other previous measurements combined. Ashutosh devised a method of using cosmic rays to pin down the positions of 30,240 sensor wires, each within a precision of one micron. Cosmic-ray muons are produced in the upper atmosphere from collisions of high-energy protons and helium nuclei coming from outer space. These muons rain down and pass through a 3m×3m cylindrical particle-tracking detector in the CDF experiment. The high-precision sensor wires, placed at high voltage in the gaseous volume of this detector, record the passage of electrons and muons coming from the W boson decay. Ashutosh used the data from these sensors to measure the momentum of each electron and muon with an accuracy of 0.004 per cent.

Understanding such a large volume of data with extreme precision is always challenging. Every time the team was faced with a puzzle, Ashutosh's philosophy was to leave no stone unturned until the mystery was solved. The journey felt like a treasure hunt. The team was so focused on the precision and robustness of the analysis that the value itself of the W boson mass, when it was decrypted, was more like a wonderful shock. Not only is this new measurement much more precise than all other measurements but it also demonstrates rigorous consistency checks. For example, Ashutosh and his team also measure the Z boson mass in both electron and muon channels and find agreement with the Large Electron Positron (LEP) collider's measurement at CERN. No other measurement of the W boson mass has performed this consistency check.

Having so far talked about the importance of the W boson mass, let me introduce you to the special characteristics of this elusive entity. Of the basic principles that physicists use to describe the beginning of the Universe, the W boson is one of the most important. Understanding it and its behaviour is central to particle physics. It is a quantum-mechanical mediator of the weak force, one of the four known forces in nature. Even today the existence of the world is dependent on the W boson having a large mass. For example, the nuclear fusion of four protons into a helium nucleus is the reaction that powers the sun. The reaction requires the conversion of protons into neutrons by the weak force at just the right rate, which is possible because the W boson has a large mass. The W boson controls the Sun's energy output—slightly more or less and the Earth's surface would be fried or frozen. This is one of the most important aspects of the Universe that is crucial for our existence. Knowing it well proves useful in a host of other investigations in nuclear physics and astrophysics, such as the creation of all heavy elements, including gold. Furthermore, the radioactivity induced by the weak force releases enough energy in the Earth's mantle to keep the Earth's iron core molten, generating a magnetic shield that protects all life on Earth from lethal solar radiation. One could say that life on Earth depends on the W boson.

What new physics principles might explain the discrepancy between the SM theory and Ashutosh's measurement? A popular hypothesis amongst string theorists has been supersymmetry. To establish new physics like supersymmetry, it was necessary to measure the mass of the W boson with as high a degree of accuracy as possible. The value of the W boson mass in nature is influenced by yet-unknown particles through quantum fluctuations in the vacuum. All known particles, including top quarks and Higgs bosons are involved in this quantum foam. If supersymmetric particles exist, they will also participate in these fluctuations and cause an additional small change in the W boson mass. With the conjecture of supersymmetric particles, the predicted mass of the W boson could increase by up to 80 MeV/c^2 relative to the Standard Model theory prediction, depending upon the properties of the new particles.

Similar calculations have been performed assuming the existence of additional Higgs-like bosons, a fifth force, or dark-matter particles, which also change the W boson mass by a similar amount. These examples illustrate how the predicted mass of the W boson changes from theory to theory. The power of the W boson mass measurement arises from its ability to adjudicate between these different hypotheses, to pass judgment and select the one closer to the truth, so to speak. The more accurate the measurement, the closer to the truth one can hone in.

Thus, establishing the mass of the W boson with utmost accuracy and comparing it with predicted values from different theories is instrumental in going beyond the Standard Model and breaking ground for new physics. It would offer proof for or against what had been conceptualized around the interactions of particles and forces at the subnuclear level. The latest mass measurement motivates an extension of our conceptual understanding at the fundamental level.

Ashutosh has initiated and led the analyses to measure the W boson mass precisely in the CDF II experiment at Fermilab. Over the last twenty-seven years, he has published five world-leading measurements of the W boson mass. He has pursued this measurement over a longer period, and published more often, than anyone else in the world. The present measurement is the most significant deviation ever observed from a fundamental prediction of the Standard Model of physics.

One of the primary goals of the Tevatron Run 2 (1999–2011) was to perform a precise measurement of the W boson mass. Ashutosh's group developed and refined the techniques for performing precise calibrations of the CDF detector over the last two decades, starting in the early 2000's. In parallel, the criteria for selecting the data for analysis were tuned up. Thirdly, they wrote sophisticated simulation codes to incorporate the minute details of the experiment and known physics effects. Prior to the 2022 publication, CDF published W boson mass measurements in 2007 and 2012, using subsets of the complete dataset and using state-of-the-art analysis techniques at the time. The latest publication is the culmination of decades of experience in this fascinating area of fundamental research.

The data from the CDF II experiment has been fully analysed. Ashutosh is engaged in discussions with colleagues on other experiments, to see if he can come up with more ideas for improvement. In parallel, he hopes that the ideas he has published can help other experiments perform a similarly precise measurement of the W boson mass. The experiments at the LHC have collected and are continuing to collect a lot of data. Even though the W bosons at LHC are produced differently than the Tevatron (the LHC is a proton-proton collider while the Tevatron was a proton-antiproton collider), the LHC experiments have the opportunity to make this measurement. If a new electron-positron collider is built, it can measure the W boson mass even more precisely—confirmation of Ashutosh's measurement is one of the best justifications for this new collider. As the world expert, the prestigious journal *Nature* invited Ashutosh to write a detailed review article on the state of the art, which was featured as their cover story in March 2024.

The theoretical physics community is taking a close look at the calculations. They are already exploring extensions of the Standard Model, that could bring the theory in line with Ashutosh's measurement. These ideas could motivate a new round of experiments that would be sensitive to the new physics. Hunting for new particles is indeed an excellent method to follow up with.

The LHC as well as smaller, specialized experiments (e.g. the muon anomalous magnetic moment measurement) are sensitive to the kinds of new particles and interactions that can influence the W boson mass. If there is new physics which could explain the difference of this measurement from the SM expectation, then the new physics could show up directly in these experiments. Looking for rare processes or processes forbidden by the Standard Model could also provide additional evidence of new physics. A new electron-positron collider would enable ultra-precise measurements and searches for rare processes in a different environment than the proton-proton collisions at the LHC.

In parallel, Ashutosh is looking to the future. He is pursuing the hypothesis that dark matter consists of particles. According to certain extensions of Standard Model, such particles could be produced at the LHC. Since their signature would be incredibly fleeting, it is a technological challenge to capture the traces of exotic particles that disappear in a nanosecond into dark matter. Ashutosh is designing electronic circuits that could capture the fleeting images created by such processes. These circuits will perform the task of identifying dark-matter production hundreds of times faster than traditional computers. Ashutosh's idea is to embed artificial intelligence in the form of unsupervised machine learning directly into silicon chips. He has published three papers describing these ideas, the latest two in prestigious Nature journals. He is working with a team of eight students from computer science, engineering, mathematics, and physics on this design project—the construction of a prototype is imminent. This device will be a breakthrough in ultra-fast, real-time computer vision, a leading area of research in artificial intelligence.

Additional Sources

Dr V.G. Bhide, *Basic Interactions and Fundamental Forces of Nature*, (Shekhar Phatak & Associates, 1998)

Brian Green, *The Elegant Universe*, (Vintage Books, 2000)

Roger S. Jones, *Physics for the Rest of Us*, (Barnes & Noble Books, 1999)

Alfred B. Bartz, PhD, *Physics Decade by Decade* (Facts on File Inc.,)

Glossary

Aai: Mother

Aaji: Grandmother

Aatya: Paternal aunt, father's sister

Abhangas: Devotional songs written by Maharashtrian saint-poets

Amsul: Dried peel of Kokum—a fruit with a pleasantly sour taste and good digestive properties

Ashutosh: Name given to Lord Shiva because he spreads happiness everywhere; also, he who is pleased

Baba: Father

Bal Gandharva: A great Maharashtrian thespian, also known for his superlative singing

Batata Wada: Spicy potato balls

Bhajias: Savoury fritters made of chickpea flour

Bhalchandra Nemade: A Jnanpith Award-winning Marathi novelist

Biryani: A delicious and aromatic dish with rice and meat

Chaitra Poornima: Full moon day of the Hindu month Chaitra, coinciding approximately with the English months of March and April

Dada: Elder brother

Datta Jayanti: An auspicious birth date of Shri Dattatraya - a revered Hindu deity

Draupadi: Heroine of the Indian epic Mahabharata

Ganapati Bappa: A deity of learning, worshipped in great style in Maharashtra

Garba Dance: Very popular folk dance of Gujarat

Gayatri Mantra: A prayer to be chanted in Sanskrit propitiating the Sun God

Gita/Shrimad Bhagavad Gita: 'Celestial Song' by Lord Krishna; a divine sermon, reflecting on human life; a spiritual discourse greatly revered by Indians

Gurukul: Abode of the guru

Holi: A popular Indian festival of colours, celebrating the onset of spring

Kaka: Paternal uncle/father's brother

Kaki: Paternal aunt/paternal uncle's wife

Kanawala: Sweet puffs made with semolina covers and sweetened coconut stuffing

K.L. Saigal: An Indian film actor and legendary singer

Kanyadaan: A rite performed by the father or brother of the bride in a Hindu wedding ceremony; the giving away of the daughter of the family in marriage

Konkani: A language spoken in western coastal regions of India

Koshimbir: Salad

Kosla: Cocoon, the name of Bhalachandra Nemade's very popular novel

Kusumagraj: Eminent Marathi poet and dramatist, Jnanpith Award-winner

Mahabharata: The epic poem by sage Vyasa, a tale of the war between two kindred families, the Kauravas and the Pandavas

Mahaprasad Lunch: An auspicious meal taken as a benediction from God after its public worship

Mama: Maternal uncle/mother's brother

Mami: Maternal aunt/maternal uncle's wife

Mangal in the horoscope: Astrological belief that the presence of the planet Mangal (Mars) in a particular place in one's horoscope is inauspicious for their future spouse

Maoshi: Maternal aunt/mother's sister

Mera Naam Joker (My Name Is Joker): A Hindi film; late Indian filmmaker Raj Kapoor's swan song

Moravala: Sweet preserve of amla (Indian gooseberry), a rich source of Vitamin C

Mothe Baba: Grandfather

Mothi Aai: Grandmother

Nishkaam Karmayogi: A selfless person doing their duty without expecting a reward

Panaji: Great-grandmother

Panchatantra: Ancient Indian book of animal fables/moral tales

Pankaj Mullick: A great singer of Hindi and Bengali films, music composer, singer of 'Rabindra Sangeet' (Nobel Poet Laureate Rabindranath Tagore's lyrics sung in a special genre of music)

Puranas: A vast body of sacred literature of India

Rajgir: A hill station in Bihar, a capital city of ancient Magadha empire, and the place where Gautam Buddha spent thirteen years of his life

Rakhi: A sacred thread tied by a sister on her brother's wrist during the festival of Rakshabandhan

Ramayana: The epic poem by sage Valmiki narrating the life story of Lord Rama

Rashtra Sewa Dal: A nationwide organization promoting the national spirit

Rishi: An Indian sage

Rudra Avatar: Lord Shiva in a furious mood is known as Rudra, so a person who is angry

Sage Jamadagni: A sage in Indian mythology known for his violent rage

Sant Ramdas: A revered saint–poet of Maharashtra from the medieval period

Sant Tukaram: A revered saint–poet of Maharashtra from the medieval period

Sattvic: Food that nourishes the body and promotes spirituality. In Ayurveda, food is divided into saatvik, rajasik and tamasik

Shivaji Maharaj: A gallant Marathi ruler of the medieval period

Shloka: Hymns from Indian scriptures

Stupa: A monument built in Buddhist style of architecture

Tai: Elder sister

Tathastu: So be it/God bless you

Tel Poli: A popular Maharashtrian sweet bread made with chickpeas, jaggery and wheat flour

Thread ceremony: A Hindu ritual in which the male child of the family is initiated into the Hindu religion and is made to take a vow of celibacy till he completes education

Three Knot Four: A trick-taking card game

Tortoise: A second avatar (incarnation) of Lord Vishnu, the protector of the world according to Hindu mythology; he appears in ten incarnations—namely, fish, tortoise, and boar as animals; Nrisimha (half man, half lion); and Vamana, Parshurama, Rama, Krishna, Buddha and Kalki as men

Upanishads: Essence of Vedas, reflections on Hindu philosophy

Ustadon ki Ustad: A person who so skilled that she is the master of other skilled persons

Vastu Puja: A house-warming ritual to propitiate the residing deity of one's new house

Vedas: Hindu religious scriptures

Vipassana: Buddhist style of meditation

Yamuna: A famous river in north India

About the Author

Mrs Manik Kotwal, mother of Prof. Ashutosh Kotwal, wrote about her son's journey from his early childhood to becoming a world-renowned particle physicist in her Marathi book *Putra Vhava Aisa* (2016), which received the Ashok Tilak Award. Prior Marathi biographies to her credit are *Doordarshi* (of Galileo, 2008), *Oppenheimer* (2011) and *Atma Siddha* (of well-known social activist Smt. Nirmala Purandare, 2015). She has translated French classics and the poetry of Nobel Laureate Rabindranath Tagore. She taught in prestigious schools in Nagpur and Mumbai. An aficionado of dramatics and theatre arts, she has directed and starred in plays performed on the Lucknow, Varanasi and Delhi stages, placing first and second in the Uttar Pradesh state competitions in 1973 and 1974. She has also worked in worked in television in Delhi and Mumbai. Over the last thirty years, she has worked as a child development activist in about 200 villages in rural Maharashtra. Manik Kotwal lives in Pune, India, with her husband, Vijay Kotwal.

About the Translator

Jerry Pinto has translated several important works from Marathi including Daya Pawar's seminal autobiography, *Baluta*, and Sachin Kundalkar's novel, *Cobalt Blue*. From Hindi he has translated Swadesh Deepak's account of his mental illness and recovery in *I Have Not Seen Mandu*. His latest translation was Jnanpith Award-winner Damodar Mauzo's Konkani novel, *Boy Unloved*. He is also the winner of the Sahitya Akademi Award, the National Award for the Best Book on Cinema and the Windham-Campbell Award for Fiction.

HarperCollins *Publishers* India

At HarperCollins India, we believe in telling the best stories and finding the widest readership for our books in every format possible. We started publishing in 1992; a great deal has changed since then, but what has remained constant is the passion with which our authors write their books, the love with which readers receive them, and the sheer joy and excitement that we as publishers feel in being a part of the publishing process.

Over the years, we've had the pleasure of publishing some of the finest writing from the subcontinent and around the world, including several award-winning titles and some of the biggest bestsellers in India's publishing history. But nothing has meant more to us than the fact that millions of people have read the books we published, and that somewhere, a book of ours might have made a difference.

As we look to the future, we go back to that one word—a word which has been a driving force for us all these years.

Read.